EVERYTHING YOU NEED TO KNOW TO SCORE HIGH ON

POSTAL CLERK AND CARRIER

John Gosney
Dawn Rosenberg McKay

ARCO
THOMSON LEARNING

Australia • Canada • Mexico • Singapore • Spain • United Kingdom • United States

An ARCO Book

ARCO is a registered trademark of Thomson Learning, Inc., and is used herein under license by Peterson's.

About Peterson's

Founded in 1966, Peterson's, a division of Thomson Learning, is the nation's largest and most respected provider of lifelong learning online resources, software, reference guides, and books. The Education Supersite^{SM} at petersons.com—the Web's most heavily traveled education resource—has searchable databases and interactive tools for contacting U.S.-accredited institutions and programs. CollegeQuest® (CollegeQuest.com) offers a complete solution for every step of the college decision-making process. GradAdvantage™ (GradAdvantage.org), developed with Educational Testing Service, is the only electronic admissions service capable of sending official graduate test score reports with a candidate's online application. Peterson's serves more than 55 million education consumers annually.

Thomson Learning is among the world's leading providers of lifelong learning, serving the needs of individuals, learning institutions, and corporations with products and services for both traditional classrooms and for online learning. For more information about the products and services offered by Thomson Learning, please visit www.thomsonlearning.com. Headquartered in Stamford, Connecticut, with offices worldwide, Thomson Learning is part of The Thomson Corporation (www.thomson.com), a leading e-information and solutions company in the business, professional, and education marketplaces. The Corporation's common shares are listed on the Toronto and London stock exchanges.

For Genna and Jackson

For more information, contact Peterson's, 2000 Lenox Drive, Lawrenceville, NJ 08648; 800-338-3282; or find us on the World Wide Web at: www.petersons.com/about

Twenty-Second Edition

Library of Congress Number available upon request.

ISBN 0-02-863737-2

Printed in the United States of America

10 9 8 7 6 5 4 3 2 1   03 02 01

CONTENTS

Introduction vi

PART ONE
A Job with the U.S. Postal Service   1

Working for the U.S. Postal Service 3

Welcome to the U.S. Postal Service 3

Salary, Benefits, and Employment Opportunities with the U.S. Postal Service 4

Training and Qualifications for U.S. Postal Service Jobs 10

Finding More Information on USPS Positions 11

Postal Service Job Descriptions 15

A Variety of Positions with the USPS 15

Post Office Clerk 15

City or Special Carrier/Special Delivery Messenger 17

Distribution Clerk, Machine 19

Flat Sorting Machine Operator 20

Mail Handler 21

Mail Processor 23

Mark-up Clerk—Automated 23

Rural Carrier 24

PART TWO
Test Preparation Strategies   27

Before You Take the Prelininary Exam 29

Directions for Taking the Preliminary Exam 29

Directions for Scoring Your Exam 29

Preliminary Model Exam Answer Sheet 31

Score Sheet 35

Preliminary Model Exam   37

Part A—Address Checking 37

Address Checking 38

Part B—Memory for Addresses 41

Memory for Addresses 49

Part C—Number Series 50

Number Series 51

Part D—Following Oral Instructions 52

Following Oral Instructions 55

Correct Answers for Preliminary Exam 61

Familiarize Yourself with the Tests   69

Get to Know the Test 69

Rules and Procedures 69

Score Determination and Reporting 71

General Test-Taking Strategies 72

Score Higher: Address Checking Strategies   75

Address Checking Strategies 75

Practice Quiz 75

Strategies to Score Higher 76

Practice Exercises 79

The Real Thing: Practice an Exam 81

Score Higher: Memory for Addresses   85

Memory Strategies 85

Practice Quiz 85

Tips and Techniques 86

The Real Thing: Practice an Exam 87

Score Higher: Strategies for Working with Number Series   91

Number Series Strategies 91

Practice Quiz 91

Strategies for Working with Number Series Questions 92

Number Series Practice I 93

Number Series Practice II 94

Score Higher: Strategies for Following Oral Instructions   99

Tips for Oral Instruction Questions 99

Practice with Oral Instruction Questions 101

PART 3
Practice Tests 121

Address Checking Practice Tests 123

Taking the Timed Practice Tests 123

Timed Practice Tests 125

Practice Test Answers 135

Self-Evaluation Chart 137

Memory for Addresses Practice Tests 139

Taking the Timed Test 139

Timed Test 140

Answers—Memory for Addresses 147

Self-Evaluation Chart 149

Number Series Practice Tests 151

Taking the Timed Test 151

Practice Test I 153

Practice Test II 154

Answers—Practice Test I 155

Answers—Practice Test II 156

Self-Evaluation Chart 157

Following Oral Instructions Practice Tests 159

Taking the Timed Test 159

The Timed Test 161

Full Length Practice Exam: Exam 470 and Exam 460 171

Part A—Address Checking 179

Part B—Memory for Addresses 183

Part C—Number Series 189

Part D—Following Oral Instructions 191

Correct Answers for Model Exam I 201

Score Sheet 208

Glossary 209

Introduction

Congratulations on selecting *ARCO Postal Clerk and Carrier!* You have in your hands a powerful tool to ensure your best chances at getting a great score on the United States Postal Exam. By working through the book, taking time to practice the sample exercises and study the various tips and techniques for tackling various question types, you can put yourself at a solid advantage for achieving your best score. Also, the book contains up-to-date information, including:

- Job requirements
- Benefits
- Working conditions
- Salaries

This is **your** book, written with **your success** in mind—enjoy reading it, and good luck on your exam!

HOW TO USE THIS BOOK

Unlike many test preparation books, you don't have to read through the book from front to back. If you prefer, you can jump right into the sample tests (Chapters 8 through 12). Or maybe you'd like to see some strategies for approaching the various exam questions. You can find these in Chapters 4 through 7. Finally, detailed, current information on jobs with the USPS can be found in the first three chapters (including World Wide Web addresses for more detailed information). Again, this is your book—use it as you like!

ACKNOWLEDGEMENTS

Thanks to everyone at ARCO for their outstanding support and professionalism on this and other projects, with a special thank you going out to Dave Henthorn for always being a true professional. Also, another big thank you is owed to Dawn Rosenberg-McKay for contributing so much great research.

ONE

A Job with the U.S. Postal Service

CONTENTS

Working for the U.S. Postal Service   3

Postal Service Job Descriptions   15

WORKING FOR THE U.S. POSTAL SERVICE

Welcome to the U.S. Postal Service

Remember when you were a kid, and you took a field trip to your local post office? More than likely, a friendly employee gave you a tour of the mail sorting area, demonstrated how the various computers are used (depending, of course, on your age at the time of the tour!), and perhaps gave you a peek into one of the mail trucks. And, if you're like many people, you left with the impression that the only thing postal employees do is "sort the mail." Maybe this impression stayed with you into adulthood.

Most people are familiar with the duties of the city carrier and post-office window clerk (the same friendly employees who may have given you the tour when you were young). However, very few people are aware of the many different tasks required in "sorting the mail," not to mention the enormous variety of occupations in the U.S. Postal Service.

Twenty-four hours a day, mail (mail consisting of packages, magazines, and other assorted papers) moves through the typical large post office. It takes a lot of hard work to keep that mail moving, and all that hard work requires the involvement of many different people performing many different tasks:

- City carriers have collected some of this mail from neighborhood mailboxes; some has been trucked in from surrounding towns or from the airport. When a truck arrives at the post office, mail handlers unload the mail.
- Postal clerks then sort it according to destination. After being sorted, outgoing mail is loaded into trucks for delivery to the airport or nearby towns. Local mail is left for carriers to deliver the next morning.
- To keep buildings and equipment clean and in good working order, the Postal Service employs a variety of service and maintenance workers, including janitors, laborers, truck mechanics, electricians, carpenters, and painters. Some workers specialize in repairing machines that process mail.
- Postal inspectors audit the operations of post offices to see that they are run efficiently, that funds are spent properly, and that postal laws and regulations are observed. They also prevent and detect crimes such as theft, forgery, and fraud involving use of the mail.
- Postmasters and supervisors are responsible for the day-to-day operation of the post office, for hiring and promoting employees, and for setting up work schedules.

Almost 85 percent of all postal workers are in jobs directly related to processing and delivering mail. This group includes postal clerks, city carriers, mail handlers, rural carriers, and truck drivers. Postmasters and supervisors make up nearly 10 percent of total employment, and maintenance workers about 4 percent. The remainder includes such workers as postal inspectors, guards, personnel workers, and secretaries.

As you can see, there are lots of exciting positions within the U.S. Postal Service. However, the focus of this book will be on the positions of Postal Clerk and Carrier. Not only will you receive up-to-date information on these positions, but you also learn specific techniques for how to get your best score on the exams (you'll also get plenty of opportunity to practice on each exam question type).

Salary, Benefits, and Employment Opportunies with the U.S. Postal Service

The United States Postal Service is an independent agency of the Federal Government. As such, employees of the Postal Service are federal employees who enjoy the generous benefits offered by the government. These benefits include an automatic raise at least once a year, regular cost-of-living adjustments, liberal paid vacation and sick leave, life insurance, hospitalization, and the opportunity to join a credit union.

At the same time, the operation of the Postal Service is businesslike and independent of politics. A postal worker's job is secure even though presidential administrations change. An examination system is used to fill vacancies. This system provides opportunities for those who are able and motivated to enter the Postal Service and to move within it.

BENEFITS

The table below illustrates the general benefits offered by the USPS.

> Post Office employees are covered by the same benefits as employees of the Federal Government, including Federal Employees Health Benefits (FEHB), Federal Employees Retirement System (FERS), and Life Insurance.

Type of Benefits	Who Is Covered	Available Options
Health: Federal Employees Health Benefits (FEHB)	Postal employees and retirees and their survivors. Coverage may include the following: • Self only • Family coverage for yourself, your spouse, and unmarried dependent children under age 22	• Managed Fee for Service Plans • Point of Service (POP) options • Health Maintenance Organizations (HMOs)
Retirement: Federal Employees Retirement System (FERS) Benefits	Almost all new employees hired after 1983 are automatically covered. Employees who leave may still qualify for benefits. Builds on the Social Security benefits employees may earn in the future, or may already have earned, from non-Federal work.	FERS is a three-tiered retirement plan, consisting of these components: • Social Security Benefits (available for those age 62 and retired) • Basic Benefits Plan (financed by a small contribution from the employee and the government)

Type of Benefits	Who Is Covered	Available Options
Retirement: (cont'd)		*A Special Retirement Supplement, for employees who meet the criteria, is paid as a monthly benefit until the employee reaches age 62.* • Thrift Savings Plan (tax-deferred retirement savings and investment plan; similar to 401(k) plans)
Life: The Federal Employees' Group Life Insurance Program *(FEGLI)*	Postal employees and retirees, as well as many of their family members, are eligible for this group life insurance program.	• Basic Insurance (automatic unless employee opts out; insured pays $2/3$ of cost and the government pays $1/3$) • Optional Insurance (not automatic; insured pays 100% of cost)

SALARIES

Salaries within the USPS are "graded." The amount of time you've been employed, any promotions you might have achieved, as well as whether or not you work full-time or part-time are all factors that determine your salary.

The following tables illustrate salary levels for various positions with the USPS. You are assigned a "Grade"(e.g., Grade 5) depending on the type of position you fill (note that each position has different grade levels). To move between steps (e.g., B to C) requires that you be in the previous position for a specified number of weeks (more details on these "step" requirements are defined after the tables).

LETTER CARRIER PAY SCHEDULE—3/14/1998 (YEARLY)

	A	B	C	D	E
Grade 5	$27,011	$29,895	$32,210	$34,443	$34,731
Grade 6	$28,585	$31,665	$32,859	$35,147	$35,462

	F	G	H	I	J
Grade 5	$35,022	$35,309	$35,600	$35,888	$36,177
Grade 6	$35,777	$36,088	$36,404	$36,718	$37,029

	K	L	M	N	O
Grade 5	$36,468	$36,755	$37,046	$37,334	$37,623
Grade 6	$37,345	$37,660	$37,973	$38,290	$38,604

MAIL HANDLERS PAY SCHEDULE—3/13/1999 (YEARLY)

	A	B	C	D	E
Grade 4	$23,808	$28,512	$30,721	$33,975	$34,237
Grade 5	$25,122	$30,149	$32,419	$34,618	$34,900

	F	G	H	I	J
Grade 4	$34,503	$34,766	$35,029	$35,293	$35,559
Grade 5	$35,187	$35,467	$35,753	$36,039	$36,320

	K	L	M	N	O
Grade 4	$35,823	$36,087	$36,350	$36,614	$36,877
Grade 5	$36,606	$36,886	$37,171	$37,455	$37,739

RURAL CARRIER EVALUATED SCHEDULE—3/13/1999
FULL-TIME ANNUAL BASIC RATES (PARTIAL SCHEDULE)

Hours	A	B	C	1	2	3	4
12	$7,768	$8,590	$9,220	$9,859	$9,952	$10,043	$10,135
18	$11,649	$12,887	$13,832	$14,788	$14,926	$15,066	$15,203
24	$15,533	$17,178	$18,439	$19,719	$19,900	$20,082	$20,266
30	$19,415	$21,480	$23,056	$24,651	$24,878	$25,111	$25,337
40	$25,887	$28,633	$30,735	$32,862	$33,167	$33,475	$33,779
48	$33,655	$37,223	$39,955	$42,721	$43,119	$43,518	$43,914

Hours	5	6	7	8	9	10	11
12	$10,226	$10,321	$10,413	$10,503	$10,597	$10,688	$10,781
18	$15,343	$15,479	$15,618	$15,756	$15,896	$16,034	$16,172
24	$20,449	$20,633	$20,817	$21,000	$21,182	$21,368	$21,550
30	$25,566	$25,796	$26,026	$26,255	$26,484	$26,714	$26,945
40	$34,087	$34,392	$34,698	$35,006	$35,310	$35,618	$35,923
48	$44,313	$44,713	$45,111	$45,509	$45,907	$46,306	$46,704

FULL-TIME REGULAR APWU SALARY SCHEDULE (PS)—9/12/1998
(MAINTENANCE EMPLOYEES, MOTOR VEHICLE EMPLOYEES, POSTAL CLERKS,
MAIL EQUIPMENT SHOPS EMPLOYEES, MATERIAL DISTRIBUTION CENTERS EMPLOYEES)

Grade	AA	A	B	C	D	E	F	G
1	$22,715	$25,041	$27,128	$29,216	$32,323	$32,536	$32,750	$32,962
2	$23,000	$25,393	$27,533	$29,667	$32,837	$33,067	$33,297	$33,527
3	$23,364	$25,771	$27,964	$30,155	$33,393	$33,641	$33,893	$34,138
4	—	$25,738	$28,434	$30,688	$33,997	$34,265	$34,536	$34,805
5	—	$27,219	$30,103	$32,418	$34,651	$34,939	$35,230	$35,517
6	—	$28,793	$31,873	$33,067	$35,355	$35,670	$35,985	$36,296
7	—	$29,392	$32,545	$33,774	$36,119	$36,457	$36,794	$37,133
8	—	—	—	$34,365	$36,937	$37,304	$37,670	$38,037
9	—	—	—	$35,191	$37,829	$38,228	$38,624	$39,021
10	—	—	—	$36,062	$38,771	$39,199	$39,625	$40,054

Grade	H	I	J	K	L	M	N	O
1	$33,174	$33,387	$33,600	$33,813	$34,027	$34,236	$34,451	$34,663
2	$33,760	$33,988	$34,219	$34,451	$34,679	$34,912	$35,142	$35,370
3	$34,389	$34,635	$34,887	$35,134	$35,383	$35,630	$35,879	$36,126
4	$35,071	$35,340	$35,609	$35,879	$36,150	$36,418	$36,686	$36,953
5	$35,808	$36,096	$36,385	$36,676	$36,963	$37,254	$37,542	$37,831
6	$36,612	$36,926	$37,237	$37,553	$37,868	$38,181	$38,498	$38,812
7	$37,474	$37,809	$38,149	$38,485	$38,823	$39,163	$39,500	$39,837
8	$38,406	$38,771	$39,141	$39,505	$39,873	$40,239	$40,605	$40,974
9	$39,415	$39,810	$40,206	$40,605	$40,999	$41,399	$41,765	$42,191
10	$40,483	$40,909	$41,337	$41,766	$42,192	$42,621	$43,049	$43,476

Again, as you advance in your selected position within the USPS, you will become eligible for pay increases.

To be eligible for a periodic step increase, an employee:

- Must have received and currently be serving under a career appointment
- Must have performed in a satisfactory or outstanding manner during the waiting period
- Cannot have received an equivalent increase during the waiting period
- Must have completed the required waiting period (see tables below)

The following are Step Increase Waiting Periods for Bargaining Unit Positions. The number under each Grade column indicates the waiting period in number of weeks.

POSTAL SERVICE (PS) SCHEDULE

Steps (From → To)	Grades 1–3	Grades 4–7	Grades 8–10	Steps (From → To)	Grades 1–3	Grades 4–7	Grades 8–10
A → B	96	—	—	H → I	44	44	44
B → C	88	96	—	I → J	44	44	44
C → D	88	44	—	J → K	34	34	34
D → E	44	44	52	K → L	34	34	34
E → F	44	44	44	L → M	26	26	26
F → G	44	44	44	M → N	26	26	26
G → H	44	44	44	N → O	24	24	24

MAIL HANDLERS' (MH) SCHEDULE

Steps (From → To)	Grade 3	Grades 4–6	Steps (From → To)	Grades 3	Grades 4–6
A → B	96	—	H → I	44	44
B → C	88	96	I → J	44	44
C → D	88	44	J → K	34	34
D → E	44	44	K → L	34	34
E → F	44	44	L → M	26	26
F → G	44	44	M → N	26	26
G → H	44	44	N → O	24	24

MAIL TRANSPORTATION EQUIPMENT CENTERS

Steps (From → To)	Grades 1–3	Grades 4–7	Grades 8–10	Steps (From → To)	Grades 1–3	Grades 4–7	Grades 8–10
A → B	96	—	—	H → I	44	44	44
B → C	88	96	—	I → J	44	44	44
C → D	88	44	—	J → K	34	34	34
D → E	44	44	52	K → L	34	34	34
E → F	44	44	44	L → M	26	26	26
F → G	44	44	44	M → N	26	26	26
G → H	44	44	44	N → O	24	24	24

MAIL EQUIPMENT SHOPS & AREA SUPPLY CENTERS

Steps (From → To)	Grades 1–3	Grades 4–7	Grades 8–10	Steps (From → To)	Grades 1–3	Grades 4–7	Grades 8–10
A → B	96	—	—	H → I	44	44	44
B → C	88	96	—	I → J	44	44	44
C → D	88	44	—	J → K	34	34	34
D → E	44	44	52	K → L	34	34	34
E → F	44	44	44	L → M	26	26	26
F → G	44	44	44	M → N	26	26	26
G → H	44	44	44	N → O	24	24	24

RURAL CARRIER SCHEDULES*

Steps (From → To)	B to C	C to 1	1 to 2	2 to 3	3 to 4	4 to 5	5 to 6	6 to 7	7 to 8	8 to 9	9 to 10	10 to 11	11 to 12
Hours/Miles	96	44	44	44	44	44	44	44	34	34	26	26	24

Waiting periods for these step increases apply to all hours on the Rural Carrier Evaluated Schedule, all miles on the Rural Mileage Schedule, and Grade 5 of the Rural Auxiliary Schedule.

HOLIDAYS

The following holidays are observed by all USPS offices:

- New Year's Day
- Martin Luther King Jr.'s Birthday
- George Washington's Birthday
- Memorial Day
- Independence Day
- Labor Day
- Columbus Day
- Veterans' Day
- Thanksgiving Day
- Christmas Day

LEAVE TIME?

In addition to the benefits listed above, employees of the postal service are also granted leave time for a variety of purposes. The following table illustrates the amount of leave time you can expect, depending on the reason for leave and your years of service.

Type of Leave	Use of This Type of Leave	Amount of Time You May Use
Annual Leave	For rest, recreation, and for personal and emergency purposes *Must be approved in advance by appropriate supervisor	Employees earn 13, 20, or 26 days of annual leave each leave year, according to their years of service.
Sick Leave	• Medical, dental, or optical examination or treatment • You are incapacitated by physical or mental illness, injury, or pregnancy or confinement • Contagious disease: If the employee himself or herself has a contagious disease or must care for a family member with a contagious disease • Medical leave for disabled veterans	Full-time employee: 13 days per year (employees accrue 4 hours for each full biweekly pay period, without limitation)
Family and Medical Leave	According to the Family and Medical Leave Act of 1993 (FMLA), employees are entitled to 12 weeks of unpaid leave for the following reasons: • the birth and care of your child • placement of a child with you for adoption or foster care • care of your spouse, child, or parent with a serious health condition • your own serious health condition *You may substitute Annual Leave for unpaid leave*	Twelve administrative work weeks during any 12-month period
Court Leave	For employees who are summoned, in connection with a judicial proceeding, to serve as a juror or to serve a witness, in a nonofficial capacity, in a case involving the Federal Government or Postal Service	

(continues)

(continues)

Type of Leave	Use of This Type of Leave	Amount of Time You May Use
Military Leave	For reservists or for members of the National Guard	Up to 15 days
Leave Sharing	Allows career postal employees to donate their leave to other career postal employees for a medical emergency when the recipient has exhausted his or her own leave	

Training and Qualifications for U.S. Postal Service Jobs

An applicant for a Postal Service job must pass an examination and meet minimum age requirements. Generally, the minimum age is 18 years, but a high school graduate may begin work at 16 years if the job is not hazardous and does not require the use of a motor vehicle. Many Postal Service jobs do not require formal education or special training. Applicants for these jobs are hired on the basis of their examination scores.

Some postal jobs do have special education or experience requirements, and some are open only to veterans. Any special requirements will be stated on the announcement of examination.

ADDITIONAL QUALIFYING ISSUES FOR USPS POSITIONS

- Male applicants born after December 31, 1959, unless for some reason they are exempt, must be registered with the Selective Service System.
- The Immigration Reform and Control Act of 1986 applies to postal workers. All postal workers must be citizens of the United States or must be able to prove identity and right to work in the United States (permanent resident alien status—Green Card).
- Applicants should apply at the post office where they wish to work and take the entrance examination for the job they want.
- A physical examination, including drug testing, is required.
- Applicants for jobs that require strength and stamina are sometimes given a special test. For example, mail handlers must be able to lift mail sacks weighing up to 70 pounds. The names of applicants who pass the examinations are placed on a list in the order of their scores.
- Examinations for most jobs include a written test.
- Five extra points are added to the score of an honorably discharged veteran and 10 extra points to the score of a veteran wounded in combat or disabled. Disabled veterans who have a compensable, service-connected disability of 10 percent or more are placed at the top of the eligibility list.

When a job opens, the appointing officer chooses one of the top three applicants. Others are left on the list to be considered for future openings.

New employees are trained either on the job by supervisors and other experienced employees, or in local training centers. Training ranges from a few days to several months, depending on the job. For example, mail handlers and mechanics' helpers can learn their jobs in a relatively short time. Postal inspectors, on the other hand, need months of training.

Advancement opportunities are available for most postal workers because there is a management commitment to provide career development. Also, employees can get preferred assignments, such as the day shift or a more desirable delivery route, as their seniority increases. When an opening occurs, employees may submit written requests, called "bids," for assignment to the vacancy. The bidder who meets the qualifications and has the most seniority gets the job.

Finding More Information on USPS Positions

National Job Listings for the United States Postal Service can be found on its Web site at www.usps.gov or on the Telephone Job Lines. These jobs include management, supervisory, administrative, professional, and technical positions, and not Craft or Bargaining Unit positions, such as clerk, carrier, or processor. The telephone numbers for these job lines are:

- **Jobs Open to the Public:**
  National Vacancies: 800-JOB-USPS
- **Jobs Open to Postal Employees:**
  National Vacancies: 800-NATL-VAC

There is no centralized listing of Craft or Bargaining Unit job openings for the local offices of the U.S. Postal Service. These job vacancies are posted on the bulletin boards of local post offices, in local newspapers, and are also available from District Offices. You can find the District Office closest to you by calling the Local Employment Hotline at 800-276-5627.

Several local post offices are accessible from the United States Postal Service Web site, which can be found at www.usps.gov. Some list job openings on the Web site. Some also have job hotlines that can be used to access vacancies in that location. Here are the telephone numbers for these job hotlines:

Salt Lake City, Utah	801-974-2209
Washington, DC	202-636-1537
Northern Virginia	703-698-6561
Imperial Valley/San Diego, CA	619-674-0577
Riverside/San Bernardino, CA	909-335-4339
Long Island, NY	516-582-7530

There are also several Internet sites you can visit for more information. Although it is by no means exhaustive, the following list should get you started in the right direction, as you learn more about what working for the USPS has to offer.

General Information

Postal Facts (http://www.usps.gov/history/pfact98.htm)
Facts and figures to help you learn more about the USPS.

USPS Annual Reports (http://www.usps.gov/history/annual.htm)

Job Listings

Federal Jobs Digest Online: Postal Exams (http://www.jobsfed.com/postal.htm)
Job listings and information about how to apply

U.S. Postal Service: Human Resources (www.usps.gov/hrisp)
Lists vacancies that include management, supervisory, administrative, professional, and technical positions only.

Online Publications

The Mail Handler and The Mail Handler Update (http://www.npmhu.org/Pubs/MailHandler.htm)
(http://www.npmhu.org/Pubs/Update.htm)
Publications from the National Mail Handlers Association

Postal Digest Reference Links from FedForce (www.clubfed.com/fedforce/fedforce.html)
Articles from *FedForce* that were cited in the Postal Employees News Digest newsletter.

Postal Life (www.usps.gov/history/plife/welcome.htm)
This publication is about Postal Service employees.

Postal News from FederalTimes.com (www.federaltimes.com/)
News of interest to those in the United States Postal Service.

Unions and Associations and Contract Information

American Postal Workers Union (APWU) Locals (http://www.apwu.org/locals.htm)

American Postal Workers Union (www.apwu.org)

National Association of Letter Carriers (http://www.nalc.org/)

National Association of Postal Supervisors (http://www.naps.org/)

National Postal Mail Handlers Union (http://www.npmhu.org/)

National Rural Letter Carriers Association (http://home.nrlca.org/nrlcainfo/)

Collective Bargaining Agreements

American Postal Workers Union 1998–2000 Agreement (http://www.apwu.org/IndRel/contractpage.htm)

National Association of Letter Carriers 1994–1998 Agreement (http://www.rollanet.org/~gary/contract.html)

National Rural Letter Carriers Association 1995–1999 Agreement (http://www.nemisys.com/RCIGinc/95-cont.htm)

Other Information about Working for the U.S. Postal Service

Letter Carrier Stuff (http://www.rollanet.org/~gary/index.html)
This site exists to promote the sharing of information among letter carriers.

Post Office Locator (http://www.usps.gov/ncsc/locators/find-po.html)
Find your local post office.

Postal Workers Web Ring (http://www.webring.org/cgi-bin/webring?ring=postalring;list)
Links to postal employees' Web sites.

The Postal Zone (http://www.geocities.com/CapitolHill/9285/)
A lot of links to information of interest to USPS employees.

What Does a Letter Carrier Do? (http://home.columbus.rr.com/angelx3/postal/faq.html)
A day-in-the-life account written by a city carrier.

POSTAL SERVICE JOB DESCRIPTIONS

A Variety of Positions with the USPS

Deciding on a job within the USPS is like deciding on any other job. Each position is unique, and appeals to different individuals for different reasons. Do you enjoy a specific type of work? If you don't really like being outdoors, then a courier route is probably not the right position for you. Perhaps you enjoy a position that is more routine from day to day, as compared to one that changes every minute? A mail sorting position might be the best fit for you. The point is that you should try to match the job descriptions listed in this chapter with your own interests, keeping in mind (of course) that all positions within the USPS are competitive, so you might want to look for two or three positions that interest you, in case your "first choice position" isn't available right away.

> Remember, your goal of landing your first-choice job must be tempered with the realities of the real world. However, career advancement is encouraged within the USPS, so you can always "work your way up" to that great job you've been dreaming of, even if you don't get it when you first start.

Post Office Clerk

JOB DUTIES

Remember that trip to the post office when you were a kid (we're not letting you forget, are we)? You might remember thinking the only duties of a postal clerk are to sell stamps and to take packages.

Actually, the majority of postal clerks are distribution clerks (see the section on distribution clerks for more information about being one) who sort incoming and outgoing mail in workrooms. Only in a small post office does a postal clerk perform "double duty" of sitting behind the counter *and* sorting mail.

Generally speaking, post office clerks perform the following tasks:

- Sort and distribute mail to post offices and to carrier routes
- May also perform a variety of services at public windows of post offices, post office branches, or stations (again, usually only in small post offices)
- Perform related duties as assigned

WORKING CONDITIONS

The postal clerk might have to perform more or less manual work, depending on the size of the post office where he/she works, as well as the equipment in place (chutes, sorting machines) to help with this task. Generally speaking, work involves continuous standing, stretching, and reaching. Additionally, the postal clerk might be required to handle heavy sacks of letter mail or parcel post weighing up to 70 pounds.

As was mentioned at the beginning of this chapter, different jobs appeal to different people, all for different reasons. However, you should be aware that some distribution clerks (which again can be the primary role of the postal clerk) can become bored with the routine of sorting mail. Also, postal clerks might be required to work at night (especially at large post offices, where sorting and distributing the mail is a "24/7" activity).

However, if your duties also include those of a window clerk, you more than likely experience a wider variety of duties. You have frequent contact with the public (which might be viewed as a benefit or drawback, depending on your personality), your work is normally not physically strenuous, and you won't have to work much at night. Again, each post office is unique in what duties are assigned to the postal clerk.

QUALIFICATION REQUIREMENTS

Qualification requirements for the position of postal clerk closely mirror the working conditions described previously.

No experience is necessary for the position of postal clerk.

A successful applicant must show, on a physical examination, that the applicant is able to perform the duties of the position:

- Prolonged standing, walking, and reaching
- Handling of heavy sacks of mail
- Distance vision must test 20/40 (Snellen) in one eye (corrective lenses permitted)
- Ability to read without strain printed material the size of typewritten characters (corrective lenses permitted)
- Ability to hear the conversational voice, with or without a hearing aid (for window positions)
- Maintain emotional and mental stability

TESTING REQUIREMENT

The testing requirement for postal clerks is *Postal Service Test 470, Configuration 1.* You must attain a rating of at least 70 out of 100.

The subjects you are tested on include:

Memory for addresses

Address checking

ADDITIONAL PROVISIONS

You should also be aware of the following additional provisions for postal clerks:

* Duties of newly appointed part-time clerks and carriers are interchangeable
* Must maintain pleasant and effective public relations with customers and others, requiring a general familiarity with postal laws, regulations, and procedures commonly used, and with the geography of the area
* Must maintain neat and proper personal attire and grooming, including wearing a uniform when required

---

Postal Clerks are represented by:
The American Postal Workers Union, AFL-CIO
1300 L Street NW
Washington, DC 20005
202-842-4200
On the Web: www.apwu.org

City or Special Carrier/ Special Delivery Messenger

Perhaps the most familiar of positions within the USPS, the role of "mailperson" brings to mind a wealth of feelings. How many times have you anxiously waited for the "postman" to deliver a letter or package? Maybe it was the results of your college entrance exams? Or perhaps one of the many items (and items of exceptionally high quality, of course) that you impulsively purchased from an advertisement you saw on television.

Indeed, the postman is a fixture in our culture, the bringer of good and bad news (and lots of junk mail, too!). All kidding aside, it is an exceptionally crucial job. Despite the rise in popularity of e-mail, can we really imagine a world where there was no daily postal delivery? Postal couriers definitely are worthy of the attention they receive.

You might be surprised to learn, however, that much of the postal carrier's work is done at the post office. Often starting as early as 6 a.m., carriers start their day at the post office, where they spend a few hours arranging their mail for delivery, re-addressing letters to be forwarded, and taking care of other details.

JOB DUTIES

A carrier typically covers his or her route on foot, toting a heavy load of mail in a satchel or pushing it in a cart. In outlying areas, a carrier might drive a car or small truck. Carriers or Special Delivery Messengers perform the following tasks:

* Promptly and efficiently deliver and collect mail on foot or by vehicle under varying conditions in a prescribed area or on various routes

- Deliver parcel post from trucks and make collections of mail from various boxes or other locations
- Maintain pleasant and effective public relations with customers

WORKING CONDITIONS

The mail is always delivered, come rain or shine. There must be an extreme weather situation for the mail to be postponed for an entire day (it might be late, of course, but that's a big difference from not going out at all).

With that thought in mind, carriers:

- May be required to drive motor vehicles in all kinds of traffic and road conditions (obviously, you need a driver's license)
- May be required to carry mail in shoulder satchels weighing as much as 35 pounds
- May be required to load and unload sacks of mail weighing up to 70 pounds
- Must serve in all kinds of weather

Despite these tough requirements, the job does have some key advantages. Carriers who begin work early in the morning are through by early afternoon. They are also free to work at their own pace as long as they cover their routes within a certain period of time.

QUALIFICATION REQUIREMENTS

As with many positions with the USPS, a carrier must be in such physical condition as to enable him or her to do potentially strenuous and physically taxing work. You must, upon physical examination, be able to perform the following duties:

- Prolonged standing, walking, and reaching
- Handling of heavy sacks of mail
- Distance vision must test 20/40 (Snellen) in one eye (corrective lenses permitted)
- Ability to read without strain printed material the size of typewritten characters (corrective lenses permitted)
- Maintain emotional and mental stability
- Must not have an irremedial defect or incurable disease that prevents efficient performance of duty that renders them a hazard to themselves, fellow employees, or others
- If driving of a vehicle weighing less than 10,000 pounds (GVW) is required, applicant must have vision of 20/40 in one eye and be able to read, without strain, printed material the size of typewritten characters (corrective lenses permitted). The ability to hear is not required to operate a vehicle weighing less than 10,000 pounds (GVW).

> No experience is necessary for the position of city or special carrier.

TESTING REQUIREMENT

The testing requirement for postal clerks is *Postal Service Test 470, Configuration 1.* You must attain a rating of at least 70 out of 100.

The subjects you will be tested on include:

Memory for addresses

Address checking

ADDITIONAL PROVISIONS

In addition to the information listed previously, you are also required to adhere to the following requirements, if you wish to be a carrier for the USPS:

- Duties of newly appointed part-time clerks and carriers are interchangeable.
- Must maintain pleasant and effective public relations with customers and others, requiring a general familiarity with postal laws, regulations, and procedures commonly used, and with the geography of the area.
- Must maintain neat and proper personal attire and grooming, including wearing a uniform when required.
- For positions requiring driving, applicants must have a valid state driver's license, and demonstrate and maintain a safe driving record. Applicants must pass the Postal Service road test to show the ability to safely drive a vehicle of the type used on the job.

City Carriers are represented by:
National Association of Letter Carriers, AFL-CIO
100 Indian Avenue, NW
Washington, DC 20001-2144
202-393-4695
On the Web: www.nalc.org

Distribution Clerk, Machine

JOB DUTIES

The work of the distribution clerk is more routine than that of other postal clerks, but the starting salary is higher. However, you should realize that as a distribution clerk, you might be on your feet all day. Additionally, you must be able to, on occasion, handle sacks of mail weighing as much as 70 pounds.

Perhaps the most challenging aspect of the job (and an aspect that will either greatly appeal to you, or greatly discourage you, depending on your personality) is the way in which you must sort mail. You must memorize a complicated scheme, which enables you to quickly and efficiently sort mail. These schemes include, for example, being able to quickly read a ZIP code and determine how the piece of mail is to be directed.

> Increasing automation within the Postal Service has made the job of the distribution clerk quite secure. Although there are never any "100 percent guarantees," this is a fact you might consider when investigating USPS positions (along with your own personal interests, of course!).

QUALIFICATION REQUIREMENTS

The distribution clerk, machine applicant must possess sufficient levels of the following KSAs (Knowledge, Skills, and Abilities):

- Knowledge of multi-position letter sorting machine
- Ability to:
  - Work without immediate supervision
  - Work in cooperation with follow employees to efficiently perform the duties of the position
  - Observe and act on visual information such as names, addresses, numbers, and shapes
  - Learn and recall pairings of addresses with numbers, letters, or positions
  - Sequence, or place mail in the proper numerical, alphabetical, or geographic order
- Must be physically able to efficiently perform the duties of the position
- Must have vision of 20/40 (Snellen) in one eye, near acuity of 7 or higher in either eye (Titmus or Bausch and Lomb), and the ability to read, without strain, printed material the size of typewritten characters (corrective lenses permitted)
- Ability to distinguish basic colors and shades is desirable

TESTING REQUIREMENT

To apply for this position, you must:

- Take *Postal Service Test 470, Configuration 1* as a requirement for the trainee position
- Successfully complete dexterity training as required by management

Distribution Clerks are represented by:
The American Postal Workers Union, AFL-CIO
1300 L Street NW
Washington, DC 20005
202-842-4200
On the Web: www.apwu.org

Flat Sorting Machine Operator
JOB DUTIES

A flat sorting machine operator's work is very similar to that of the Distribution Clerk position. However, as a flat sorting machine operator, you work with large, bulky packages.

You might guess that, with this requirement, you have to possess greater physical strength and stamina. Like the Distribution Clerk machine operator's position, increasing automation adds a good degree of security to this position, which is a definite plus that might offset the "physically taxing" requirements of the position.

QUALIFICATION REQUIREMENTS

In order to qualify for this position, you must possess sufficient levels of the following KSAs (Knowledge, Skills, and Abilities):

- Work without immediate supervision
- Work in cooperation with fellow employees to efficiently perform the duties of the position
- Observe and act on visual information such as names, addresses, numbers, and shapes
- Learn and recall pairings of addresses with numbers, letters, or positions
- Sequence, or place mail in the proper numerical, alphabetical, or geographic order
- Perform routine troubleshooting, such as removing jams
- Must be physically able to efficiently perform the duties of the position
- Must have vision of 20/40 (Snellen) in one eye, near acuity of 7 or higher in either eye (Titmus or Bausch and Lomb), and the ability to read, without strain, printed material the size of typewritten characters (corrective lenses permitted)
- Ability to distinguish basic colors and shades is desirable

TESTING REQUIREMENT

The testing requirements for this position include:

- Take *Postal Service Test 470, Configuration 1* as a requirement for the trainee position
- Successfully complete the appropriate training program for the flat sorting machine operation
- Demonstrate the ability to key at 45 items per minute with 98 percent accuracy

Flat Sorting Machine Operators are represented by:
The American Postal Workers Union, AFL-CIO
1300 L Street NW
Washington, DC 20005
202-842-4200
On the Web: www.apwu.org

Mail Handler

JOB DUTIES

As a mail handler, you unload and move bulk mail, and perform other duties incidental to the movement and processing of mail.

QUALIFICATION REQUIREMENTS

You must:

- Demonstrate sufficient levels of Knowledge, Skills, and Abilities (KSAs), which include at least minimum competency for senior-qualified positions
- Demonstrate these KSAs by describing examples of experience, education, or training, any of which may be non-postal
- Be physically able to perform effiently the duties of the position

> Because of the extreme physical nature of this job, if you have certain physical conditions you won't be permitted to take the strength and stamina test without prior approval of your doctor (which is a requirement for this position). These conditions include hernia or rupture, back trouble, heart trouble, pregnancy, or any other condition that makes it dangerous for you to lift and carry 70-pound weights.

- Have vision of 20/40 (Snellen) in one eye and the ability to read, without strain, printed material the size of typewritten characters (corrective lenses are permitted)
- Be able to hear the conversational voice in at least one ear (hearing aid permitted)

TESTING REQUIREMENT

Testing requirements for the position of mail handler include that you must:

- Successfully complete the *Postal Service Test 470, Configuration 2*, which measures the applicant's ability to understand simple word meanings, check names and numbers, and follow oral directions.
- Pass a test of physical abilities prior to appointment.

> If you fail to qualify on the strength and stamina test, you won't be tested again in the same group of hires. If you fail this test a second time, your eligibility for the position is canceled.

> Mail Handlers are represented by:
> **National Postal Mail Handlers Union, AFL-CIO**
> 1101 Connecticut Avenue, NW, Suite 500
> Washington, DC 20036
> 202-833-9095
> On the Web: www.npmhu.org

Mail Processor

JOB DUTIES

You are required to perform a combination of tasks that are used to process the mail, by utilizing a variety of mail-processing equipment, if you choose the path of mail processor.

WORKING CONDITIONS

The physical requirements for this position are not as tough as those required for mail handlers (but you also won't start at the same salary as that of a mail handler).

QUALIFICATION REQUIREMENTS

- Must be physically able to perform efficiently the duties of the position
- Vision of 20/40 (Snellen) in one eye and the ability to read, without strain, printed material the size of typewritten characters (corrective lenses permitted)
- Ability to distinguish basic colors and shades is desirable

TESTING REQUIREMENT

You must successfully complete *Postal Service Test 470, Configuration 2*, which tests your ability to understand simple word meanings, check names and numbers, and follow oral directions.

Mail Processors are represented by:
The American Postal Workers Union, AFL-CIO
1300 L Street NW
Washington, DC 20005
202-842-4200
On the Web: www.apwu.org

Mark-up Clerk—Automated

JOB DUTIES

A mark-up clerk, automated, operates an electro-mechanical operator-paced machine to process mail as undeliverable as addressed. In doing this, you operate the keyboard of a computer terminal to enter and extract dates to several databases. Although you don't have to be a computer programmer to qualify for this position, you should feel comfortable working with computers, as you need to enter into several potentially different programs in order to enter, view, and change data.

QUALIFICATION REQUIREMENTS

Qualifications include:

- Must demonstrate a sufficient level of the following KSAs (Knowledge, Skills, and Abilities):
- Ability to:
  - Use reference materials and manuals relevant to the position
  - Perform effectively under the pressures of the position
  - Operate any office equipment appropriate to the position
  - Work with others
- Six months of clerical or office machine operating experience

> The ability to type will prove invaluable for your role as a mark-up clerk, automated.

- Successful completion of a four-year high school course or successful completion of business school may be substituted for the six months of clerical or office machine operating requirements
- Must be physically able to perform efficiently the duties of the position
- Vision of 20/40 (Snellen) in one eye and the ability to read, without strain, printed material the size of typewritten characters (corrective lenses permitted)
- Ability to distinguish basic colors and shades is desirable

TESTING REQUIREMENT

Given the clerically oriented requirements of this position, you need to demonstrate the ability to key data codes on a computer terminal at a rate of 14 correct lines per minute, which must be demonstrated by successful completion of *Postal Service Test 715*. You also need to successfully complete *Postal Service Test 470, Configuration 2*.

> Markup Clerks are represented by:
> **The American Postal Workers Union, AFL-CIO**
> 1300 L Street NW
> Washington, DC 20005
> 202-842-4200
> On the Web: www.apwu.org

Rural Carrier

JOB DUTIES

The work of the rural carrier combines the work of the window clerk and the letter carrier. However, the job also has special characteristics of its own.

As a rural carrier, you begin the day with sorting and loading the mail for delivery. Then comes your drive (which might be over tough roads—during tough weather). Given the "rural" nature of your job, you deliver most of your mail from the car. At the end of your day, you return to the post office with outgoing mail and money collected in various transactions.

As you might guess, you enjoy a great deal of independence with this position, as there is no one "looking over your shoulder." However, the work can be taxing, and you have to endure the inherent dilemmas that come with spending lots of time in the car.

> Because many of your patrons live in remote locations (hence "rural" in your job title), you are also required, on occasion, to perform all the duties of a window clerk, including accepting, collecting, and delivering all classes of mail and selling stamp supplies and money orders.

WORKING CONDITIONS

In general, you should expect the following working conditions:

- Must load and deliver parcels weighing up to 70 pounds
- Placing letters and parcels in mail boxes requires careful handling of the vehicle, and frequent shifting from one side of the vehicle to the other
- Working with the public requires maintaining pleasant and effective working relations with customers and an acceptable appearance

QUALIFICATION REQUIREMENTS

Requirements for this position include that you have the ability to:

- Read, understand, and apply written instructions
- Perform basic arithmetic computations
- Prepare reports and maintain records
- Communicate effectively with customers
- Work effectively without close supervision

You must also:

- Be physically able to perform efficiently the arduous duties of the position
- Have vision of 20/40 (Snellen) in one eye and the ability to read, without strain, printed material the size of typewritten characters (corrective lenses permitted)

> The ability to hear is not required for this position.

TESTING REQUIREMENT

You must successfully complete *Postal Service Test 460*.

ADDITIONAL PROVISIONS

In addition to the requirements listed previously, you must have a valid state driver's license and a safe driving record, and must pass the Postal Service road test, which shows the ability to safely drive the type of vehicle used on the job.

Additionally, rural carriers furnish all necessary vehicle equipment for prompt handling of the mail, unless supplied by the employer (you are paid for equipment maintenance).

Rural Carriers are represented by:
National Rural Letter Carriers Association
Fourth Floor
1630 Duke Street
Alexandria, VA 22314-3465
703-684-5545
On the Web: www.nrlca.org

TWO

Test Preparation Strategies

CONTENTS

Before You Take the Preliminary Exam   29

Preliminary Model Exam   37

Familiarize Yourself with the Tests   69

Score Higher: Address Checking Strategies   75

Score Higher: Memory for Addresses   85

Score Higher: Strategies for Working with Number Series   91

Score Higher: Strategies for Following Oral Instructions   99

BEFORE YOU TAKE THE PRELIMINARY EXAM

The purpose of the Preliminary Exam is to establish a base upon which you can build your studies for your postal exam. The preliminary exam will give you an idea of the demands of the exam, of how well you can meet these demands now, and of how far you need to go to succeed on the exam. By starting out with a full-length exam, you see from the beginning how many questions you must answer and how quickly you must work to score high on this exam.

Directions for Taking the Preliminary Exam

- Arrange for a friend or family member to read the oral instructions for Part D. If you are unable to find a reader, skip ahead and read the chapter entitled "Strategies for Following Oral Instructions." Prepare a tape according to the instructions in that chapter.
- Choose a workspace that is quiet and well lit.
- Clear the desk or tabletop of all clutter.
- Bring a stopwatch or kitchen timer and two or three number-two pencils with good erasers to your work area. Although the pencils should have plenty of exposed lead, you will find that it is easier and doesn't take as long to fill in the answer circles if the pencils are not razor sharp. The little circles on the answer sheet must be completely filled in, and the fewer strokes needed to fill them, the faster you will be able to work. Scribble a bit to dull the points now. At the actual exam, you will dull the points as you fill out the grids before the exam begins.
- Tear out the answer sheets for the preliminary exam and place them on the desk or table beside your book, to the right if you are right-handed, to the left if you are left-handed.
- Read page 37 and answer the Address Checking sample questions. Then set the timer and begin work on Part A.
- Stop as soon as time is up and draw a line on your answer sheet at your stopping place. You want an accurate measure of how many questions you were able to answer correctly within the time limit. However, you may go back and get extra practice later on by answering the remaining questions without including them in your score.
- Proceed through the entire exam in this manner. First, answer the sample questions for the part just as you will at the exam site; then set the timer and answer as many questions as possible within the time limit. Mark your stopping place on the answer sheet and move on.

Directions for Scoring Your Exam

- When you have completed the entire preliminary exam, check your answers against the correct answer key on pages 61–64. Circle all wrong answers in red so that you can easily locate them when you analyze your errors.
- Calculate your raw score for each part of the exam as instructed on the score sheet on page 35.
- Check to see where your scores fall on the self-evaluation chart on page 35.
- Now analyze your errors and begin to learn from them. You might be able to identify a pattern of errors in address checking and in following oral instructions. And you might be able to begin developing expertise at number series as you study the explanations.

After you have completed the preliminary exam and have analyzed your results, you should have a good idea of where you stand and of how much you need to do to prepare for the exam. Plan to spend many hours with the four instructional chapters in Part II. Each will give you valuable help with answering the four distinct question types. Absorb all the information. Follow through with the drills and exercises. Do not jump ahead to the model exams until you are really prepared. Then go on and develop skill and speed with the model exams.

Preliminary Model Exam Answer Sheet

PART A—ADDRESS CHECKING

1. Ⓐ Ⓓ
2. Ⓐ Ⓓ
3. Ⓐ Ⓓ
4. Ⓐ Ⓓ
5. Ⓐ Ⓓ
6. Ⓐ Ⓓ
7. Ⓐ Ⓓ
8. Ⓐ Ⓓ
9. Ⓐ Ⓓ
10. Ⓐ Ⓓ
11. Ⓐ Ⓓ
12. Ⓐ Ⓓ
13. Ⓐ Ⓓ
14. Ⓐ Ⓓ
15. Ⓐ Ⓓ
16. Ⓐ Ⓓ
17. Ⓐ Ⓓ
18. Ⓐ Ⓓ
19. Ⓐ Ⓓ

20. Ⓐ Ⓓ
21. Ⓐ Ⓓ
22. Ⓐ Ⓓ
23. Ⓐ Ⓓ
24. Ⓐ Ⓓ
25. Ⓐ Ⓓ
26. Ⓐ Ⓓ
27. Ⓐ Ⓓ
28. Ⓐ Ⓓ
29. Ⓐ Ⓓ
30. Ⓐ Ⓓ
31. Ⓐ Ⓓ
32. Ⓐ Ⓓ
33. Ⓐ Ⓓ
34. Ⓐ Ⓓ
35. Ⓐ Ⓓ
36. Ⓐ Ⓓ
37. Ⓐ Ⓓ
38. Ⓐ Ⓓ

39. Ⓐ Ⓓ
40. Ⓐ Ⓓ
41. Ⓐ Ⓓ
42. Ⓐ Ⓓ
43. Ⓐ Ⓓ
44. Ⓐ Ⓓ
45. Ⓐ Ⓓ
46. Ⓐ Ⓓ
47. Ⓐ Ⓓ
48. Ⓐ Ⓓ
49. Ⓐ Ⓓ
50. Ⓐ Ⓓ
51. Ⓐ Ⓓ
52. Ⓐ Ⓓ
53. Ⓐ Ⓓ
54. Ⓐ Ⓓ
55. Ⓐ Ⓓ
56. Ⓐ Ⓓ
57. Ⓐ Ⓓ

58. Ⓐ Ⓓ
59. Ⓐ Ⓓ
60. Ⓐ Ⓓ
61. Ⓐ Ⓓ
62. Ⓐ Ⓓ
63. Ⓐ Ⓓ
64. Ⓐ Ⓓ
65. Ⓐ Ⓓ
66. Ⓐ Ⓓ
67. Ⓐ Ⓓ
68. Ⓐ Ⓓ
69. Ⓐ Ⓓ
70. Ⓐ Ⓓ
71. Ⓐ Ⓓ
72. Ⓐ Ⓓ
73. Ⓐ Ⓓ
74. Ⓐ Ⓓ
75. Ⓐ Ⓓ
76. Ⓐ Ⓓ

77. Ⓐ Ⓓ
78. Ⓐ Ⓓ
79. Ⓐ Ⓓ
80. Ⓐ Ⓓ
81. Ⓐ Ⓓ
82. Ⓐ Ⓓ
83. Ⓐ Ⓓ
84. Ⓐ Ⓓ
85. Ⓐ Ⓓ
86. Ⓐ Ⓓ
87. Ⓐ Ⓓ
88. Ⓐ Ⓓ
89. Ⓐ Ⓓ
90. Ⓐ Ⓓ
91. Ⓐ Ⓓ
92. Ⓐ Ⓓ
93. Ⓐ Ⓓ
94. Ⓐ Ⓓ
95. Ⓐ Ⓓ

PART B—MEMORY FOR ADDRESSES

1 Ⓐ Ⓑ Ⓒ Ⓓ Ⓔ	23 Ⓐ Ⓑ Ⓒ Ⓓ Ⓔ	45 Ⓐ Ⓑ Ⓒ Ⓓ Ⓔ	67 Ⓐ Ⓑ Ⓒ Ⓓ Ⓔ
2 Ⓐ Ⓑ Ⓒ Ⓓ Ⓔ	24 Ⓐ Ⓑ Ⓒ Ⓓ Ⓔ	46 Ⓐ Ⓑ Ⓒ Ⓓ Ⓔ	68 Ⓐ Ⓑ Ⓒ Ⓓ Ⓔ
3 Ⓐ Ⓑ Ⓒ Ⓓ Ⓔ	25 Ⓐ Ⓑ Ⓒ Ⓓ Ⓔ	47 Ⓐ Ⓑ Ⓒ Ⓓ Ⓔ	69 Ⓐ Ⓑ Ⓒ Ⓓ Ⓔ
4 Ⓐ Ⓑ Ⓒ Ⓓ Ⓔ	26 Ⓐ Ⓑ Ⓒ Ⓓ Ⓔ	48 Ⓐ Ⓑ Ⓒ Ⓓ Ⓔ	70 Ⓐ Ⓑ Ⓒ Ⓓ Ⓔ
5 Ⓐ Ⓑ Ⓒ Ⓓ Ⓔ	27 Ⓐ Ⓑ Ⓒ Ⓓ Ⓔ	49 Ⓐ Ⓑ Ⓒ Ⓓ Ⓔ	71 Ⓐ Ⓑ Ⓒ Ⓓ Ⓔ
6 Ⓐ Ⓑ Ⓒ Ⓓ Ⓔ	28 Ⓐ Ⓑ Ⓒ Ⓓ Ⓔ	50 Ⓐ Ⓑ Ⓒ Ⓓ Ⓔ	72 Ⓐ Ⓑ Ⓒ Ⓓ Ⓔ
7 Ⓐ Ⓑ Ⓒ Ⓓ Ⓔ	29 Ⓐ Ⓑ Ⓒ Ⓓ Ⓔ	51 Ⓐ Ⓑ Ⓒ Ⓓ Ⓔ	73 Ⓐ Ⓑ Ⓒ Ⓓ Ⓔ
8 Ⓐ Ⓑ Ⓒ Ⓓ Ⓔ	30 Ⓐ Ⓑ Ⓒ Ⓓ Ⓔ	52 Ⓐ Ⓑ Ⓒ Ⓓ Ⓔ	74 Ⓐ Ⓑ Ⓒ Ⓓ Ⓔ
9 Ⓐ Ⓑ Ⓒ Ⓓ Ⓔ	31 Ⓐ Ⓑ Ⓒ Ⓓ Ⓔ	53 Ⓐ Ⓑ Ⓒ Ⓓ Ⓔ	75 Ⓐ Ⓑ Ⓒ Ⓓ Ⓔ
10 Ⓐ Ⓑ Ⓒ Ⓓ Ⓔ	32 Ⓐ Ⓑ Ⓒ Ⓓ Ⓔ	54 Ⓐ Ⓑ Ⓒ Ⓓ Ⓔ	76 Ⓐ Ⓑ Ⓒ Ⓓ Ⓔ
11 Ⓐ Ⓑ Ⓒ Ⓓ Ⓔ	33 Ⓐ Ⓑ Ⓒ Ⓓ Ⓔ	55 Ⓐ Ⓑ Ⓒ Ⓓ Ⓔ	77 Ⓐ Ⓑ Ⓒ Ⓓ Ⓔ
12 Ⓐ Ⓑ Ⓒ Ⓓ Ⓔ	34 Ⓐ Ⓑ Ⓒ Ⓓ Ⓔ	56 Ⓐ Ⓑ Ⓒ Ⓓ Ⓔ	78 Ⓐ Ⓑ Ⓒ Ⓓ Ⓔ
13 Ⓐ Ⓑ Ⓒ Ⓓ Ⓔ	35 Ⓐ Ⓑ Ⓒ Ⓓ Ⓔ	57 Ⓐ Ⓑ Ⓒ Ⓓ Ⓔ	79 Ⓐ Ⓑ Ⓒ Ⓓ Ⓔ
14 Ⓐ Ⓑ Ⓒ Ⓓ Ⓔ	36 Ⓐ Ⓑ Ⓒ Ⓓ Ⓔ	58 Ⓐ Ⓑ Ⓒ Ⓓ Ⓔ	80 Ⓐ Ⓑ Ⓒ Ⓓ Ⓔ
15 Ⓐ Ⓑ Ⓒ Ⓓ Ⓔ	37 Ⓐ Ⓑ Ⓒ Ⓓ Ⓔ	59 Ⓐ Ⓑ Ⓒ Ⓓ Ⓔ	81 Ⓐ Ⓑ Ⓒ Ⓓ Ⓔ
16 Ⓐ Ⓑ Ⓒ Ⓓ Ⓔ	38 Ⓐ Ⓑ Ⓒ Ⓓ Ⓔ	60 Ⓐ Ⓑ Ⓒ Ⓓ Ⓔ	82 Ⓐ Ⓑ Ⓒ Ⓓ Ⓔ
17 Ⓐ Ⓑ Ⓒ Ⓓ Ⓔ	39 Ⓐ Ⓑ Ⓒ Ⓓ Ⓔ	61 Ⓐ Ⓑ Ⓒ Ⓓ Ⓔ	83 Ⓐ Ⓑ Ⓒ Ⓓ Ⓔ
18 Ⓐ Ⓑ Ⓒ Ⓓ Ⓔ	40 Ⓐ Ⓑ Ⓒ Ⓓ Ⓔ	62 Ⓐ Ⓑ Ⓒ Ⓓ Ⓔ	84 Ⓐ Ⓑ Ⓒ Ⓓ Ⓔ
19 Ⓐ Ⓑ Ⓒ Ⓓ Ⓔ	41 Ⓐ Ⓑ Ⓒ Ⓓ Ⓔ	63 Ⓐ Ⓑ Ⓒ Ⓓ Ⓔ	85 Ⓐ Ⓑ Ⓒ Ⓓ Ⓔ
20 Ⓐ Ⓑ Ⓒ Ⓓ Ⓔ	42 Ⓐ Ⓑ Ⓒ Ⓓ Ⓔ	64 Ⓐ Ⓑ Ⓒ Ⓓ Ⓔ	86 Ⓐ Ⓑ Ⓒ Ⓓ Ⓔ
21 Ⓐ Ⓑ Ⓒ Ⓓ Ⓔ	43 Ⓐ Ⓑ Ⓒ Ⓓ Ⓔ	65 Ⓐ Ⓑ Ⓒ Ⓓ Ⓔ	87 Ⓐ Ⓑ Ⓒ Ⓓ Ⓔ
22 Ⓐ Ⓑ Ⓒ Ⓓ Ⓔ	44 Ⓐ Ⓑ Ⓒ Ⓓ Ⓔ	66 Ⓐ Ⓑ Ⓒ Ⓓ Ⓔ	88 Ⓐ Ⓑ Ⓒ Ⓓ Ⓔ

PART C—NUMBER SERIES

1. Ⓐ Ⓑ Ⓒ Ⓓ Ⓔ	7. Ⓐ Ⓑ Ⓒ Ⓓ Ⓔ	13. Ⓐ Ⓑ Ⓒ Ⓓ Ⓔ	19. Ⓐ Ⓑ Ⓒ Ⓓ Ⓔ
2. Ⓐ Ⓑ Ⓒ Ⓓ Ⓔ	8. Ⓐ Ⓑ Ⓒ Ⓓ Ⓔ	14. Ⓐ Ⓑ Ⓒ Ⓓ Ⓔ	20. Ⓐ Ⓑ Ⓒ Ⓓ Ⓔ
3. Ⓐ Ⓑ Ⓒ Ⓓ Ⓔ	9. Ⓐ Ⓑ Ⓒ Ⓓ Ⓔ	15. Ⓐ Ⓑ Ⓒ Ⓓ Ⓔ	21. Ⓐ Ⓑ Ⓒ Ⓓ Ⓔ
4. Ⓐ Ⓑ Ⓒ Ⓓ Ⓔ	10. Ⓐ Ⓑ Ⓒ Ⓓ Ⓔ	16. Ⓐ Ⓑ Ⓒ Ⓓ Ⓔ	22. Ⓐ Ⓑ Ⓒ Ⓓ Ⓔ
5. Ⓐ Ⓑ Ⓒ Ⓓ Ⓔ	11. Ⓐ Ⓑ Ⓒ Ⓓ Ⓔ	17. Ⓐ Ⓑ Ⓒ Ⓓ Ⓔ	23. Ⓐ Ⓑ Ⓒ Ⓓ Ⓔ
6. Ⓐ Ⓑ Ⓒ Ⓓ Ⓔ	12. Ⓐ Ⓑ Ⓒ Ⓓ Ⓔ	18. Ⓐ Ⓑ Ⓒ Ⓓ Ⓔ	24. Ⓐ Ⓑ Ⓒ Ⓓ Ⓔ

PART D—FOLLOWING ORAL INSTRUCTIONS

1 Ⓐ Ⓑ Ⓒ Ⓓ Ⓔ   23 Ⓐ Ⓑ Ⓒ Ⓓ Ⓔ   45 Ⓐ Ⓑ Ⓒ Ⓓ Ⓔ   67 Ⓐ Ⓑ Ⓒ Ⓓ Ⓔ

2 Ⓐ Ⓑ Ⓒ Ⓓ Ⓔ   24 Ⓐ Ⓑ Ⓒ Ⓓ Ⓔ   46 Ⓐ Ⓑ Ⓒ Ⓓ Ⓔ   68 Ⓐ Ⓑ Ⓒ Ⓓ Ⓔ

3 Ⓐ Ⓑ Ⓒ Ⓓ Ⓔ   25 Ⓐ Ⓑ Ⓒ Ⓓ Ⓔ   47 Ⓐ Ⓑ Ⓒ Ⓓ Ⓔ   69 Ⓐ Ⓑ Ⓒ Ⓓ Ⓔ

4 Ⓐ Ⓑ Ⓒ Ⓓ Ⓔ   26 Ⓐ Ⓑ Ⓒ Ⓓ Ⓔ   48 Ⓐ Ⓑ Ⓒ Ⓓ Ⓔ   70 Ⓐ Ⓑ Ⓒ Ⓓ Ⓔ

5 Ⓐ Ⓑ Ⓒ Ⓓ Ⓔ   27 Ⓐ Ⓑ Ⓒ Ⓓ Ⓔ   49 Ⓐ Ⓑ Ⓒ Ⓓ Ⓔ   71 Ⓐ Ⓑ Ⓒ Ⓓ Ⓔ

6 Ⓐ Ⓑ Ⓒ Ⓓ Ⓔ   28 Ⓐ Ⓑ Ⓒ Ⓓ Ⓔ   50 Ⓐ Ⓑ Ⓒ Ⓓ Ⓔ   72 Ⓐ Ⓑ Ⓒ Ⓓ Ⓔ

7 Ⓐ Ⓑ Ⓒ Ⓓ Ⓔ   29 Ⓐ Ⓑ Ⓒ Ⓓ Ⓔ   51 Ⓐ Ⓑ Ⓒ Ⓓ Ⓔ   73 Ⓐ Ⓑ Ⓒ Ⓓ Ⓔ

8 Ⓐ Ⓑ Ⓒ Ⓓ Ⓔ   30 Ⓐ Ⓑ Ⓒ Ⓓ Ⓔ   52 Ⓐ Ⓑ Ⓒ Ⓓ Ⓔ   74 Ⓐ Ⓑ Ⓒ Ⓓ Ⓔ

9 Ⓐ Ⓑ Ⓒ Ⓓ Ⓔ   31 Ⓐ Ⓑ Ⓒ Ⓓ Ⓔ   53 Ⓐ Ⓑ Ⓒ Ⓓ Ⓔ   75 Ⓐ Ⓑ Ⓒ Ⓓ Ⓔ

10 Ⓐ Ⓑ Ⓒ Ⓓ Ⓔ   32 Ⓐ Ⓑ Ⓒ Ⓓ Ⓔ   54 Ⓐ Ⓑ Ⓒ Ⓓ Ⓔ   76 Ⓐ Ⓑ Ⓒ Ⓓ Ⓔ

11 Ⓐ Ⓑ Ⓒ Ⓓ Ⓔ   33 Ⓐ Ⓑ Ⓒ Ⓓ Ⓔ   55 Ⓐ Ⓑ Ⓒ Ⓓ Ⓔ   77 Ⓐ Ⓑ Ⓒ Ⓓ Ⓔ

12 Ⓐ Ⓑ Ⓒ Ⓓ Ⓔ   34 Ⓐ Ⓑ Ⓒ Ⓓ Ⓔ   56 Ⓐ Ⓑ Ⓒ Ⓓ Ⓔ   78 Ⓐ Ⓑ Ⓒ Ⓓ Ⓔ

13 Ⓐ Ⓑ Ⓒ Ⓓ Ⓔ   35 Ⓐ Ⓑ Ⓒ Ⓓ Ⓔ   57 Ⓐ Ⓑ Ⓒ Ⓓ Ⓔ   79 Ⓐ Ⓑ Ⓒ Ⓓ Ⓔ

14 Ⓐ Ⓑ Ⓒ Ⓓ Ⓔ   36 Ⓐ Ⓑ Ⓒ Ⓓ Ⓔ   58 Ⓐ Ⓑ Ⓒ Ⓓ Ⓔ   80 Ⓐ Ⓑ Ⓒ Ⓓ Ⓔ

15 Ⓐ Ⓑ Ⓒ Ⓓ Ⓔ   37 Ⓐ Ⓑ Ⓒ Ⓓ Ⓔ   59 Ⓐ Ⓑ Ⓒ Ⓓ Ⓔ   81 Ⓐ Ⓑ Ⓒ Ⓓ Ⓔ

16 Ⓐ Ⓑ Ⓒ Ⓓ Ⓔ   38 Ⓐ Ⓑ Ⓒ Ⓓ Ⓔ   60 Ⓐ Ⓑ Ⓒ Ⓓ Ⓔ   82 Ⓐ Ⓑ Ⓒ Ⓓ Ⓔ

17 Ⓐ Ⓑ Ⓒ Ⓓ Ⓔ   39 Ⓐ Ⓑ Ⓒ Ⓓ Ⓔ   61 Ⓐ Ⓑ Ⓒ Ⓓ Ⓔ   83 Ⓐ Ⓑ Ⓒ Ⓓ Ⓔ

18 Ⓐ Ⓑ Ⓒ Ⓓ Ⓔ   40 Ⓐ Ⓑ Ⓒ Ⓓ Ⓔ   62 Ⓐ Ⓑ Ⓒ Ⓓ Ⓔ   84 Ⓐ Ⓑ Ⓒ Ⓓ Ⓔ

19 Ⓐ Ⓑ Ⓒ Ⓓ Ⓔ   41 Ⓐ Ⓑ Ⓒ Ⓓ Ⓔ   63 Ⓐ Ⓑ Ⓒ Ⓓ Ⓔ   85 Ⓐ Ⓑ Ⓒ Ⓓ Ⓔ

20 Ⓐ Ⓑ Ⓒ Ⓓ Ⓔ   42 Ⓐ Ⓑ Ⓒ Ⓓ Ⓔ   64 Ⓐ Ⓑ Ⓒ Ⓓ Ⓔ   86 Ⓐ Ⓑ Ⓒ Ⓓ Ⓔ

21 Ⓐ Ⓑ Ⓒ Ⓓ Ⓔ   43 Ⓐ Ⓑ Ⓒ Ⓓ Ⓔ   65 Ⓐ Ⓑ Ⓒ Ⓓ Ⓔ   87 Ⓐ Ⓑ Ⓒ Ⓓ Ⓔ

22 Ⓐ Ⓑ Ⓒ Ⓓ Ⓔ   44 Ⓐ Ⓑ Ⓒ Ⓓ Ⓔ   66 Ⓐ Ⓑ Ⓒ Ⓓ Ⓔ   88 Ⓐ Ⓑ Ⓒ Ⓓ Ⓔ

Score Sheet

ADDRESS CHECKING: Your score on the Address Checking section is based on the number of questions you answered correctly minus the number of questions you answered incorrectly. To determine your score, subtract the number of wrong answers from the number of correct answers.

Number Right   –   Number Wrong   =   Raw Score

_____   –   _____.   =   _____

MEMORY FOR ADDRESSES: Your score on the Memory for Addresses section is based upon the number of questions you answered correctly minus one-fourth of the questions you answered incorrectly (number wrong divided by 4). Calculate this now:

Number Wrong ÷ 4 = _____.

Number Right   –   Number Wrong ÷ 4   =   Raw Score

_____   –   _____   =   _____

NUMBER SERIES: Your score on the Number Series section is based only on the number of questions you answered correctly. Wrong answers do not count against you.

Number Right   =   Raw Score

_____   =   _____

FOLLOWING ORAL INSTRUCTIONS: Your score on the Following Oral Instructions section is based only upon the number of questions you marked correctly on the answer sheet. The worksheet is not scored, and wrong answers on the answer sheet do not count against you.

Number Right   =   Raw Score

_____   =   _____

TOTAL SCORE: To find your total raw score, add together the raw scores for each section of the exam.

Address Checking Score   _____

\+

Memory for Addresses Score   _____

\+

Number Series Score   _____

\+

Following Oral Instructions Score   _____

=   _____

Total Raw Score   _____

Self-Evaluation Chart

Calculate your raw score for each test as shown above. Then check to see where your score falls on the scale from Poor to Excellent. Lightly shade in the boxes in which your scores fall.

Part	Excellent	Good	Average	Fair	Poor
Address Checking	80–95	65–79	50–64	35–49	1–34
Memory for Addresses	75–88	60–74	45–59	30–44	1–29
Number Series	21–24	18–20	14–17	11–13	1–10
Following Oral Instructions	27–31	23–26	19–22	14–18	1–13

PRELIMINARY MODEL EXAM

Part A—Address Checking
SAMPLE QUESTIONS

You will be allowed three minutes to read the directions and answer the five sample questions that follow. On the actual test, however, you will have only 6 minutes to answer 95 questions, so see how quickly you can compare addresses and still get the correct answer.

Directions: Each question consists of two addresses. If the two addresses are alike in EVERY way, mark A on your answer sheet. If the two addresses are different in ANY way, mark D on your answer sheet.

1 ... 3380 Federal Street	3380 S Federal Street
2 ... 1618 Highland Way	1816 Highland Way
3 ... Greenvale NY 11548	Greenvale NY 11548
4 ... Ft. Collins CO 80523	Ft. Collings CO 80523
5 ... 7214 NW 83rd St	7214 NW 83rd St

```
+-------------------------------+    +-------------------------------+
|     SAMPLE ANSWER SHEET       |    |      CORRECT ANSWERS          |
|                               |    |                               |
|  1. (A)(D)     4. (A)(D)      |    |  1. (A)●     4. (A)●           |
|  2. (A)(D)     5. (A)(D)      |    |  2. (A)●     5. ●(D)           |
|  3. (A)(D)                    |    |  3. ●(D)                       |
+-------------------------------+    +-------------------------------+
```

Address Checking

Time: 6 Minutes • 95 Questions

Directions: For each question, compare the address in the left column with the address in the right column. If the two addresses are ALIKE IN EVERY WAY, blacken space A on your answer sheet. If the two addresses are DIFFERENT IN ANY WAY, blacken space D on your answer sheet. Correct answers for this test are on page 61.

1...197 Wonderview Dr NW	197 Wonderview Dr NW
2...243 S Capistano Ave	234 S Capistrano Ave
3...4300 Las Pillas Rd	4300 Las Pillas Rd
4...5551 N Ramara Ave	5551 N Ramara St
5...Walden Col 80480	Waldon Col 80480
6...2200 E Dunnington St	2200 E Dowington St
7...2700 Helena Way	2700 Helena Way
8...3968 S Zeno Ave	3968 S Zemo Ave
9...14011 Costilla Ave NE	14011 Costilla Ave SE
10...1899 N Dearborn Dr	1899 N Dearborn Dr
11...8911 Scranton Way	8911 Scranton Way
12...365 Liverpool St	356 Liverpool St
13...1397 Lewiston Pl	1297 Lewiston Pl
14...4588 Crystal Way	4588 Crystal Rd
15...Muscle Shoals AL 35660	Muscle Shoals AL 35660
16...988 Larkin Johson Ave SE	988 Larkin Johnson Ave SE
17...5501 Greenville Blvd NE	5501 Greenview Blvd NE
18...7133 N Baranmor Pky	7133 N Baranmor Pky
19...10500 Montana Rd	10500 Montana Rd
20...4769 E Kalispell Dr	4769 E Kalispell Cir
21...Daytona Beach Fla 32016	Daytona Beach FL 32016
22...2227 W 94th Ave	2272 W 94th Ave
23...6399 E Ponce De Leon St	6399 E Ponce De Leon Ct
24...20800 N Rainbow Pl	20800 N Rainbow Pl
25...Sasser GA 31785	Sasser GA 31785
26...Washington DC 20018	Washington DC 20013
27...6500 Milwaukee NE	6500 Milwaukee SE
28...1300 Strasburg Dr	1300 Strasburg Dr

29…Burnettsville IN 47926	Bornettsville IN 47926
30…1594 S Frontage St	1594 S Frontage Ave
31…37099 Oliphant Ln	37909 Oliphant Ln
32…2248 Avonsdale Cir NW	2248 Avonsdale Cir NE
33…1733 Norlander Dr SE	1733 Norlander Dr SW
34…15469 W Oxalida Dr	15469 W Oxalido Dr
35…4192 E Commonwealth Ave	4192 E Commonwealth Ave
36…Kingsfield Maine 04947	Kingsfield Maine 04947
37…246 East Ramsdell Rd	246 East Ramsdale Rd
38…8456 Vina Del Maro Blvd	8456 Vina Del Maro Blvd
39…6688 N 26th Street	6888 N 26th Street
40…1477 Woodrow Wilson Blvd	1477 Woodrow Wilson Blvd
41…3724 S 18th Ave	3724 S 18th Ave
42…11454 S Lake Maggiore Blvd	11454 S Lake Maggiore Blvd
43…4832 N Bougainnvilla Ave	4832 N Bougainnvillia Ave
44…3713 Coffee Pot Riviera	3773 Coffee Pot Riviera
45…2800 S Freemont Ter	2800 S Freemond Ter
46…3654 S Urbane Dr	3654 S Urbane Cir
47…1408 Oklahoma Ave NE	1408 Oklahoma Ave NE
48…6201 Meadowland Ln	6201 Meadowlawn Ln
49…5799 S Augusta Ln	15799 S Augusta Ln
50…5115 Winchester Rd	5115 Westchester Rd
51…4611 N Kendall Pl	4611 N Kenall Pl
52…17045 Dormieone Cir	17045 Dormieone Cir
53…3349 Palma Del Mar Blvd	3345 Palma Del Mar Blvd
54…13211 E 182nd Ave	12311 E 182nd Ave
55…Evansville WY 82636	Evansville WI 82636
56…6198 N Albritton Rd	6198 N Albretton Rd
57…11230 Twinflower Cir	11230 Twintower Cir
58…6191 Lockett Station Rd	6191 Lockett Station Rd
59…1587 Vanderbilt Dr N	1587 Vanderbilt Dr S
60…Ontarioville IL 60103	Ontarioville IL 60103
61…4204 Bridgeton Ave	4204 Bridgeton Ave
62…31215 N Emerald Dr	31215 N Emerald Cir

63...4601 N Peniman Ave	4601 N Peniman Ave
64...3782 SE Verrazanna Bay	3782 SE Verrazana Bay
65...2766 N Thunderbird Ct	2766 N Thunderbird Ct
66...2166 N Elmorado Ct	2166 N Eldorado Ct
67...10538 Innsbruck Ln	1058 Innsbruck Ln
68...888 Lonesome Rd	8888 Lonesome Rd
69...4023 N Brainbridge Ave	4023 N Brainbridge Ave
70...3000 E Roberta Rd	30000 E Roberta Rd
71...Quenemo KS 66528	Quenemo KS 66528
72...13845 Donahoo St	13345 Donahoo St
73...10466 Gertrude NE	10466 Gertrude NE
74...2733 N 105th Ave	2733 S 105th Ave
75...3100 N Wyandotte Cir	3100 N Wyandotte Ave
76...11796 Summittcrest Dr	11769 Summittcrest Dr
77...Viburnum Miss 65566	Viburnom Miss 65566
78...9334 Kindleberger Rd	9334 Kindleberger Road
79...4801 Armourdale Pky	8401 Armourdale Pky
80...9392 Northrup Ave	9392 Northrop Ave
81...11736 Rottinghaus Rd	11736 Rottinghaus Rd
82...3878 Flammang Dr	3878 Flammang Dr
83...2101 Johnstontown Way	2101 Johnsontown Way
84...1177 Ghentwoodrow St	1177 Ghentwoodrow Ct
85...888 Onadaga Ct	888 Onadaga Ct
86...3205 N Rastetter Ave	3205 N Rastetter Ave
87...1144 Yellowsands Dr NE	1144 Yellowsands Dr NW
88...3197 Clerkenwell Ct	3197 Clerkenwell Ct
89...3021 Pemaquid Way	3210 Pemaquid Way
90...1398 Angelina Rd	1398 Angelino Rd
91...4331 NW Zoeller Ave	4881 NW Zoeller Ave
92...1805 Jeassamine Ln	1805 Jassamine Ln
93...14411 Bellemeade Ave	14411 Bellemeade Ave
94...Noquochoke MA 02790	Noguochoke MA 02790
95...11601 Hagamann Cir	11601 Hagamann Ct

END OF ADDRESS CHECKING

Part B—Memory for Addresses

SAMPLE QUESTIONS

The sample questions for this part are based upon the addresses in the five boxes below. Your task is to mark on your answer sheet the letter of the box in which each address belongs. You will have five minutes now to study the locations of the addresses. Cover the boxes and try to mark the location of the sample questions. You may look back at the boxes if you cannot yet mark the address locations from memory.

The exam itself provides three practice sessions before the question set that really counts. Practice I and Practice III supply you with the boxes and permit you to refer to them if necessary. Practice II and the Memory for Addresses test themselves do not permit you to look at the boxes. The test itself is based on memory.

A	B	C	D	E
8300–8699 Ball	9100–9799 Ball	9800–9999 Ball	8200–8299 Ball	8700–9099 Ball
Meadow	Swing	Winter	Checker	Ford
9800–9999 Wren	8700–9099 Wren	8300–8699 Wren	9100–9799 Wren	8200–8299 Wren
Denim	Vapor	Artisan	Zenith	Hammock
8200–8299 Slug	9800–9999 Slug	8700–9099 Slug	8300–8699 Slug	9100–9799 Slug

1. 8700–9099 Wren

2. 9100–9799 Slug

3. Denim

4. 9800–9999 Ball

5. Checker

6. Hammock

7. 9800–9999 Slug

8. 8300–8699 Ball

9. 8200–8299 Wren

10. Vapor

11. 8700–9099 Slug

12. Artisan

13. 8200–8299 Ball

14. 9100–9799 Wren

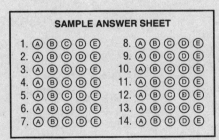

PRACTICE FOR MEMORY FOR ADDRESSES

Directions: *The five boxes below are labeled A, B, C, D, and E. In each box are three sets of number spans with names and two names that are not associated with numbers. In the next THREE MINUTES, you must try to memorize the box location of each name and number span. The position of a name or number span within its box is not important. You need only remember the letter of the box in which the item is to be found. You will use these names and numbers to answer three sets of practice questions that are NOT scored and one actual test that IS scored. Correct answers are on pages 62 and 63.*

A	B	C	D	E
8300–8699 Ball	9100–9799 Ball	9800–9999 Ball	8200–8299 Ball	8700–9099 Ball
Meadow	Swing	Winter	Checker	Ford
9800–9999 Wren	8700–9099 Wren	8300–8699 Wren	9100–9799 Wren	8200–8299 Wren
Denim	Vapor	Artisan	Zenith	Hammock
8200–8299 Slug	9800–9999 Slug	8700–9099 Slug	8300–8699 Slug	9100–9799 Slug

PRACTICE I

Directions: *Use the next THREE MINUTES to mark on the answer sheet at the end of Practice I the letter of the box in which each item that follows is to be found. Try to mark each item without looking back at the boxes. If, however, you get stuck, you may refer to the boxes during this practice exercise. If you find that you must look at the boxes, try to memorize as you do so. This test is for practice only. It will not be scored.*

1. 9100–9799 Wren
2. 8700–9099 Slug
3. Winter
4. 8700–9099 Ball
5. 9800–9999 Wren
6. 9800–9999 Slug
7. 8700–9099 Wren
8. Meadow
9. Vapor
10. 9100–9799 Ball
11. 9100–9799 Slug
12. 8700–9099 Wren
13. 9800–9999 Ball
14. 8200–8299 Wren
15. Checker
16. Hammock
17. 8300–8699 Ball

18. 9100–9799 Wren
19. 8300–8699 Slug
20. 8700–9099 Wren
21. 8200–8299 Slug
22. Ford
23. Denim
24. 9800–9999 Wren
25. 9100–9799 Ball
26. Artisan
27. 8700–9099 Ball
28. 8200–8299 Ball
29. 8200–8299 Wren
30. Zenith
31. Vapor
32. Meadow
33. 8700–9099 Slug
34. 9800–9999 Slug

35. 9800–9999 Wren
36. Winter
37. Swing
38. 9100–9799 Slug
39. 9800–9999 Ball
40. 8300–8699 Wren
41. 8300–8699 Ball
42. Swing
43. Zenith
44. 9100–9799 Slug
45. 8700–9099 Ball
46. Checker
47. 8300–8699 Wren
48. Vapor
49. 8200–8299 Slug
50. 9800–9999 Wren
51. 9100–9799 Wren

52. Artisan

53. Swing

54. Hammock

55. 8300–8699 Slug

56. 8300–8699 Ball

57. 9800–9999 Ball

58. 8700–9099 Slug

59. Meadow

60. Denim

61. 9100–9799 Ball

62. 8200–8299 Ball

63. Ford

64. 9100–9799 Slug

65. 9800–9999 Slug

66. Winter

67. Zenith

68. 8700–9099 Wren

69. 8200–8299 Wren

70. Checker

71. 8700–9099 Ball

72. 8300–8699 Slug

73. 9100–9799 Wren

74. 9800–9999 Ball

75. Meadow

76. 8700–9099 Wren

77. 8300–8699 Ball

78. 9100–9799 Slug

79. Hammock

80. Vapor

81. 9800–9999 Slug

82. 8200–8299 Wren

83. Artisan

84. Swing

85. 9800–9999 Ball

86. 9100–9799 Wren

87. 8200–8299 Slug

88. 8700–9099 Ball

PRACTICE I ANSWER SHEET

1 Ⓐ Ⓑ Ⓒ Ⓓ Ⓔ   23 Ⓐ Ⓑ Ⓒ Ⓓ Ⓔ   45 Ⓐ Ⓑ Ⓒ Ⓓ Ⓔ   67 Ⓐ Ⓑ Ⓒ Ⓓ Ⓔ

2 Ⓐ Ⓑ Ⓒ Ⓓ Ⓔ   24 Ⓐ Ⓑ Ⓒ Ⓓ Ⓔ   46 Ⓐ Ⓑ Ⓒ Ⓓ Ⓔ   68 Ⓐ Ⓑ Ⓒ Ⓓ Ⓔ

3 Ⓐ Ⓑ Ⓒ Ⓓ Ⓔ   25 Ⓐ Ⓑ Ⓒ Ⓓ Ⓔ   47 Ⓐ Ⓑ Ⓒ Ⓓ Ⓔ   69 Ⓐ Ⓑ Ⓒ Ⓓ Ⓔ

4 Ⓐ Ⓑ Ⓒ Ⓓ Ⓔ   26 Ⓐ Ⓑ Ⓒ Ⓓ Ⓔ   48 Ⓐ Ⓑ Ⓒ Ⓓ Ⓔ   70 Ⓐ Ⓑ Ⓒ Ⓓ Ⓔ

5 Ⓐ Ⓑ Ⓒ Ⓓ Ⓔ   27 Ⓐ Ⓑ Ⓒ Ⓓ Ⓔ   49 Ⓐ Ⓑ Ⓒ Ⓓ Ⓔ   71 Ⓐ Ⓑ Ⓒ Ⓓ Ⓔ

6 Ⓐ Ⓑ Ⓒ Ⓓ Ⓔ   28 Ⓐ Ⓑ Ⓒ Ⓓ Ⓔ   50 Ⓐ Ⓑ Ⓒ Ⓓ Ⓔ   72 Ⓐ Ⓑ Ⓒ Ⓓ Ⓔ

7 Ⓐ Ⓑ Ⓒ Ⓓ Ⓔ   29 Ⓐ Ⓑ Ⓒ Ⓓ Ⓔ   51 Ⓐ Ⓑ Ⓒ Ⓓ Ⓔ   73 Ⓐ Ⓑ Ⓒ Ⓓ Ⓔ

8 Ⓐ Ⓑ Ⓒ Ⓓ Ⓔ   30 Ⓐ Ⓑ Ⓒ Ⓓ Ⓔ   52 Ⓐ Ⓑ Ⓒ Ⓓ Ⓔ   74 Ⓐ Ⓑ Ⓒ Ⓓ Ⓔ

9 Ⓐ Ⓑ Ⓒ Ⓓ Ⓔ   31 Ⓐ Ⓑ Ⓒ Ⓓ Ⓔ   53 Ⓐ Ⓑ Ⓒ Ⓓ Ⓔ   75 Ⓐ Ⓑ Ⓒ Ⓓ Ⓔ

10 Ⓐ Ⓑ Ⓒ Ⓓ Ⓔ   32 Ⓐ Ⓑ Ⓒ Ⓓ Ⓔ   54 Ⓐ Ⓑ Ⓒ Ⓓ Ⓔ   76 Ⓐ Ⓑ Ⓒ Ⓓ Ⓔ

11 Ⓐ Ⓑ Ⓒ Ⓓ Ⓔ   33 Ⓐ Ⓑ Ⓒ Ⓓ Ⓔ   55 Ⓐ Ⓑ Ⓒ Ⓓ Ⓔ   77 Ⓐ Ⓑ Ⓒ Ⓓ Ⓔ

12 Ⓐ Ⓑ Ⓒ Ⓓ Ⓔ   34 Ⓐ Ⓑ Ⓒ Ⓓ Ⓔ   56 Ⓐ Ⓑ Ⓒ Ⓓ Ⓔ   78 Ⓐ Ⓑ Ⓒ Ⓓ Ⓔ

13 Ⓐ Ⓑ Ⓒ Ⓓ Ⓔ   35 Ⓐ Ⓑ Ⓒ Ⓓ Ⓔ   57 Ⓐ Ⓑ Ⓒ Ⓓ Ⓔ   79 Ⓐ Ⓑ Ⓒ Ⓓ Ⓔ

14 Ⓐ Ⓑ Ⓒ Ⓓ Ⓔ   36 Ⓐ Ⓑ Ⓒ Ⓓ Ⓔ   58 Ⓐ Ⓑ Ⓒ Ⓓ Ⓔ   80 Ⓐ Ⓑ Ⓒ Ⓓ Ⓔ

15 Ⓐ Ⓑ Ⓒ Ⓓ Ⓔ   37 Ⓐ Ⓑ Ⓒ Ⓓ Ⓔ   59 Ⓐ Ⓑ Ⓒ Ⓓ Ⓔ   81 Ⓐ Ⓑ Ⓒ Ⓓ Ⓔ

16 Ⓐ Ⓑ Ⓒ Ⓓ Ⓔ   38 Ⓐ Ⓑ Ⓒ Ⓓ Ⓔ   60 Ⓐ Ⓑ Ⓒ Ⓓ Ⓔ   82 Ⓐ Ⓑ Ⓒ Ⓓ Ⓔ

17 Ⓐ Ⓑ Ⓒ Ⓓ Ⓔ   39 Ⓐ Ⓑ Ⓒ Ⓓ Ⓔ   61 Ⓐ Ⓑ Ⓒ Ⓓ Ⓔ   83 Ⓐ Ⓑ Ⓒ Ⓓ Ⓔ

18 Ⓐ Ⓑ Ⓒ Ⓓ Ⓔ   40 Ⓐ Ⓑ Ⓒ Ⓓ Ⓔ   62 Ⓐ Ⓑ Ⓒ Ⓓ Ⓔ   84 Ⓐ Ⓑ Ⓒ Ⓓ Ⓔ

19 Ⓐ Ⓑ Ⓒ Ⓓ Ⓔ   41 Ⓐ Ⓑ Ⓒ Ⓓ Ⓔ   63 Ⓐ Ⓑ Ⓒ Ⓓ Ⓔ   85 Ⓐ Ⓑ Ⓒ Ⓓ Ⓔ

20 Ⓐ Ⓑ Ⓒ Ⓓ Ⓔ   42 Ⓐ Ⓑ Ⓒ Ⓓ Ⓔ   64 Ⓐ Ⓑ Ⓒ Ⓓ Ⓔ   86 Ⓐ Ⓑ Ⓒ Ⓓ Ⓔ

21 Ⓐ Ⓑ Ⓒ Ⓓ Ⓔ   43 Ⓐ Ⓑ Ⓒ Ⓓ Ⓔ   65 Ⓐ Ⓑ Ⓒ Ⓓ Ⓔ   87 Ⓐ Ⓑ Ⓒ Ⓓ Ⓔ

22 Ⓐ Ⓑ Ⓒ Ⓓ Ⓔ   44 Ⓐ Ⓑ Ⓒ Ⓓ Ⓔ   66 Ⓐ Ⓑ Ⓒ Ⓓ Ⓔ   88 Ⓐ Ⓑ Ⓒ Ⓓ Ⓔ

PRACTICE II

Directions: The next 88 questions constitute another practice exercise. Mark your answers on the Practice II answer sheet. Again, the time limit is THREE MINUTES. This time, however, you must NOT look at the boxes while answering the questions. You must rely on your memory in marking the box location of each item. This practice test will not be scored.

1. 8200–8299 Ball
2. 8300–8699 Wren
3. 9800–9999 Slug
4. Hammock
5. Meadow
6. 8700–9099 Ball
7. 8700–9099 Slug
8. 9800–9999 Wren
9. Zenith
10. Swing
11. 8200–8299 Wren
12. 8200–8299 Slug
13. 8300–8699 Slug
14. 9100–9799 Ball
15. Ford
16. Checker
17. Artisan
18. 8300–8699 Ball
19. 8700–9099 Wren
20. 9800–9999 Wren
21. Vapor
22. Meadow
23. 8200–8299 Ball
24. Winter
25. Ford
26. 8300–8699 Ball
27. 8700–9099 Wren
28. 8700–9099 Slug
29. Zenith
30. Checker

31. 8700–9099 Ball
32. 9100–9799 Wren
33. 9800–9999 Slug
34. 8200–8299 Slug
35. Denim
36. Winter
37. Hammock
38. 9100–9799 Slug
39. 9100–9799 Ball
40. 9800–9999 Ball
41. Artisan
42. Meadow
43. 9800–9999 Wren
44. 8300–8699 Wren
45. 8300–8699 Slug
46. 8300–8699 Ball
47. Swing
48. Vapor
49. 9800–9999 Ball
50. 9100–9799 Wren
51. 9100–9799 Slug
52. 8700–9099 Wren
53. 8300–8699 Ball
54. Swing
55. Zenith
56. Hammock
57. Denim
58. 8700–9099 Ball
59. 8300–8699 Slug
60. 9800–9999 Slug

61. 9800–9999 Wren
62. 8700–9099 Slug
63. Meadow
64. 8200–8299 Ball
65. 9100–9799 Ball
66. Ford
67. 8200–8299 Wren
68. 8300–8699 Wren
69. 8300–8699 Slug
70. Checker
71. Artisan
72. 8700–9099 Wren
73. 8200–8299 Slug
74. 8700–9099 Slug
75. Winter
76. Vapor
77. 8300–8699 Ball
78. 8700–9099 Ball
79. 8700–9099 Slug
80. Vapor
81. Swing
82. 9800–9999 Wren
83. 9800–9999 BAll
84. 8300–8699 Wren
85. 8300–8699 Ball
86. 8300–8699 Slug
87. Hammock
88. Denim

PRACTICE II ANSWER SHEET

1 Ⓐ Ⓑ Ⓒ Ⓓ Ⓔ	23 Ⓐ Ⓑ Ⓒ Ⓓ Ⓔ	45 Ⓐ Ⓑ Ⓒ Ⓓ Ⓔ	67 Ⓐ Ⓑ Ⓒ Ⓓ Ⓔ
2 Ⓐ Ⓑ Ⓒ Ⓓ Ⓔ	24 Ⓐ Ⓑ Ⓒ Ⓓ Ⓔ	46 Ⓐ Ⓑ Ⓒ Ⓓ Ⓔ	68 Ⓐ Ⓑ Ⓒ Ⓓ Ⓔ
3 Ⓐ Ⓑ Ⓒ Ⓓ Ⓔ	25 Ⓐ Ⓑ Ⓒ Ⓓ Ⓔ	47 Ⓐ Ⓑ Ⓒ Ⓓ Ⓔ	69 Ⓐ Ⓑ Ⓒ Ⓓ Ⓔ
4 Ⓐ Ⓑ Ⓒ Ⓓ Ⓔ	26 Ⓐ Ⓑ Ⓒ Ⓓ Ⓔ	48 Ⓐ Ⓑ Ⓒ Ⓓ Ⓔ	70 Ⓐ Ⓑ Ⓒ Ⓓ Ⓔ
5 Ⓐ Ⓑ Ⓒ Ⓓ Ⓔ	27 Ⓐ Ⓑ Ⓒ Ⓓ Ⓔ	49 Ⓐ Ⓑ Ⓒ Ⓓ Ⓔ	71 Ⓐ Ⓑ Ⓒ Ⓓ Ⓔ
6 Ⓐ Ⓑ Ⓒ Ⓓ Ⓔ	28 Ⓐ Ⓑ Ⓒ Ⓓ Ⓔ	50 Ⓐ Ⓑ Ⓒ Ⓓ Ⓔ	72 Ⓐ Ⓑ Ⓒ Ⓓ Ⓔ
7 Ⓐ Ⓑ Ⓒ Ⓓ Ⓔ	29 Ⓐ Ⓑ Ⓒ Ⓓ Ⓔ	51 Ⓐ Ⓑ Ⓒ Ⓓ Ⓔ	73 Ⓐ Ⓑ Ⓒ Ⓓ Ⓔ
8 Ⓐ Ⓑ Ⓒ Ⓓ Ⓔ	30 Ⓐ Ⓑ Ⓒ Ⓓ Ⓔ	52 Ⓐ Ⓑ Ⓒ Ⓓ Ⓔ	74 Ⓐ Ⓑ Ⓒ Ⓓ Ⓔ
9 Ⓐ Ⓑ Ⓒ Ⓓ Ⓔ	31 Ⓐ Ⓑ Ⓒ Ⓓ Ⓔ	53 Ⓐ Ⓑ Ⓒ Ⓓ Ⓔ	75 Ⓐ Ⓑ Ⓒ Ⓓ Ⓔ
10 Ⓐ Ⓑ Ⓒ Ⓓ Ⓔ	32 Ⓐ Ⓑ Ⓒ Ⓓ Ⓔ	54 Ⓐ Ⓑ Ⓒ Ⓓ Ⓔ	76 Ⓐ Ⓑ Ⓒ Ⓓ
11 Ⓐ Ⓑ Ⓒ Ⓓ Ⓔ	33 Ⓐ Ⓑ Ⓒ Ⓓ Ⓔ	55 Ⓐ Ⓑ Ⓒ Ⓓ Ⓔ	77 Ⓐ Ⓑ Ⓒ Ⓓ Ⓔ
12 Ⓐ Ⓑ Ⓒ Ⓓ Ⓔ	34 Ⓐ Ⓑ Ⓒ Ⓓ Ⓔ	56 Ⓐ Ⓑ Ⓒ Ⓓ Ⓔ	78 Ⓐ Ⓑ Ⓒ Ⓓ Ⓔ
13 Ⓐ Ⓑ Ⓒ Ⓓ Ⓔ	35 Ⓐ Ⓑ Ⓒ Ⓓ Ⓔ	57 Ⓐ Ⓑ Ⓒ Ⓓ Ⓔ	79 Ⓐ Ⓑ Ⓒ Ⓓ Ⓔ
14 Ⓐ Ⓑ Ⓒ Ⓓ Ⓔ	36 Ⓐ Ⓑ Ⓒ Ⓓ Ⓔ	58 Ⓐ Ⓑ Ⓒ Ⓓ Ⓔ	80 Ⓐ Ⓑ Ⓒ Ⓓ Ⓔ
15 Ⓐ Ⓑ Ⓒ Ⓓ Ⓔ	37 Ⓐ Ⓑ Ⓒ Ⓓ Ⓔ	59 Ⓐ Ⓑ Ⓒ Ⓓ Ⓔ	81 Ⓐ Ⓑ Ⓒ Ⓓ Ⓔ
16 Ⓐ Ⓑ Ⓒ Ⓓ Ⓔ	38 Ⓐ Ⓑ Ⓒ Ⓓ Ⓔ	60 Ⓐ Ⓑ Ⓒ Ⓓ Ⓔ	82 Ⓐ Ⓑ Ⓒ Ⓓ Ⓔ
17 Ⓐ Ⓑ Ⓒ Ⓓ Ⓔ	39 Ⓐ Ⓑ Ⓒ Ⓓ Ⓔ	61 Ⓐ Ⓑ Ⓒ Ⓓ Ⓔ	83 Ⓐ Ⓑ Ⓒ Ⓓ Ⓔ
18 Ⓐ Ⓑ Ⓒ Ⓓ Ⓔ	40 Ⓐ Ⓑ Ⓒ Ⓓ Ⓔ	62 Ⓐ Ⓑ Ⓒ Ⓓ Ⓔ	84 Ⓐ Ⓑ Ⓒ Ⓓ Ⓔ
19 Ⓐ Ⓑ Ⓒ Ⓓ Ⓔ	41 Ⓐ Ⓑ Ⓒ Ⓓ Ⓔ	63 Ⓐ Ⓑ Ⓒ Ⓓ Ⓔ	85 Ⓐ Ⓑ Ⓒ Ⓓ Ⓔ
20 Ⓐ Ⓑ Ⓒ Ⓓ Ⓔ	42 Ⓐ Ⓑ Ⓒ Ⓓ Ⓔ	64 Ⓐ Ⓑ Ⓒ Ⓓ Ⓔ	86 Ⓐ Ⓑ Ⓒ Ⓓ Ⓔ
21 Ⓐ Ⓑ Ⓒ Ⓓ Ⓔ	43 Ⓐ Ⓑ Ⓒ Ⓓ Ⓔ	65 Ⓐ Ⓑ Ⓒ Ⓓ Ⓔ	87 Ⓐ Ⓑ Ⓒ Ⓓ Ⓔ
22 Ⓐ Ⓑ Ⓒ Ⓓ Ⓔ	44 Ⓐ Ⓑ Ⓒ Ⓓ Ⓔ	66 Ⓐ Ⓑ Ⓒ Ⓓ Ⓔ	88 Ⓐ Ⓑ Ⓒ Ⓓ Ⓔ

PRACTICE III

Directions: The names and addresses are repeated for you in the boxes below. Each name and each number span is in the same box in which you found it in the original set. You will now be allowed FIVE MINUTES to study the locations again. Do your best to memorize the letter of the box in which each item is located. This is your last chance to see the boxes.

A	B	C	D	E
8300–8699 Ball Meadow 9800–9999 Wren Denim 8200–8299 Slug	9100–9799 Ball Swing 8700–9099 Wren Vapor 9800–9999 Slug	9800–9999 Ball Winter 8300–8699 Wren Artisan 8700–9099 Slug	8200–8299 Ball Checker 9100–9799 Wren Zenith 8300–8699 Slug	8700–9099 Ball Ford 8200–8299 Wren Hammock 9100–9799 Slug

Directions: This is your last practice test. Mark the location of each of the 88 items on the Practice III answer sheet. You will have FIVE MINUTES to answer these questions. Do NOT look back at the boxes. This practice test will not be scored.

1. 8200–8299 Ball
2. 9100–9799 Wren
3. 8300–8699 Slug
4. 8700–9099 Wren
5. Denim
6. Ford
7. 8300–8699 Ball
8. 9100–9799 Slug
9. 8200–8299 Slug
10. Meadow
11. Zenith
12. 8700–9099 Slug
13. 9800–9999 Ball
14. 9100–9799 Ball
15. 8700–9099 Wren
16. 9100–9799 Slug
17. 9100–9799 Ball
18. 9100–9799 Wren
19. Artisan
20. Vapor
21. 8300–8699 Wren
22. Meadow

23. 9800–9999 Slug
24. 8700–9099 Wren
25. 8700–9099 Ball
26. Winter
27. Denim
28. 8200–8299 Ball
29. 8300–8699 Slug
30. Hammock
31. Ford
32. 8300–8699 Ball
33. 8700–9099 Wren
34. 8700–9099 Slug
35. Meadow
36. Vapor
37. 8700–9099 Ball
38. 9100–9799 Wren
39. 9800–9999 Ball
40. 9800–9999 Slug
41. Hammock
42. Winter
43. Swing
44. 9100–9799 Ball

45. 9100–9799 Slug
46. 8300–8699 Wren
47. 8200–8299 Wren
48. Ford
49. Zenith
50. 8200–8299 Slug
51. 8300–8699 Slug
52. Denim
53. 8200–8299 Ball
54. 9800–9999 Wren
55. Artisan
56. Checker
57. 9100–9799 Slug
58. 9700–9799 Ball
59. 8200–8299 Wren
60. 8300–8699 Wren
61. 9800–9999 Ball
62. 8200–8299 Wren
63. 8200–8299 Slug
64. 8700–9099 Wren
65. Hammock
66. Zenith

67. 9100–9799 Ball

68. 9800–9999 Slug

69. 8300–8699 Ball

70. 8300–8699 Wren

71. Denim

72. Meadow

73. 9800–9999 Wren

74. 8200–8299 Ball

75. 8300–8699 Slug

76. Checker

77. Winter

78. Vapor

79. 9100–9799 Slug

80. 9100–9799 Wren

81. 8700–9099 Ball

82. 8700–9099 Slug

83. Swing

84. Artisan

85. Ford

86. 9800–9999 Ball

87. 8200–8299 Wren

88. 8300–8699 Ball

PRACTICE III ANSWER SHEET

1 Ⓐ Ⓑ Ⓒ Ⓓ Ⓔ   23 Ⓐ Ⓑ Ⓒ Ⓓ Ⓔ   45 Ⓐ Ⓑ Ⓒ Ⓓ Ⓔ   67 Ⓐ Ⓑ Ⓒ Ⓓ Ⓔ

2 Ⓐ Ⓑ Ⓒ Ⓓ Ⓔ   24 Ⓐ Ⓑ Ⓒ Ⓓ Ⓔ   46 Ⓐ Ⓑ Ⓒ Ⓓ Ⓔ   68 Ⓐ Ⓑ Ⓒ Ⓓ Ⓔ

3 Ⓐ Ⓑ Ⓒ Ⓓ Ⓔ   25 Ⓐ Ⓑ Ⓒ Ⓓ Ⓔ   47 Ⓐ Ⓑ Ⓒ Ⓓ Ⓔ   69 Ⓐ Ⓑ Ⓒ Ⓓ Ⓔ

4 Ⓐ Ⓑ Ⓒ Ⓓ Ⓔ   26 Ⓐ Ⓑ Ⓒ Ⓓ Ⓔ   48 Ⓐ Ⓑ Ⓒ Ⓓ Ⓔ   70 Ⓐ Ⓑ Ⓒ Ⓓ Ⓔ

5 Ⓐ Ⓑ Ⓒ Ⓓ Ⓔ   27 Ⓐ Ⓑ Ⓒ Ⓓ Ⓔ   49 Ⓐ Ⓑ Ⓒ Ⓓ Ⓔ   71 Ⓐ Ⓑ Ⓒ Ⓓ Ⓔ

6 Ⓐ Ⓑ Ⓒ Ⓓ Ⓔ   28 Ⓐ Ⓑ Ⓒ Ⓓ Ⓔ   50 Ⓐ Ⓑ Ⓒ Ⓓ Ⓔ   72 Ⓐ Ⓑ Ⓒ Ⓓ Ⓔ

7 Ⓐ Ⓑ Ⓒ Ⓓ Ⓔ   29 Ⓐ Ⓑ Ⓒ Ⓓ Ⓔ   51 Ⓐ Ⓑ Ⓒ Ⓓ Ⓔ   73 Ⓐ Ⓑ Ⓒ Ⓓ Ⓔ

8 Ⓐ Ⓑ Ⓒ Ⓓ Ⓔ   30 Ⓐ Ⓑ Ⓒ Ⓓ Ⓔ   52 Ⓐ Ⓑ Ⓒ Ⓓ Ⓔ   74 Ⓐ Ⓑ Ⓒ Ⓓ Ⓔ

9 Ⓐ Ⓑ Ⓒ Ⓓ Ⓔ   31 Ⓐ Ⓑ Ⓒ Ⓓ Ⓔ   53 Ⓐ Ⓑ Ⓒ Ⓓ Ⓔ   75 Ⓐ Ⓑ Ⓒ Ⓓ Ⓔ

10 Ⓐ Ⓑ Ⓒ Ⓓ Ⓔ   32 Ⓐ Ⓑ Ⓒ Ⓓ Ⓔ   54 Ⓐ Ⓑ Ⓒ Ⓓ Ⓔ   76 Ⓐ Ⓑ Ⓒ Ⓓ Ⓔ

11 Ⓐ Ⓑ Ⓒ Ⓓ Ⓔ   33 Ⓐ Ⓑ Ⓒ Ⓓ Ⓔ   55 Ⓐ Ⓑ Ⓒ Ⓓ Ⓔ   77 Ⓐ Ⓑ Ⓒ Ⓓ Ⓔ

12 Ⓐ Ⓑ Ⓒ Ⓓ Ⓔ   34 Ⓐ Ⓑ Ⓒ Ⓓ Ⓔ   56 Ⓐ Ⓑ Ⓒ Ⓓ Ⓔ   78 Ⓐ Ⓑ Ⓒ Ⓓ Ⓔ

13 Ⓐ Ⓑ Ⓒ Ⓓ Ⓔ   35 Ⓐ Ⓑ Ⓒ Ⓓ Ⓔ   57 Ⓐ Ⓑ Ⓒ Ⓓ Ⓔ   79 Ⓐ Ⓑ Ⓒ Ⓓ Ⓔ

14 Ⓐ Ⓑ Ⓒ Ⓓ Ⓔ   36 Ⓐ Ⓑ Ⓒ Ⓓ Ⓔ   58 Ⓐ Ⓑ Ⓒ Ⓓ Ⓔ   80 Ⓐ Ⓑ Ⓒ Ⓓ Ⓔ

15 Ⓐ Ⓑ Ⓒ Ⓓ Ⓔ   37 Ⓐ Ⓑ Ⓒ Ⓓ Ⓔ   59 Ⓐ Ⓑ Ⓒ Ⓓ Ⓔ   81 Ⓐ Ⓑ Ⓒ Ⓓ Ⓔ

16 Ⓐ Ⓑ Ⓒ Ⓓ Ⓔ   38 Ⓐ Ⓑ Ⓒ Ⓓ Ⓔ   60 Ⓐ Ⓑ Ⓒ Ⓓ Ⓔ   82 Ⓐ Ⓑ Ⓒ Ⓓ Ⓔ

17 Ⓐ Ⓑ Ⓒ Ⓓ Ⓔ   39 Ⓐ Ⓑ Ⓒ Ⓓ Ⓔ   61 Ⓐ Ⓑ Ⓒ Ⓓ Ⓔ   83 Ⓐ Ⓑ Ⓒ Ⓓ Ⓔ

18 Ⓐ Ⓑ Ⓒ Ⓓ Ⓔ   40 Ⓐ Ⓑ Ⓒ Ⓓ Ⓔ   62 Ⓐ Ⓑ Ⓒ Ⓓ Ⓔ   84 Ⓐ Ⓑ Ⓒ Ⓓ Ⓔ

19 Ⓐ Ⓑ Ⓒ Ⓓ Ⓔ   41 Ⓐ Ⓑ Ⓒ Ⓓ Ⓔ   63 Ⓐ Ⓑ Ⓒ Ⓓ Ⓔ   85 Ⓐ Ⓑ Ⓒ Ⓓ Ⓔ

20 Ⓐ Ⓑ Ⓒ Ⓓ Ⓔ   42 Ⓐ Ⓑ Ⓒ Ⓓ Ⓔ   64 Ⓐ Ⓑ Ⓒ Ⓓ Ⓔ   86 Ⓐ Ⓑ Ⓒ Ⓓ Ⓔ

21 Ⓐ Ⓑ Ⓒ Ⓓ Ⓔ   43 Ⓐ Ⓑ Ⓒ Ⓓ Ⓔ   65 Ⓐ Ⓑ Ⓒ Ⓓ Ⓔ   87 Ⓐ Ⓑ Ⓒ Ⓓ Ⓔ

22 Ⓐ Ⓑ Ⓒ Ⓓ Ⓔ   44 Ⓐ Ⓑ Ⓒ Ⓓ Ⓔ   66 Ⓐ Ⓑ Ⓒ Ⓓ Ⓔ   88 Ⓐ Ⓑ Ⓒ Ⓓ Ⓔ

Memory for Addresses

Time: 5 minutes • 88 Questions

Directions: *Mark your answers on the answer sheet in the section headed "MEMORY FOR ADDRESSES." This test will be scored. You are NOT permitted to look at the boxes. Work from memory, as quickly and as accurately as you can. Correct answers are on page 63.*

1. 9800–9999 Wren
2. 9100–9799 Ball
3. Meadow
4. Hammock
5. 9100–9799 Slug
6. 8200–8299 Ball
7. 9800–9999 Slug
8. Zenith
9. Vapor
10. 8200–8299 Wren
11. 8300–8699 Wren
12. 9800–9999 Ball
13. 8300–8699 Slug
14. Ford
15. Artisan
16. Denim
17. 9800–9999 Slug
18. 8200–8299 Slug
19. 8700–9099 Wren
20. 9100–9799 Wren
21. Checker
22. Swing
23. 8300–8699 Slug
24. Winter
25. 9100–9799 Ball
26. 8700–9099 Wren
27. 9100–9799 Slug
28. 8300–8699 Wren
29. Artisan
30. Ford

31. 8300–8699 Ball
32. 8700–9099 Ball
33. 9100–9799 Wren
34. Denim
35. Checker
36. 8200–8299 Slug
37. 8700–9099 Slug
38. 8200–8299 Wren
39. Zenith
40. Hammock
41. 8200–8299 Ball
42. Swing
43. 9800–9999 Slug
44. 9800–9999 Ball
45. Vapor
46. 8700–9099 Ball
47. 9100–9799 Wren
48. 8700–9099 Slug
49. 8700–9099 Wren
50. 8300–8699 Ball
51. Winter
52. Hammock
53. Meadow
54. 8200–8299 Slug
55. 8300–8699 Wren
56. 9100–9799 Slug
57. Denim
58. Swing
59. Ford
60. 9100–9799 Ball

61. 8200–8299 Ball
62. 9100–9799 Wren
63. Checker
64. 9800–9999 Slug
65. 8200–8299 Wren
66. 8300–8699 Slug
67. Vapor
68. Zenith
69. 9800–9999 Ball
70. 9800–9999 Wren
71. Artisan
72. 8200–8299 Ball
73. 8300–8699 Slug
74. 9100–9799 Ball
75. Vapor
76. Meadow
77. 8200–8299 Wren
78. 8700–9099 Slug
79. 9100–9799 Ball
80. Swing
81. Artisan
82. 9800–9999 Wren
83. Hammock
84. 8300–8699 Wren
85. 8300–8699 Ball
86. 9100–9799 Slug
87. Checker
88. Ford

END OF MEMORY FOR ADDRESSES

Part C—Number Series

SAMPLE QUESTIONS

The following sample questions show you the type of question that will be used in Part C. You will have three minutes to answer the sample questions below and to study the explanations.

Directions: *Each number series question consists of a series of numbers that follows some definite order. The numbers progress from left to right according to some rule. One pair of numbers to the right of the series comprises the next two numbers in the series. Study each series to try to find a pattern to the series and to figure out the rule that governs the progression. Choose the answer pair that continues the series according to the pattern established and mark its letter on your answer sheet.*

1. 21 21 19 17 17 15 13 ...... (A) 11 11   (B) 13 11   (C) 11 9   (D) 9 7   (E) 13 13

The pattern of this series is: repeat the number, then subtract 2 and subtract 2 again; repeat the number, then subtract 2 and subtract 2 again and so on. Following the pattern, the series should continue with (B) 13 11 and then go on 9 9 7 5 5 3 1 1.

2. 23 22 20 19 16 15 11 ...... (A) 6 5   (B) 10 9   (C) 6 1   (D) 10 6   (E) 10 5

If you write in the changes between the numbers of the series, you can see that the pattern being established is: $-1, -2, -1, -3, -1, -4, -1, -5...$. Fitting the pattern to the remaining numbers, it is apparent that (E) is the answer because $11 - 1 = 10$ and $10 - 5 = 5$.

3. 5 6 8 9 11 12 14 .... (A) 15 16   (B) 16 17   (C) 15 17   (D) 16 18   (E) 17 19

The pattern here is: $+1, +2; +1, +2; +1, +2$, and so on. The answer is (C) because $14 + 1 = 15$ and $15 + 2 = 17$.

4. 7 10 8 13 16 8 19 .... (A) 22 8   (B) 8 22   (C) 20 21   (D) 22 25   (E) 8 25

Marking the changes between numbers is not sufficient for solving this series. You must first notice that the number 8 is repeated after each two numbers. If you disregard the 8's, you can see that the series is increasing by a factor of $+3$. With this information, you can choose (A) as the correct answer because $19 + 3 = 22$, and the two numbers, 19 and 22, are then followed by 8.

5. 1 35 2 34 3 33 4 .... (A) 4 5   (B) 32 31   (C) 32 5   (D) 5 32   (E) 31 6

This series is, in reality, two alternating series. One series, beginning with 1, increases at the rate of $+1$. The other series alternates with the first. It begins with 35 and decreases by -1. The answer is (C) because the next number in the decreasing series is 32 and the next number in the increasing series is 5.

SAMPLE ANSWER SHEET	CORRECT ANSWERS
1. Ⓐ Ⓑ Ⓒ Ⓓ Ⓔ	1. Ⓐ ● Ⓒ Ⓓ Ⓔ
2. Ⓐ Ⓑ Ⓒ Ⓓ Ⓔ	2. Ⓐ Ⓑ Ⓒ Ⓓ ●
3. Ⓐ Ⓑ Ⓒ Ⓓ Ⓔ	3. Ⓐ Ⓑ ● Ⓓ Ⓔ
4. Ⓐ Ⓑ Ⓒ Ⓓ Ⓔ	4. ● Ⓑ Ⓒ Ⓓ Ⓔ
5. Ⓐ Ⓑ Ⓒ Ⓓ Ⓔ	5. Ⓐ Ⓑ ● Ⓓ Ⓔ

Number Series

Time: 20 Minutes • 24 Questions

Directions: *Each number series question consists of a series of numbers that follows some definite order. The numbers progress from left to right according to some rule. One pair of numbers to the right of the series comprises the next two numbers in the series. Study each series to try to find a pattern to the series and to figure out the rule that governs the progression. Choose the answer pair that continues the series according to the pattern established and mark its letter on your answer sheet. Correct answers are on page 63 and 64.*

1. 8 9 10 8 9 10 8 .... (A)8 9   (B)9 10   (C)9 8   (D)10 8   (E)8 10

2. 3 4 4 3 5 5 3 .... (A)3 3   (B)6 3   (C)3 6   (D)6 6   (E)6 7

3. 7 7 3 7 7 4 7 .... (A)7 7   (B)7 8   (C)5 7   (D)8 7   (E)7 5

4. 18 18 19 20 20 21 22 ..... (A)22 23   (B)23 24   (C)23 23   (D)22 22   (E)21 22

5. 2 6 10 3 7 11 4 .... (A)12 16   (B)5 9   (C)8 5   (D)12 5   (E)8 12

6. 11 8 15 12 19 16 23 .... (A)27 20   (B)24 20   (C)27 24   (D)20 24   (E)20 27

7. 16 8 15 9 14 10 13 .... (A)12 11   (B)13 12   (C)11 13   (D)11 12   (E)11 14

8. 4 5 13 6 7 12 8 .... (A)9 11   (B)13 9   (C)9 13   (D)11 9   (E)11 10

9. 19 24 20 25 21 26 22 ..... (A)18 27   (B)22 24   (C)23 29   (D)27 23   (E)28 32

10. 25 25 22 22 19 19 16 ..... (A)18 18   (B)16 16   (C)16 13   (D)15 15   (E)15 13

11. 1 1 2 3 5 8 13 .... (A)21 29   (B)21 34   (C)18 27   (D)21 27   (E)24 32

12. 1 3 2 4 3 5 4 .... (A)6 5   (B)5 6   (C)3 1   (D)3 5   (E)4 3

13. 1 2 2 3 3 3 4 .... (A)4 5   (B)5 5   (C)3 5   (D)4 4   (E)4 3

14. 9 17 24 30 35 39 42 .... (A)43 44   (B)44 46   (C)44 45   (D)45 49   (E)46 50

15. 1 4 9 16 25 36 49 .... (A)56 64   (B)60 65   (C)62 75   (D)64 80   (E)64 81

16. 8 12 17 24 28 33 40 .... (A)47 53   (B)45 50   (C)43 49   (D)48 54   (E)44 49

17. 28 31 34 37 40 43 46 ..... (A)49 52   (B)47 49   (C)50 54   (D)49 53   (E)51 55

18. 17 17 24 24 31 31 38 ..... (A)38 39   (B)38 17   (C)38 45   (D)38 44   (E)39 50

19. 3 12 6 24 12 48 24 .... (A)96 48   (B)56 23   (C)64 12   (D)52 36   (E)64 48

20. 87 83 79 75 71 67 63 ..... (A)62 61   (B)63 59   (C)60 56   (D)59 55   (E)59 54

21. 10 2 8 2 6 2 4 .... (A)4 4   (B)2 2   (C)3 3   (D)4 2   (E)5 2

22. 8 9 11 14 18 23 29 .... (A)35 45   (B)32 33   (C)38 48   (D)34 40   (E)36 44

23. 11 14 12 15 13 16 14 ..... (A)14 17   (B)15 16   (C)16 20   (D)17 15   (E)18 13

24. 14 2 12 4 10 6 8 .... (A)10 12   (B)6 8   (C)12 10   (D)8 6   (E)10 14

END OF NUMBER SERIES

Part D—Following Oral Instructions

DIRECTIONS AND SAMPLE QUESTIONS

Listening to Instructions: When you are ready to try these sample questions, give the following instructions to a friend and have the friend read them aloud to you at the rate of 80 words per minute. Do not read them to yourself. Your friend will need a watch with a second hand. Listen carefully and do exactly what your friend tells you to do with the worksheet and answer sheet. Your friend will tell you some things to do with each item on the worksheet. After each set of instructions, your friend will give you time to mark your answer by darkening a circle on the sample answer sheet. Because B and D sound very much alike, your friend will say "B as in baker" when he or she means B, and "D as in dog" when he or she means D.

Before proceeding further, tear out the worksheet on page 53. Then hand this book to your friend.

To the Person Who Is to Read the Instructions: The instructions are to be read at the rate of 80 words per minute. Do not read aloud the material that is in parentheses. Do not repeat any instructions.

READ ALOUD TO THE CANDIDATE

Look at line 1 on the worksheet. (Pause slightly.) Write a D as in dog in the fourth box. (Pause 2 seconds.) Now, on your answer sheet, find the number in that box and darken space D as in dog for that number. (Pause 5 seconds.)

Look at line 2. The number in each circle is the number of employees in a post office. In the circle holding the largest number of employees, write a B as in baker. (Pause 2 seconds.) Now, on your answer sheet, darken the space for the number-letter combination that is in the circle you just wrote in. (Pause 5 seconds.)

Look at line 3 on the worksheet. (Pause slightly.) Write the letter C on the blank next to the right-hand number. (Pause 2 seconds.) Now, on your answer sheet, find the number beside which you just wrote and darken space C. (Pause 5 seconds.)

Look at line 3 again. (Pause slightly.) Write the letter B as in baker on the blank next to the left-hand number. (Pause 2 seconds.) Now, on your answer sheet, find the number beside which you just wrote and darken space B as in baker. (Pause 5 seconds.)

Look at line 4 on your worksheet. (Pause slightly.) Draw a line under every "X" in the line. (Pause 5 seconds.) Count the number of lines that you have drawn, divide by 2, and write that number at the end of the line. (Pause 5 seconds.) Now, on your answer sheet, find that number and darken space C for that number. (Pause 5 seconds.)

SAMPLE WORKSHEET

Directions: *Listening carefully to each set of instructions, mark each item on this worksheet as directed. Then complete each question by marking the sample answer sheet below as directed. For each answer you will darken the answer for a number-letter combination. Should you fall behind and miss an instruction, don't become excited. Let that one go and listen for the next one. If, when you start to darken a space for a number, you find that you have already darkened another space for that number, either erase the first mark and darken the space for the new combination or let the first mark stay and do not darken a space for the new combination. Write with a pencil that has a clean eraser. When you finish, you should have no more than one space darkened for each number.*

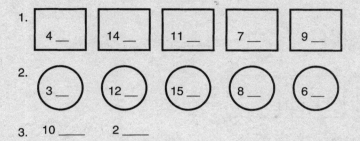

1. | 4 __ | 14 __ | 11 __ | 7 __ | 9 __ |

2. (3 __) (12 __) (15 __) (8 __) (6 __)

3. 10 ____   2 ____

4. X O X X X X O O X O X O X X O X

SAMPLE ANSWER SHEET

1. Ⓐ Ⓑ Ⓒ Ⓓ Ⓔ   6. Ⓐ Ⓑ Ⓒ Ⓓ Ⓔ   11. Ⓐ Ⓑ Ⓒ Ⓓ Ⓔ
2. Ⓐ Ⓑ Ⓒ Ⓓ Ⓔ   7. Ⓐ Ⓑ Ⓒ Ⓓ Ⓔ   12. Ⓐ Ⓑ Ⓒ Ⓓ Ⓔ
3. Ⓐ Ⓑ Ⓒ Ⓓ Ⓔ   8. Ⓐ Ⓑ Ⓒ Ⓓ Ⓔ   13. Ⓐ Ⓑ Ⓒ Ⓓ Ⓔ
4. Ⓐ Ⓑ Ⓒ Ⓓ Ⓔ   9. Ⓐ Ⓑ Ⓒ Ⓓ Ⓔ   14. Ⓐ Ⓑ Ⓒ Ⓓ Ⓔ
5. Ⓐ Ⓑ Ⓒ Ⓓ Ⓔ   10. Ⓐ Ⓑ Ⓒ Ⓓ Ⓔ   15. Ⓐ Ⓑ Ⓒ Ⓓ Ⓔ

CORRECTLY FILLED ANSWER SHEET

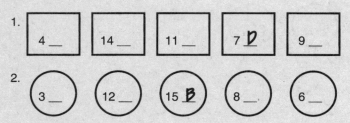

CORRECT ANSWERS TO SAMPLE QUESTIONS

1. Ⓐ Ⓑ Ⓒ Ⓓ Ⓔ   6. Ⓐ Ⓑ Ⓒ Ⓓ Ⓔ   11. Ⓐ Ⓑ Ⓒ Ⓓ Ⓔ
2. Ⓐ Ⓑ ● Ⓓ Ⓔ   7. Ⓐ Ⓑ Ⓒ ● Ⓔ   12. Ⓐ Ⓑ Ⓒ Ⓓ Ⓔ
3. Ⓐ Ⓑ Ⓒ Ⓓ Ⓔ   8. Ⓐ Ⓑ Ⓒ Ⓓ Ⓔ   13. Ⓐ Ⓑ Ⓒ Ⓓ Ⓔ
4. Ⓐ Ⓑ Ⓒ Ⓓ Ⓔ   9. Ⓐ Ⓑ Ⓒ Ⓓ Ⓔ   14. Ⓐ Ⓑ Ⓒ Ⓓ Ⓔ
5. Ⓐ Ⓑ ● Ⓓ Ⓔ   10. Ⓐ ● Ⓒ Ⓓ Ⓔ   15. Ⓐ ● Ⓒ Ⓓ Ⓔ

CORRECTLY FILLED WORKSHEET

1.
| 4 __ | 14 __ | 11 __ | 7 _D_ | 9 __ |

2. (3 __) (12 __) (15 _B_) (8 __) (6 __)

3.   10 _B_   2 _C_

4.   X̲ O X̲ X̲ X̲ X̲ O O X̲ O X̲ O X̲ X̲ O X̲   **5**

Following Oral Instructions

Time: 25 Minutes

LISTENING TO INSTRUCTIONS

Directions: *When you are ready to try this test of the Model Exam, give the following instructions to a friend and have the friend read them aloud to you at the rate of 80 words per minute. Do not read them to yourself. Your friend will need a watch with a second hand. Listen carefully and do exactly what your friend tells you to do with the worksheet and answer sheet. Your friend will tell you some things to do with each item on the worksheet. After each set of instructions, your friend will give you time to mark your answer by darkening a circle on the sample answer sheet. Because B and D sound very much alike, your friend will say "B as in baker" when he or she means B, and "D as in dog" when he or she means D.*

Before proceeding further, tear out the worksheet on page 59 and 60. Then hand this book to your friend.

To the Person Who Is to Read the Instructions: *The instructions are to be read at the rate of 80 words per minute. Do not read aloud the material that is in parentheses. After you have begun the test itself, do not repeat any instructions. The next three paragraphs consist of approximately 120 words. Read these three paragraphs aloud to the candidate in about one and one-half minutes. You may reread these paragraphs as often as necessary to establish an 80-words per minute reading speed.*

READ ALOUD TO THE CANDIDATE

On the job you will have to listen to directions and then do what you have been told to do. In this test, I will read instructions to you. Try to understand them as I read them; I cannot repeat them. After we begin, you may not ask any questions until the end of the test.

On the job you won't have to deal with pictures, numbers and letters like those in the test, but you will have to listen to instructions and follow them. We are using this test to see how well you can follow instructions.

You are to mark your test booklet according to the instructions that I'll read to you. After each set of instructions, I'll give you time to record your answers on the separate answer sheet.

The actual test begins now.

Look at line 1 on the worksheet. (Pause slightly.) Draw a line under the fourth number in the line. (Pause 2 seconds.) Now, on your answer sheet, find the number under which you just drew the line and darken space A for that number. (Pause 5 seconds.)

Look at the letters in line 2 on the worksheet. (Pause slightly.) Draw a line under the fifth letter in the line. Now, on your answer sheet, find number 59 (pause 2 seconds) and darken the space for the letter under which you drew a line. (Pause 5 seconds.)

Look at the letters in line 2 on the worksheet again. (Pause slightly.) Now draw two lines under the third letter in the line. (Pause 2 seconds.) Now, on your answer sheet, find number 65 (pause 2 seconds) and darken the space for the letter under which you drew two lines. (Pause 5 seconds.)

Look at line 3 on the worksheet. (Pause slightly.) Write an E in the last box. (Pause 2 seconds.) Now, on your answer sheet, find the number in that box and darken space E for that number. (Pause 5 seconds.)

Now look at line 3 again. (Pause slightly.) Write an A in the first box. (Pause 2 seconds.) Now, on your answer sheet, find the number in that box and darken space A for that number. (Pause 5 seconds.)

Look at line 4. (Pause slightly.) The number in each circle is the number of packages in a mail sack. In the circle for the sack holding the largest number of packages, write a B as in baker. (Pause 2 seconds.) Now, on your answer sheet, darken the space for the number-letter combination that is in the circle you just wrote in. (Pause 5 seconds.)

Look at line 4 again. In the circle for the sack holding the smallest number of packages, write an E. (Pause 2 seconds.) Now, on your answer sheet, darken the space for the number-letter combination that is in the circle you just wrote in. (Pause 5 seconds.)

Look at the drawings on line 5 on the worksheet. The four boxes are trucks for carrying mail. (Pause 2 seconds.) The truck with the highest number is to be loaded first. Write a B as in baker on the line beside the highest number. (Pause 2 seconds.) Now, on your answer sheet, darken the space for the number-letter combination that is in the box you just wrote in. (Pause 5 seconds.)

Look at line 6 on the worksheet. (Pause slightly.) Next to the middle number, write the letter D as in dog. (Pause 2 seconds.) Now, on your answer sheet, find the space for the number beside which you wrote and darken space D as in dog.

Look at the five circles in line 7 on the worksheet. Write B as in baker on the blank in the second circle. (Pause 2 seconds.) Now, on your answer sheet, darken the space for the number-letter combination that is in the circle you just wrote in. (Pause 5 seconds.)

Now take the worksheet again and write C on the blank in the third circle on line 7. (Pause 2 seconds.) Now, on your answer sheet, darken the space for the number-letter combination that is in the circle you just wrote in. (Pause 5 seconds.)

Now look at line 8 on the worksheet. (Pause slightly.) Write an A on the line next to the right-hand number. (Pause 2 seconds.) Now, on your answer sheet, find the space for the number beside which you wrote and darken box A. (Pause 5 seconds.)

Look at line 9 on the worksheet. (Pause slightly.) Draw a line under every number that is more the 60 but less than 70. (Pause 12 seconds.) Now, on your answer sheet, for each number that you drew a line under, darken space C. (Pause 25 seconds.)

Look at line 10 on the worksheet. (Pause slightly.) Draw a line under every number that is more than 5 and less than 15. (Pause 10 seconds.) Now, on your answer sheet, for each number that you drew a line under, darken space D as in dog. (Pause 25 seconds.)

Look at line 11 on the worksheet. (Pause slightly.) In each circle there is a time when the mail must leave. In the circle for the latest time, write on the line the last two figures of the time. (Pause 5 seconds.) Now, on your answer sheet, darken the space for the number-letter combination that is in the circle you just wrote in. (Pause 5 seconds.)

Look at the five boxes in line 12 on your worksheet. (Pause slightly.) If 6 is less than 3, put an E in the fourth box. (Pause slightly.) If 6 is not less than 3, put a B as in baker in the first box. (Pause 10 seconds.) Now, on your answer sheet, darken the space for the number-letter combination that is in the circle you just wrote in. (Pause 5 seconds.)

Now look at line 13 on the worksheet. (Pause slightly.) There are five circles. Each circle has a letter. (Pause slightly.) In the second circle, write the answer to this question: Which of the following numbers is smallest: 72, 51, 88, 71, 58? (Pause 10 seconds.) Now, on your answer sheet, darken the space for the number-letter combination that is in the circle you wrote in. (Pause 5 seconds.) In the third circle on the same line, write 28. (Pause 2 seconds.) Now, on your answer sheet, darken the space for the number-letter combination that is in the circle you just wrote in. (Pause 5 seconds.) In the fourth circle do nothing. In the fifth circle write the answer to this question: How many months are there in a year? (Pause 5 seconds.) Now, on your answer sheet, darken the space for the number-letter combination that is in the circle you just wrote in. (Pause 5 seconds.)

Look at line 14 on your worksheet. (Pause slightly.) There are two circles and two boxes of different sizes with numbers in them. (Pause slightly.) If 2 is smaller than 4, and 7 is less than 3, write A in the larger circle. (Pause slightly.) Otherwise, write B as in baker in the smallest box. (Pause 10 seconds.) Now, on your answer sheet, darken the space for the number-letter combination in the box or circle in which you just wrote. (Pause 5 seconds.)

Look at the boxes and words in line 15 on the worksheet. (Pause slightly.) Write the second letter of the first word in the third box. (Pause 5 seconds.) Write the first letter of the second word in the first box. (Pause 5 seconds.) Write the first letter of the third word in the second box. (Pause 5 seconds.) Now, on your answer sheet, darken the spaces for the number-letter combinations that are in the three boxes you just wrote in. (Pause 15 seconds.)

Look at line 16 on the worksheet. (Pause slightly.) Draw a line under every "O" in the line. (Pause 5 seconds.) Count the number of lines that you have drawn, subtract 2, and write that number at the end of the line. (Pause 5 seconds.) Now, on your answer sheet, find that number and darken space D as in dog for that number. (Pause 5 seconds.)

Look at line 17 on the worksheet. (Pause slightly.) If the number in the left-hand circle is smaller than the number in the right-hand circle, add 2 to the number in the left-hand circle, and change the number in that circle to this number. (Pause 8 seconds.) Then write B as in baker next to the new number. (Pause slightly.) Next, write E beside the number in the smallest box. (Pause 3 seconds.) Then, on your answer sheet, darken the spaces for the number-letter combinations that are in the box and circle you just wrote in. (Pause 5 seconds.)

Look at line 18 on the worksheet. (Pause slightly.) If in a year October comes before September, write A in the box with the smallest number. (Pause slightly.) If it does not, write C in the box with the largest number. (Pause 10 seconds.) Now, on your answer sheet, darken the space for the number-letter combination that is in the box you just wrote in. (Pause 5 seconds.)

Look at line 19 on the worksheet. (Pause slightly.) On the line beside the second letter, write the highest of these numbers: 12, 56, 42, 39, 8. (Pause 2 seconds.) Now, on your answer sheet, darken the space of the number-letter combination you just wrote. (Pause 5 seconds.)

Following Oral Instructions
WORKSHEET

Directions: *Listening carefully to each set of instructions, mark each item on this worksheet as directed. Then complete each question by marking the sample answer sheet below as directed. For each answer you will darken the answer for a number-letter combination. Should you fall behind and miss an instruction, don't become excited. Let that one go and listen for the next one. If, when you start to darken a space for a number, you find that you have already darkened another space for that number, either erase the first mark and darken the space for the new combination or let the first mark stay and do not darken a space for the new combination. Write with a pencil that has a clean eraser. When you finish, you should have no more than one space darkened for each number. Correct answers are on page 65–67.*

1.　13　　23　　2　　　19　　6

2.　E　　B　　D　　E　　C　　A　　B

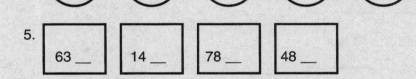

3.　| 30 __ | 18 __ | 5 __ | 14 __ | 7 __ |

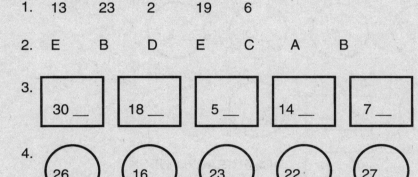

4.　26 __　16 __　23 __　22 __　27 __

5.　| 63 __ | 14 __ | 78 __ | 48 __ |

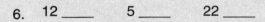

6.　12 ____　5 ____　22 ____

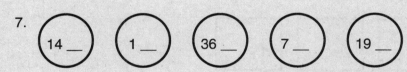

7.　14 __　1 __　36 __　7 __　19 __

8.　26 ____　86 ____

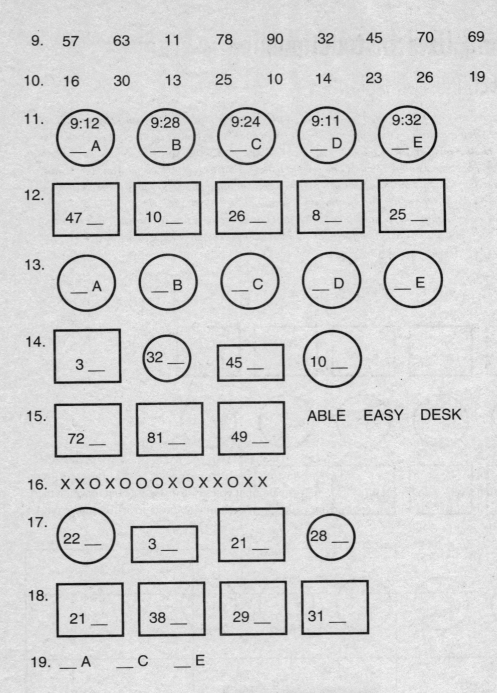

9. 57   63   11   78   90   32   45   70   69

10. 16   30   13   25   10   14   23   26   19

11. 9:12 __A   9:28 __B   9:24 __C   9:11 __D   9:32 __E

12. 47 __   10 __   26 __   8 __   25 __

13. __A   __B   __C   __D   __E

14. 3 __   32 __   45 __   10 __

15. 72 __   81 __   49 __   ABLE   EASY   DESK

16. X X O X O O O X O X X O X X

17. 22 __   3 __   21 __   28 __

18. 21 __   38 __   29 __   31 __

19. __A   __C   __E

END OF EXAMINATION

Correct Answers for Preliminary Exam

PART A—ADDRESS CHECKING

1. A	13. D	25. A	37. D	49. D	61. A	73. A	85. A
2. D	14. D	26. D	38. A	50. D	62. D	74. D	86. A
3. A	15. A	27. D	39. D	51. A	63. A	75. D	87. D
4. D	16. A	28. A	40. A	52. A	64. D	76. D	88. A
5. D	17. D	29. D	41. A	53. D	65. A	77. D	89. D
6. D	18. A	30. D	42. A	54. D	66. D	78. D	90. D
7. A	19. A	31. D	43. D	55. D	67. D	79. D	91. D
8. D	20. D	32. D	44. D	56. D	68. D	80. D	92. D
9. D	21. D	33. D	45. D	57. D	69. A	81. A	93. A
10. A	22. D	34. D	46. D	58. A	70. D	82. A	94. D
11. A	23. D	35. A	47. A	59. D	71. A	83. D	95. D
12. D	24. A	36. A	48. D	60. A	72. D	84. D	

ANALYZING YOUR ERRORS

The Address Checking Test of the Preliminary Exam contains 35 addresses that are exactly alike and 60 addresses that are different. The chart below shows what kind of difference occurs in each of the addresses that contains a difference. Check your answers against this chart to see which kind of difference you missed most often. Note also the questions in which you thought you saw a difference but in which there really was none. Becoming aware of your errors will help you eliminate those errors on future model exams and on the actual exam.

Type of Difference	Question Numbers	Number of Questions You Missed
Difference in NUMBERS	2, 12, 13, 22, 26, 31,39, 44, 49, 53, 54, 67, 68, 70, 72, 76, 79, 89, 91	
Difference in ABBREVIATIONS	4, 9, 14, 20, 21, 23, 27, 30, 32, 33, 46, 55, 59, 62, 74, 75, 78, 84, 87, 95	
Difference in NAMES	5, 6, 8, 17, 29, 34, 37, 43, 45, 48, 50, 56, 57, 64, 66, 77, 80, 83, 90, 92, 94	
No Difference	1, 3, 7, 10, 11, 15, 16, 18, 19, 24, 25, 28, 35, 36, 38, 40, 41, 42, 47, 51, 52, 58, 60, 61, 63, 65, 69, 71, 73, 81, 82, 85, 86, 88, 93	

Part B—Memory for Addresses

PRACTICE I

1. D	12. B	23. A	34. B	45. E	56. A	67. D	78. E
2. C	13. C	24. A	35. A	46. D	57. C	68. B	79. E
3. C	14. E	25. B	36. C	47. C	58. C	69. E	80. B
4. E	15. D	26. C	37. B	48. B	59. A	70. D	81. B
5. A	16. E	27. E	38. E	49. A	60. A	71. E	82. A
6. B	17. A	28. D	39. C	50. A	61. B	72. D	83. C
7. B	18. D	29. E	40. C	51. D	62. D	73. D	84. B
8. A	19. D	30. D	41. A	52. C	63. E	74. C	85. C
9. B	20. B	31. B	42. B	53. B	64. E	75. A	86. D
10. B	21. A	32. A	43. D	54. E	65. B	76. B	87. A
11. E	22. E	33. C	44. E	55. D	66. C	77. A	88. E

PRACTICE II

1. D	12. A	23. D	34. A	45. D	56. E	67. E	78. E
2. C	13. D	24. C	35. A	46. A	57. A	68. C	79. C
3. B	14. B	25. E	36. C	47. B	58. E	69. D	80. B
4. E	15. E	26. A	37. E	48. B	59. D	70. D	81. B
5. A	16. D	27. B	38. E	49. C	60. B	71. C	82. A
6. E	17. C	28. C	39. B	50. D	61. A	72. B	83. C
7. C	18. A	29. D	40. C	51. E	62. C	73. A	84. C
8. A	19. B	30. D	41. C	52. B	63. A	74. C	85. A
9. D	20. A	31. E	42. A	53. A	64. D	75. C	86. D
10. B	21. B	32. D	43. A	54. B	65. B	76. B	87. E
11. E	22. A	33. B	44. C	55. D	66. E	77. A	88. A

PRACTICE III

1. D	12. C	23. B	34. C	45. E	56. D	67. B	78. B
2. D	13. C	24. B	35. A	46. C	57. E	68. B	79. E
3. D	14. B	25. E	36. B	47. E	58. B	69. A	80. D
4. B	15. B	26. C	37. E	48. E	59. E	70. C	81. E
5. A	16. E	27. A	38. D	49. D	60. C	71. A	82. C
6. E	17. B	28. D	39. C	50. A	61. C	72. A	83. B
7. A	18. D	29. D	40. B	51. D	62. E	73. A	84. C
8. E	19. C	30. E	41. E	52. A	63. A	74. D	85. E
9. A	20. B	31. E	42. C	53. D	64. B	75. D	86. C
10. A	21. C	32. A	43. B	54. A	65. E	76. D	87. E
11. D	22. A	33. B	44. B	55. C	66. D	77. C	88. A

MEMORY FOR ADDRESSES

1. A	12. C	23. D	34. A	45. B	56. E	67. B	78. C
2. B	13. D	24. C	35. D	46. E	57. A	68. D	79. B
3. A	14. E	25. B	36. A	47. D	58. B	69. C	80. B
4. E	15. C	26. B	37. C	48. C	59. E	70. A	81. C
5. E	16. A	27. E	38. E	49. B	60. B	71. C	82. A
6. D	17. B	28. C	39. D	50. A	61. D	72. D	83. E
7. B	18. A	29. C	40. E	51. C	62. D	73. D	84. C
8. D	19. B	30. E	41. D	52. E	63. D	74. B	85. A
9. B	20. D	31. A	42. B	53. A	64. B	75. B	86. E
10. E	21. D	32. E	43. B	54. A	65. E	76. A	87. D
11. C	22. B	33. D	44. C	55. C	66. D	77. E	88. E

Part C—Number Series

1. B	4. A	7. D	10. C	13. D	16. E	19. A	22. E
2. D	5. E	8. A	11. B	14. C	17. A	20. D	23. D
3. E	6. E	9. D	12. A	15. E	18. C	21. B	24. D

EXPLANATIONS

1. **(B)** The series is simply a repetition of the sequence 8 9 10.
2. **(D)** You can feel the rhythm of this series if you read it aloud. Beginning with 4, doubled numbers are progressing upwards by +1, separated by the number 3.
3. **(E)** In this series, two 7's separate numbers that are increasing by +1.
4. **(A)** In this series, the numbers are increasing by +1. Every other number is repeated before it increases.
5. **(E)** This series is made up of a number of mini-series. In each mini-series the numbers increase by +4. After each mini-series of three numbers, a new mini-series begins, each time with a number one higher than the beginning number of the previous mini-series.
6. **(E)** This pattern is not as easy to spot as the ones in the previous questions. If you write in the direction and degree of change between each number, you can see that the rule is −3, +7, −3, +7, and so on.
7. **(D)** This series consists of two alternating series. One series begins with 16 and decreases by −1. The alternating series begins with 8 and increases by +1.
8. **(A)** Again, we have alternating series. This time the ascending series consists of two numbers increasing by +1 before being interrupted by one number of the descending series that is decreasing by −1.
9. **(D)** You may see this series as following the rule: +5, −4, +5, −4…or you may see two alternating series, one beginning with 19, the other with 24.
10. **(C)** Repeat, −3, repeat, −3, repeat, −3…
11. **(B)** Each number is reached by adding together the two previous numbers. Thus, 1 + 1 = 2; 1 + 2 = 3; 2 + 3 = 5; 5 + 8 = 13; 8 + 13 = 21; 13 + 21 = 34.
12. **(A)** You might see two alternating series increasing by +1, or you might see a rule: +2, −1, +2, −1.
13. **(D)** In this series, each number appears as often as its name implies: one 1, two 2's, three 3's, four 4's.
14. **(C)** The rule here is: +8, +7, +6, +5, +4, +3, +2....
15. **(E)** The elements of this series are the squares of successive numbers: 1^2, 2^2, 3^2, 4^2, and so on.
16. **(E)** The rule is: +4, +5, +7 and repeat +4, +5, +7....
17. **(A)** This question uses a simple +3 rule.
18. **(C)** Each number repeats itself, then increases by +7.
19. **(A)** You might see this as two alternating parallel series. In each series, the next number is the previous number multiplied by 2.
20. **(D)** Here the rule is: −4.
21. **(B)** Basically, the series descends by −2: 10 8 6 4 2. The number 2 appears between terms of the series.
22. **(E)** The rule is: +1, +2, +3, +4, +5, +6, +7, +8.
23. **(D)** Parallel ascending series alternate or the series follows the rule: +3, −2, +3, −2, +3....
24. **(D)** The first series decreases by −2. The alternating series increases by +2.

Part D—Following Oral Instructions
CORRECTLY FILLED ANSWER GRID

1 Ⓐ ● Ⓒ Ⓓ Ⓔ	23 Ⓐ Ⓑ Ⓒ Ⓓ Ⓔ	45 Ⓐ ● Ⓒ Ⓓ Ⓔ	67 Ⓐ Ⓑ Ⓒ Ⓓ Ⓔ
2 Ⓐ Ⓑ Ⓒ Ⓓ Ⓔ	24 Ⓐ ● Ⓒ Ⓓ Ⓔ	46 Ⓐ Ⓑ Ⓒ Ⓓ Ⓔ	68 Ⓐ Ⓑ Ⓒ Ⓓ Ⓔ
3 Ⓐ Ⓑ Ⓒ Ⓓ ●	25 Ⓐ Ⓑ Ⓒ Ⓓ Ⓔ	47 Ⓐ ● Ⓒ Ⓓ Ⓔ	69 Ⓐ Ⓑ ● Ⓓ Ⓔ
4 Ⓐ Ⓑ Ⓒ ● Ⓔ	26 Ⓐ Ⓑ Ⓒ Ⓓ Ⓔ	48 Ⓐ Ⓑ Ⓒ Ⓓ Ⓔ	70 Ⓐ Ⓑ Ⓒ Ⓓ Ⓔ
5 Ⓐ Ⓑ Ⓒ ● Ⓔ	27 Ⓐ ● Ⓒ Ⓓ Ⓔ	49 Ⓐ ● Ⓒ Ⓓ Ⓔ	71 Ⓐ Ⓑ Ⓒ Ⓓ Ⓔ
6 Ⓐ Ⓑ Ⓒ Ⓓ Ⓔ	28 Ⓐ Ⓑ ● Ⓓ Ⓔ	50 Ⓐ Ⓑ Ⓒ Ⓓ Ⓔ	72 Ⓐ Ⓑ Ⓒ Ⓓ ●
7 Ⓐ Ⓑ Ⓒ Ⓓ ●	29 Ⓐ Ⓑ Ⓒ Ⓓ Ⓔ	51 Ⓐ ● Ⓒ Ⓓ Ⓔ	73 Ⓐ Ⓑ Ⓒ Ⓓ Ⓔ
8 Ⓐ Ⓑ Ⓒ Ⓓ Ⓔ	30 ● Ⓑ Ⓒ Ⓓ Ⓔ	52 Ⓐ Ⓑ Ⓒ Ⓓ Ⓔ	74 Ⓐ Ⓑ Ⓒ Ⓓ Ⓔ
9 Ⓐ Ⓑ Ⓒ Ⓓ Ⓔ	31 Ⓐ Ⓑ Ⓒ Ⓓ Ⓔ	53 Ⓐ Ⓑ Ⓒ Ⓓ Ⓔ	75 Ⓐ Ⓑ Ⓒ Ⓓ Ⓔ
10 Ⓐ Ⓑ Ⓒ ● Ⓔ	32 Ⓐ Ⓑ Ⓒ Ⓓ ●	54 Ⓐ Ⓑ Ⓒ Ⓓ Ⓔ	76 Ⓐ Ⓑ Ⓒ Ⓓ Ⓔ
11 Ⓐ Ⓑ Ⓒ Ⓓ Ⓔ	33 Ⓐ Ⓑ Ⓒ Ⓓ Ⓔ	55 Ⓐ Ⓑ Ⓒ Ⓓ Ⓔ	77 Ⓐ Ⓑ Ⓒ Ⓓ Ⓔ
12 Ⓐ Ⓑ Ⓒ Ⓓ ●	34 Ⓐ Ⓑ Ⓒ Ⓓ Ⓔ	56 Ⓐ Ⓑ ● Ⓓ Ⓔ	78 Ⓐ ● Ⓒ Ⓓ Ⓔ
13 Ⓐ Ⓑ Ⓒ ● Ⓔ	35 Ⓐ Ⓑ Ⓒ Ⓓ Ⓔ	57 Ⓐ Ⓑ Ⓒ Ⓓ Ⓔ	79 Ⓐ Ⓑ Ⓒ Ⓓ Ⓔ
14 Ⓐ Ⓑ Ⓒ ● Ⓔ	36 Ⓐ Ⓑ ● Ⓓ Ⓔ	58 Ⓐ Ⓑ Ⓒ Ⓓ Ⓔ	80 Ⓐ Ⓑ Ⓒ Ⓓ Ⓔ
15 Ⓐ Ⓑ Ⓒ Ⓓ Ⓔ	37 Ⓐ Ⓑ Ⓒ Ⓓ Ⓔ	59 Ⓐ Ⓑ ● Ⓓ Ⓔ	81 Ⓐ Ⓑ Ⓒ ● Ⓔ
16 Ⓐ Ⓑ Ⓒ Ⓓ ●	38 Ⓐ Ⓑ ● Ⓓ Ⓔ	60 Ⓐ Ⓑ Ⓒ Ⓓ Ⓔ	82 Ⓐ Ⓑ Ⓒ Ⓓ Ⓔ
17 Ⓐ Ⓑ Ⓒ Ⓓ Ⓔ	39 Ⓐ Ⓑ Ⓒ Ⓓ Ⓔ	61 Ⓐ Ⓑ Ⓒ Ⓓ Ⓔ	83 Ⓐ Ⓑ Ⓒ Ⓓ Ⓔ
18 Ⓐ Ⓑ Ⓒ Ⓓ Ⓔ	40 Ⓐ Ⓑ Ⓒ Ⓓ Ⓔ	62 Ⓐ Ⓑ Ⓒ Ⓓ Ⓔ	84 Ⓐ Ⓑ Ⓒ Ⓓ Ⓔ
19 ● Ⓑ Ⓒ Ⓓ Ⓔ	41 Ⓐ Ⓑ Ⓒ Ⓓ Ⓔ	63 Ⓐ Ⓑ ● Ⓓ Ⓔ	85 Ⓐ Ⓑ Ⓒ Ⓓ Ⓔ
20 Ⓐ Ⓑ Ⓒ Ⓓ Ⓔ	42 Ⓐ Ⓑ Ⓒ Ⓓ Ⓔ	64 Ⓐ Ⓑ Ⓒ Ⓓ Ⓔ	86 ● Ⓑ Ⓒ Ⓓ Ⓔ
21 Ⓐ Ⓑ Ⓒ Ⓓ Ⓔ	43 Ⓐ Ⓑ Ⓒ Ⓓ Ⓔ	65 Ⓐ Ⓑ Ⓒ ● Ⓔ	87 Ⓐ Ⓑ Ⓒ Ⓓ Ⓔ
22 Ⓐ Ⓑ Ⓒ Ⓓ Ⓔ	44 Ⓐ Ⓑ Ⓒ Ⓓ Ⓔ	66 Ⓐ Ⓑ Ⓒ Ⓓ Ⓔ	88 Ⓐ Ⓑ Ⓒ Ⓓ Ⓔ

CORRECTLY FILLED WORKSHEET

1. 13   23   2   <u>19</u>   6

2. E   B   <u>D</u>   E   <u>C</u>   A   B

3.

| 30 <u>A</u> | 18 __ | 5 __ | 14 __ | 7 <u>E</u> |

4.

(26 __)   (16 <u>E</u>)   (23 __)   (22 __)   (27 <u>B</u>)

5.

| 63 __ | 14 __ | 78 <u>B</u> | 48 __ |

6. 12 ____   5 <u>D</u>   22 ____

7.

(14 __)   (1 <u>B</u>)   (36 <u>C</u>)   (7 __)   (19 __)

8. 26 ____   86 <u>A</u>

9. 57   <u>63</u>   11   78   90   32   45   70   <u>69</u>

10. 16   30   <u>13</u>   25   <u>10</u>   <u>14</u>   23   26   19

11.

(9:12 __ A)   (9:28 __ B)   (9:24 __ C)   (9:11 __ D)   (9:32 32 E)

12.

| 47 <u>B</u> | 10 __ | 26 __ | 8 __ | 25 __ |

13.

(__ A)   (51 B)   (28 C)   (__ D)   (12 E)

14.

| 3 __ | (32 __) | 45 <u>B</u> | (10 __)

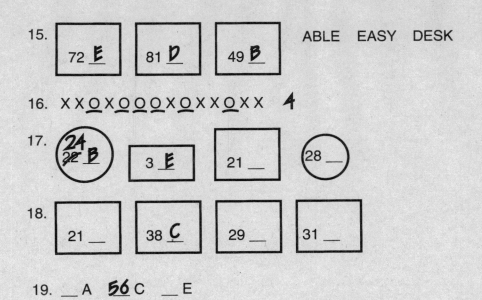

15.   72 _E_   81 _D_   49 _B_   ABLE   EASY   DESK

16.   X X O X O O O X O X X O X X   4

17.   24 / 22 _B_   3 _E_   21 __   28 __

18.   21 __   38 _C_   29 __   31 __

19.   __ A   **56** C   __ E

FAMILIARIZE YOURSELF WITH THE TESTS

Feeling anxious before you take a test is a normal reaction. You've spent many hours studying and preparing for the exam, and you want to get the best score possible. In addition, you probably think (and rightly so) that this test might be just a bit more important than some of those spelling tests you took back in elementary school. This is your career, and you want to prove to yourself and others that you're capable of achieving the highest performance.

Well, you can relax! Although the postal exams are a bit unusual (as compared to other tests), there really is no reason for you to be overly nervous. If you put in the time studying for the exam, use common sense, and don't panic, you'll be well on your way to achieving a good score.

This chapter is designed to help alleviate even more of your pre-test anxiety by introducing you to the format of the tests. Then, as you study the rest of this book, you have plenty of opportunity to practice the various question types. By test day, you still might be a bit nervous, but you shouldn't encounter any surprises.

Get to Know the Test

The four-part U.S. Postal Examination is structured as follows:

Question Type	Part Number	Number of Questions	Time Allowed
Address Checking	A	95	6 minutes
Memory for Addresses	B	88	5 minutes*
Number Series	C	24	20 minutes
Following Oral Instructions	D	20–25 (will vary)	25 minutes (approximately)

*Does not include the time allowed for memorizing addresses

> Test 470 is used by the Postal Service to evaluate job-related skills. However, it is not a true aptitude test of your abilities. Don't fall into the trap of thinking you must possess certain innate talents to get a high score. On the contrary, preparing for this test will definitely increase your chances for doing well on it. The four question types are extremely coachable and get easier with practice. Use your desire for getting hired as a key motivator throughout the test-preparation process.

The remaining chapters of this book, as well as the full-length sample exams, will give you the opportunity to practice the various question types.

Rules and Procedures

You must not underestimate the importance of following all of the rules and procedures required at the test center. This includes following all of the examiner's test-taking instructions and filling in the answer sheets correctly.

TEST-TAKING INSTRUCTIONS

Instructions read by the examiner are intended to ensure that you and all the other applicants have the same fair and objective opportunity to compete in the examination. All of you are expected to play on a level playing field. Any infraction of the rules is considered cheating. If you cheat, your test paper is not scored and you are not eligible for appointment.

- Listen to what the examiner says at all times. Be prepared to immediately act on any exam changes to content, question type, directions, or time limits.
- Follow all instructions the examiner gives you. If you do not understand any of the examiner's instructions, ask questions.
- Don't begin working on any part of the test until told to do so.
- Stop working on any part of the test when told to do so. Stop working as soon as the examiner tells you to do so. Remember that your ability to follow instructions is considered in the hiring process.
- Review your work for a test part if you finish that test part before time is called. Although you cannot go on or back to any other part of the test, you have the chance to review answers of which you are unsure or guess if guessing is a good strategy for that test part. Use the extra time you have wisely.
- Don't work on any part of the test other than the one you are told to work on. Be certain to make sure you're working on the correct test part immediately after starting. Although working in the wrong section could be an inadvertent error on your part, it would not leave a favorable impression on the examiner and would probably put you out of the running.

FILLING IN ANSWER SHEETS

You are required to fill in required personal information on the sample answer sheet sent to you by the Postal Service to be admitted to the test center. You cannot take the test without doing this. At the center, you are instructed to transfer the personal information you filled in on the sample answer sheet to the actual answer sheet.

HOW TO ENTER YOUR ANSWERS

Because Test 470 is machine scored, you must be careful to fill in your answer sheets clearly and accurately. You are given instructions concerning this in the test kit sent to you by the Postal Service. And you are given ample opportunity to perfect your skills in the practice material in this book.

> You cannot afford to lose precious exam time erasing and re-entering incorrectly entered answers. Therefore, as you answer each question for Parts A– C, look at its number and check that you are marking your answer in the space with the same number. If you cannot do this after each question, then remember to check yourself after every five questions. Either way, plan your strategy and *stick to it*.

Score Determination and Reporting

When the exam is over, the examiner collects your test booklet and answer sheet. Your answer sheet is then sent to the National Test Administration Center in Merrifield, Virginia, where a machine scans your answers and marks them as either right or wrong. Then your raw score is calculated according to the steps described in "Determining Your Raw Score" in Chapter 8, "Address Checking Practice Tests."

REPORTING OF SCALED SCORES

Your raw score is not your final score. The Postal Service:

1. Records your raw scores for each test part
2. Combines the raw test scores according to a formula
3. Converts the result to a scaled score, on a scale of 1 to 100

The entire process of conversion from raw to scaled score is confidential information.

A total scaled score of 70 is a passing score. The names of all persons with 70 or more are placed on an eligibility list (called the register) that remains valid for two years. The register is ordered according to score rankings—the names of individuals with the highest scores are at the top of the list. Hiring then takes place from the top of the list as vacancies occur.

> Although a total scaled score 70 is considered passing, it probably won't get you hired. Many candidates prepare rigorously for this test and strive for perfect scores. In fact, most applicants who are hired score between 90–100%.

LEARNING HOW YOU DID

The scoring process might take 6 to 10 weeks or even longer. Be patient. The process could take many months, but you remain eligible for employment for two years after taking the test. If you pass the exam, you receive notice of your scaled score. As the hiring process nears your number, you are notified to appear for the remaining steps of the hiring process:

1. Drug testing
2. Psychological interview
3. Physical performance tests according to the requirements of the position
4. Alpha-numeric typing test

If you fail the exam, you are not informed of your score. You are simply notified that you have failed and are not being considered for postal employment.

> You should know that as many as 50% of applicants fail Test 470. This number, of course, varies per exam administration. Use this number as a reality check for setting a serious study schedule. And even though this is a high failure rate, don't let it shake your confidence. Your preparation gives you better odds of getting a higher score than many of the candidates.

General Test-Taking Strategies

KNOW DIRECTIONS FOR EACH QUESTION TYPE

Don't waste time during the test reading directions. You are given the instructions by the Postal Service in your exam kit. Know them inside and out. This book also gives you the most recent directions used on Test 470. Remember, though, to listen to the examiner for an announcement that something has changed.

SKIP QUESTIONS WHEN STUMPED

When you cannot answer a question in Parts A–C, skip the question and come back to it after finishing the other questions in the part of the test. Circle the number of the question in your test booklet to indicate the question skipped and remember to skip the appropriate space on your answer sheet. Whether you should or should not guess is discussed in the following sections.

AVOID PERFECTIONISM

You are not expected to answer every question in Parts A and B. Don't be a perfectionist and waste time on questions you cannot answer. This kind of attitude restricts the number of questions you attempt to answer, which lowers your score. Come back to the difficult questions if you have extra time to spare.

> Use the practice tests in this book to get used to the quick pace of the test and the stringent time limitations for each test part. Adhere to these time limitations without exception. Use a stopwatch or kitchen timer for accurate measurement. This gives you a sense of your optimal pace to apply on the actual test. Not doing this handicaps your chances for a higher score.

KNOW HOW MUCH TIME YOU HAVE

To do well on Test 470, you must work quickly within the time limits allowed you. The examiner will probably inform you at periodic intervals of how much time you have left. Check your wristwatch as a backup; however, don't become obsessed by clock watching. Your time is better spent answering the questions.

> Keeping track of time does not imply you should rush through a section and answer questions carelessly. You have to be in control of the situation to do your best. This means practicing for the test as much as possible, knowing what to expect, and following the strategies provided in this book.

BUILD A TEST-SMART ATTITUDE

By practicing as much as possible for Test 470, you gain confidence in yourself, which in turn helps you succeed on the actual test. Having a test-smart attitude helps build your competitive spirit, an essential factor in doing well on this highly competitive examination.

USE THE TEST BOOKLET AS SCRATCH PAPER

You might find it beneficial to make notes or draw lines or arrows in the test booklet in pencil to help solve certain test questions. This can focus your thoughts and channel your energy to solve the question. However, don't spend too much time doing this. If it doesn't help you, stop, and go on to the next question.

ELIMINATE OBVIOUSLY INCORRECT ANSWERS

This common test-taking strategy can be used to different degrees on each test part except Part A, which only has two answer choices. To use this strategy, you must usually read all the answer choices listed to eliminate incorrect answers before choosing the correct answer. This prevents your picking a red herring (a deliberately misleading answer choice) as the answer.

SCORE HIGHER: ADDRESS CHECKING STRATEGIES

Address Checking Strategies

Of all the questions on Test 470, the address checking questions are probably the easiest. However, you should realize that these questions also carry the highest penalties for guessing. So, you should treat this question type as you would any other question—with the highest degree of speed and accuracy you can muster.

Take a look at the following "address checking" quiz, and don't worry about timing yourself. In fact, go through this quiz at your own pace, taking time to become familiar with the question type. When you're done, check your answers against the answer key provided after the quiz.

> When you are finished with the quiz, take time to review the questions you missed. If you can spot your errors, you learn to avoid them in the future.

Practice Quiz

Directions: For each question, compare the address in the left column with the address in the right column. If the two addresses are ALIKE in every way, write A next to the question number. If the two addresses are DIFFERENT in any way, write D next to the question number.

1...197 Apple Ridge Dr NW	197 Apple Ridge Dr NW
2...243 S Calumet Ave	234 S Calumet Ave
3...4300 Las Pillas Rd	4300 Las Pillas Rd
4...5551 N Summit Ave	5551 N Summit St
5...Walden CO 80480	Waldon CO 80480
6...2200 E Beach St	2200 E Beech St
7...2700 Helena Way	2700 Helena Way
8...3968 S Kingsberry Ave	3698 S Kingsbury Ave
9...14011 Costilla Ave NE	14011 Costilla Ave SE
10...1899 N Dearborn Dr	1899 N Dearborn Dr
11...8911 Scranton Way	8911 Scranton Way
12...3653 Hummingbird St	3563 Hummingbird St
13...1397 Lewiston Pl	1297 Lewiston Pl

14...4588 Crystal Way	4588 Crystal Rd
15...Muscle Shoals AL 35660	Muscle Shoals AL 35660
16...988 Larkin Johnson Ave SE	988 Larkin Johnson Ave SE
17...5501 Greenville Blvd NE	5501 Greenview Blvd NE
18...7133 N Baranmor Pky	7133 N Baranmor Pky
19...10500 Montana Rd	10500 Montana Rd
20...4769 E Fox Hollow Dr	4769 E Fox Hollow Cir
21...Daytona Beach Fla 32016	Daytona Beach FL 32016
22...2227 W 94th Ave	2272 W 94th Ave
23...6399 E Ponce De Leon St	6399 E Ponce De Leon Ct
24...20800 N Rainbow Pl	20800 N Rainbow Pl
25...Hammond GA 31785	Hammond GA 31785

ANSWERS

1. A	5. D	8. D	11. A	14. D	17. D	20. D	23. D
2. D	6. D	9. D	12. D	15. A	18. A	21. D	24. A
3. A	7. A	10. A	13. D	16. A	19. A	22. D	25. A
4. D						

Strategies to Score Higher

How did you do on the quiz? Remember to take time to review the questions you answered incorrectly.

> There is a severe penalty for guessing on this question type. The total number of wrong answers is subtracted from the total number of correct answers. If you start to run out of time, don't panic and start filling in answers at random. Instead, relax and try and remember the tips and guidelines in the rest of this chapter—you might find you have more time to finish than you thought!

Although everyone responds to the tests differently, you can use the following tips and guidelines to assist you in answering these questions. In fact, you might read through the following sections, and then try the quiz above again. Does your score improve?

- **Read for differences only!** When you spot a difference between the two given addresses, mark your answer sheet with a "D" and go immediately to the next question.
- **Vocalize your reading**. This doesn't mean simply "reading out loud," but rather reading **exactly** what is listed. For example, if you see "St." don't read it as "Street" but as "ess t." This helps you to focus on the exact details.

Know Your State and Territory Abbreviations

You should be familiar with conventional abbreviations as well as the two-letter capitalized abbreviations used with ZIP codes.

Don't worry about memorizing this list. The point of having it included here is to demonstrate how easy it is to mistake one abbreviation for another. If you vocalize what you see, you should (hopefully) "hear" the differences. And remember: your task is not to read for meaning, but to spot differences!

Alabama	Ala.	AL
Alaska	n/a	AK
American Samoa	Amer. Samoa	AS
Arizona	Ariz.	AZ
Arkansas	Ark.	AR
California	Calif.	CA
Colorado	Colo.	CO
Connecticut	Conn.	CT
Delaware	Del.	DE
District of Columbia	D.C.	DC
Florida	Fla.	FL
Georgia	Ga.	GA
Guam	n/a	GU
Hawaii	n/a	HI
Idaho	n/a	ID
Illinois	Ill.	IL
Indiana	Ind.	IN
Iowa	n/a	IA
Kansas	Kans.	KS
Kentucky	Ky.	KY
Louisiana	La.	LA
Maine	n/a	ME
Maryland	Md.	MD
Massachusetts	Mass.	MA
Michigan	Mich.	MI
Minnesota	Minn.	MN
Missouri	Mo.	MO
Montana	Mont.	MT
Nebraska	Nebr.	NE
Nevada	Nev.	NV
New Hampshire	N.H.	NH
New Jersey	N.J.	NJ

(continues)

(continues)

New Mexico	N. Mex.	NM
New York	N.Y.	NY
North Carolina	N.C.	NC
North Dakota	N.Dak.	ND
Ohio	n/a	OH
Oklahoma	Okla.	OK
Oregon	Oreg.	OR
Pennsylvania	Pa.	PA
Puerto Rico	P.R.	PR
Rhode Island	R.I.	RI
South Carolina	S.C.	SC
South Dakota	S.Dak.	SD
Tennessee	Tenn.	TN
Texas	Tex.	TX
Utah	n/a	UT
Vermont	Vt.	VT
Virginia	Va.	VA
Virgin Islands	V.I.	VI
Washington	Wash.	WA
West Virginia	W.Va.	WV
Wisconsin	Wis.	WI
Wyoming	Wyo.	WY

- **Use your hands.** Don't be afraid to use your index finger under or alongside the addresses being compared. This helps you keep your place and to focus on just one line at a time.
- **Take the question apart.** Try to break the addresses into parts; for example, first compare the street name, then the ZIP code, and so on of each of the items to be compared. This helps to make the comparison more manageable.
- **Read from right to left.** It might be very difficult for some people (remember, English speakers read left to right, so this might take some practice if English—or another left-to-right language—is your natural tongue!) You might be surprised how this forces your brain to focus on the details and not, for all practical purposes, "extraneous" information (the extraneous part being the parts of the two items that are the same).
- **Play the numbers game.** You can expect to find many differences in numbers, so keep a close eye on this when you make your comparison. Questions with two items that are not alike often have differences in the number of digits as well as differences in the order of digits.
- **Watch for differences in abbreviations.** Similar to differences in numbers, you'll find many different types of standard abbreviations; you'll also find that it's very easy to misread these, especially when comparing two items.

> Remember, you aren't expected to answer all the questions in the time given. Just try to work as quickly and as accurately as possible, and avoid guessing if you start to run out of time (instead, rely on the tips above).

Practice Exercises

Use the following practice exercises to try out the tips and techniques listed in the previous bulleted list to score the highest on Address Checking questions.

VOCALIZING TECHNIQUES

Try sounding out the following abbreviations and numbers:

NY	VA	MT	TX	10001	Pkw
CA	AL	MA	68919	3694	Cir
OR	HA	IL	828	Ct	

INDEX FINGER AS RULER OR POINTER

Try using your index finger or pointer and compare the following addresses. Are they alike or different?

1....5115 Colchester Rd	5115 Calchester Rd
2....4611 N Randall Pl	4611 N Randall Pl
3....17045 Pascack Cir	17045 Pascack Cir
4....3349 Palma del Mar Blvd	3346 Palma del Mar Blvd
5....13211 E 182nd Ave	13211 E 182nd Ave
6....Francisco WY 82636	Francisco WI 82636
7....6198 N Albritton Rd	6198 N Albretton Rd
8....11230 Twinflower Cir	11230 Twintower Cir
9....6191 MacDonald Station Rd	6191 MacDonald Station Rd
10....1587 Vanderbilt Dr N	1587 Vanderbilt Dr S

Answers

1. D   3. A   5. A   6. D   7. D   8. D   9. A   10. D

2. A   4. D

BREAK THE ADDRESS INTO PARTS

Try this technique on the following addresses. Are they alike or different?

1...3993 S Freemont Ter	3993 S Freemount Ter
2...3654 S Urbane Dr	3564 S Urbane Cir

3...1408 Oklahoma Ave NE	1408 Oklahoma Ave NE
4...6201 Meadowland Ln	6201 Meadowlawn Ln
5...5799 S Rockaway Ln	15799 S Rockaway Ln
6...3782 SE Verrazanno Bay	37872 SE Verrazanno Bay
7...2766 N Thunderbird Ct	2766 N Thunderbird Ct
8...2166 N Elmmorado Ct	2166 N Eldorado Ct
9...10538 Innsbruck Ln	10538 Innsbruck Ln
10...888 Powerville Rd	883 Powerville Rd

Answers

1. D   3. A   5. D   6. D   7. A   8. D   9. A   10. D

2. D   4. D

READ FROM RIGHT TO LEFT

Compare the following addresses using this technique.

1 ...4202 N Bainbridge Rd	4202 N Bainbridge Rd
2 ...300 E Roberta Ave	3000 E Roberta Ave
3 ...Quenemo KS 66528	Quenemo KS 66528
4 ...13845 Donahoo St	13345 Donahoo St
5 ...10466 Gertrude NE	10466 Gertrude NE
6 ...2733 N 105th Ave	2773 N 105th Ave
7 ...3100 N Wyandotte Cir	3100 N Wyandottte Ave
8 ...11796 Summerville Dr	11769 Summerville Dr
9 ...Wilburnum Miss 65566	Vilburnum Miss 65566
10 ...9334 Kindleberger Rd	9334 Kindleberger Rd

Answers

1. A   3. A   5. A   6. D   7. D   8. D   9. D   10. A

2. D   4. D

DIFFERENCES IN NUMBERS

Answer (A) if the two numbers are exactly alike, (D) if the two numbers are different in any way.

1. 2003		2003
2. 75864		75864
3. 7300		730
4. 50105		5016
5. 2184		2184
6. 8789		8789
7. 36001		3601
8. 1112		1112
9. 89900		8990
10. 07035		07035

Answers

1. A   3. D   5. A   6. A   7. D   8. A   9. D   10. A

2. A   4. D

The Real Thing: Practice an Exam

Use the following practice exam to try out the techniques you learned in this chapter, as well as give you a good idea of how it will feel on test day to confront this number of address checking questions. Go through the practice at a steady pace. When you're finished check your answers.

Directions: *For each question, compare the address in the left column with the address in the right column. If the two addresses are ALIKE in every way, write A next to the question number. If the two addresses are DIFFERENT in any way, write D next to the question number.*

1...8690 W 134th St	8960 W 134th St
2...1912 Berkshire Rd	1912 Berkshire Wy
3...5331 W Professor St	5331 W Proffesor St
4...Philadelphia PA 19124	Philadelphia PN 19124
5...7450 Gaguenay St	7450 Saguenay St
6...8650 Christy St	8650 Christey St
7...Lumberville PA 18933	Lumberville PA 1998333
8...114 Alabama Ave NW	114 Alabama Av NW
9...1756 Waterford St	1756 Waterville St

10...2214 Wister Wy	2214 Wister Wy
11...2974 Repplier Rd	2974 Repplier Dr
12...Essex CT 06426	Essex CT 06426
13...7676 N Bourbon St	7616 N Bourbon St
14...2762 Rosengarten Wy	2762 Rosengarden Wy
15...239 Windell Ave	239 Windell Ave
16...4667 Edgeworth Rd	4677 Edgeworth Rd
17...2661 Kennel St Se	2661 Kennel St Sw
18...Alamo TX 78516	Alamo TX 78516
19...3709 Columbine St	3709 Columbine St
20...9699 W 14th St	9699 W 14th Rd
21...2207 Markland Ave	2207 Markham Ave
22...Los Angeles CA 90013	Los Angeles CA 90018
23...4608 N Warnock St	4806 N Warnock St
24...7718 S Summer St	7718 S Sumner St
25...New York NY 10016	New York NY 10016
26...4514 Ft Hamilton Pk	4514 Ft Hamilton Pk
27...5701 Kosciusko St	5701 Koscusko St
28...5422 Evergreen St	4522 Evergreen St
29...Gainsville FL 43611	Gainsville FL 32611
30...5018 Church St	5018 Church Ave
31...1079 N Blake St	1097 N Blake St
32...8072 W 20th Rd	80702 W 20th Dr
33...Onoro ME 04473	Orono ME 04473
34...2175 Kimbell Rd	2175 Kimball Rd
35...1243 Mermaid St	1243 Mermaid St
36...4904 SW 134th St	4904 SW 134th St
37...1094 Hancock St	1049 Hancock St
38...Des Moines IA 50311	Des Moines IA 50311
39...4832 S Rinaldi Rd	48323 S rinaldo Rd
40...2015 Dorchester Rd	2015 Dorchester Rd
41...5216 Woodbine St	5216 Woodburn St
42...Boulder CO 80302	Boulder CA 80302
43...4739 N Marion St	479 N Marion St

44...3720 Nautilus Wy	3270 Nautilus Way
45...3636 Gramercy Pk	3636 Gramercy Pk
46...757 Johnson Ave	757 Johnston Ave
47...3045 Brighton 12th St	3045 Brighton 12th St
48...237 Ovington Ave	237 Ovington Ave
49...Kalamazoo MI 49007	Kalamazoo MI 49007
50...Lissoula MT 59812	Missoula MS59812
51...Stillwater OK 74704	Stillwater OK 47404
52...47446 Empire Blvd	4746 Empire Bldg
53...6321 St Johns Pl	6321 St Johns Pl
54...2242 Vanderbilt Ave	2242 Vanderbilt Ave
55...542 Ditmas Blvd	542 Ditmars Blvd
56...4603 W Argyle Rd	4603 W Argyle Rd
57...653 Knickerbocker Ave NE	653 Knickerbocker Ave NE
58...3651 Midwood Terr	3651 Midwood Terr
59...Chapel Hill NC 27514	Chaple Hill NC 27514
60...3217 Vernon Pl NW	3217 Vernon Dr NW
61...1094 Rednor Pkwy	1049 Rednor Pkwy
62...986 S Doughty Blvd	986 S Douty Blvd
63...Lincoln NE 68508	Lincoln NE 65808
64...1517 LaSalle Ave	1517 LaSalle Ave
65...3857 S Morris St	3857 S Morriss St
66...6104 Saunders Expy	614 Saunders Expy
67...2541 Appleton St	2541 Appleton Rd
68...Washington DC 20052	Washington DC 20052
69...6439 Kessler Blvd S	6439 Kessler Blvd S
70...4786 Catalina Dr	4786 Catalana Dr
71...132 E Hampton Pkwy	1322 E Hampton Pkwy
72...1066 Goethe Sq S	1066 Geothe Sq S
73...1118 Jerriman Wy	1218 Jerriman Wy
74...5798 Grand Central Pkwy	57998 Grand Central Pkwy
75...Delaware OH 43015	Delaware OK 43015
76...Corvallis OR 97331	Corvallis OR 97331
77...4231 Keating Ave N	4231 Keating Av N

78...5689 Central Pk Pl	5869 Central Pk Pl
79...1108 Lyndhurst Dr	1108 Lyndhurst Dr
80...842 Chambers Ct	842 Chamber Ct
81...Athens OH 45701	Athens GA 45701
82...Tulsa OK 74171	Tulsa OK 71471
83...6892 Beech Grove Ave	6892 Beech Grove Ave
84...2939 E Division St	2929 W Division St
85...1554 Pitkin Ave	1554 Pitkin Ave
86...905 St Edwards Plz	950 St Edwards Plz
87...1906 W 152nd St	1906 W 152nd St
88...3466 Glenmore Ave	3466 Glenville Ave
89...Middlebury VT 05753	Middleberry VT 05753
90...Evanston IL 60201	Evanston IN 60201
91...9401 W McDonald Ave	9401 W MacDonald Ave
92...55527 Albermarle Rd	5527 Albermarle Rd
93...9055 Carter Dr	9055 Carter Dr
94...Greenvale NY 11548	Greenvale NY 11458
95...1149 Cherry Gr S	1149 Cherry Gr S

ANSWERS

1. D	13. D	25. A	37. D	49. A	61. D	73. D	85. A
2. D	14. D	26. A	38. A	50. D	62. D	74. D	86. D
3. D	15. A	27. D	39. D	51. D	63. D	75. D	87. A
4. D	16. D	28. D	40. A	52. D	64. A	76. A	88. D
5. D	17. D	29. D	41. D	53. A	65. D	77. D	89. D
6. D	18. A	30. D	42. D	54. A	66. D	78. D	90. D
7. D	19. A	31. D	43. D	55. D	67. D	79. A	91. D
8. D	20. D	32. D	44. D	56. A	68. A	80. D	92. D
9. D	21. D	33. D	45. A	57. A	69. A	81. D	93. A
10. A	22. D	34. D	46. D	58. A	70. D	82. D	94. D
11. D	23. D	35. A	47. A	59. D	71. D	83. A	95. A
12. A	24. D	36. A	48. A	60. D	72. D	84. D	

Memory Strategies

Compared to address checking questions, "Memory for Addresses" are often considered one of the hardest types of questions on the exam. However, as with most exam questions on standardized tests, the questions **look** harder than they really are.

This chapter introduces you to some techniques that help you score higher on this question type. To begin, take the following quiz (which consists of an official set of sample questions). Take your time, become familiar with the question type and what it asks of you.

Practice Quiz

Directions: The five boxes below are labeled A, B, C, D, and E. In each box are five addresses: three are street addresses with number ranges and two are unnumbered place names. The position of an address within a box is not important. You need only remember the letter of the box in which the address is found. After memorizing the addresses, cover up the boxes and answer the questions. Take as much time as you need to answer the questions.

A	B	C	D	E
4700–5599 Table	6800–6999 Table	5600–6499 Table	6500–6799 Table	4400–4699 Table
Lismore	Kelford	Joel	Tatum	Ruskin
5600–6499 West	6500–6799 West	6800–6999 West	4400–4699 West	4700–5599 West
Hesper	Musella	Sardis	Porter	Nathan
4400–4699 Blake	5600–6499 Blake	6500–6799 Blake	4700–5599 Blake	6800–6999 Blake

Directions: For each of the following addresses, select the letter of the box in which each addresses is found. Write in the letter next to the question number.

1. Sardis

2. 4700–5599 Table

3. 4700–5599 Blake

4. Porter

5. 4400–4699 West

6. Tatum

7. Hesper

8. Musella

9. 6500–6799 West

10. Ruskin

ANSWERS

1. C 3. D 5. D 6. D 7. A 8. B 9. B 10. E

2. A 4. D

Tips and Techniques

Did you find this quiz difficult? If you did, don't worry. Even though some people have great visual memory (that is, they can look at a page and remember what the information said, as well as how it looked), most of us don't have this skill (at least not to a "prodigy"-like degree).

The actual test requires you to answer up to 88 questions in 5 minutes without referring back to the original boxes. You are, however, given extensive unscored pretest practice with these boxes (like the one you saw in the sample quiz) to help you memorize what's in each box.

This extensive pretest practice, while perhaps daunting at first glance, can really pay off. Basically, it gives you time to memorize the information you need. If you can use the techniques described in this chapter to help you during this "practice time," you can turn a very difficult section of the test into one that is, perhaps, a little more manageable. Read through the tips and techniques listed in this chapter to help you improve your memory techniques.

- **Memorize single names first.** First, take a good look at the five boxes. You should notice that in each box there are two single names and three sets of number spans with names. Single names usually are easier to memorize than the name/number combinations, so memorize these single names first.
- **Combine name pairs into key words.** This is a good way of memorizing large chunks of information, as you "combine" information into one single piece. For example, if one of the boxes had the names "Tatum" and "Porter"(let's say box "C"), you could combine this into "TaP." Hopefully, this combination of words triggers the association to "Tatum" and "Porter" in your mind, when you need to recall the information.
- **Use word associations.** In the example above, we combine "Tatum" and "Porter" into TaP. Don't just leave it at that—go ahead and associate "TaP" with "Tap Dancing" or "Tap Water"—the point is to make your word combination as useful as possible, so your mind can better associate it with the original information you are attempting to memorize.
- **Use the information to make up sentences or phrases.** Again, drawing on our "Tatum" and "Porter" example, it might be easier for you to simply combine the information to make a sentence (this might prove much more useful if you are struggling with short word combinations). For example, you might end up an associative sentence like, "Porter found the Tatum Hotel very nice."
- **Focus on number spans.** If you look again at the five sample lettered boxes used in the practice quiz, you will find five different number spans paired with three street names. In other words, each street name has the same five number spans.

Table	4400–4699, 4700–5599, 5600–6499, 6500–6799, 6800–6999
West	4400–4699, 4700–5599, 5600–6499, 6500–6799, 6800–6999
Blake	4400–4699, 4700–5599, 5600–6499, 6500–6799, 6800–6999

Remember, though, that you have 15 different addresses to remember, not 5, because each number span is paired with three different names in three different locations.

- **Shorten the numbers.** If you look at the number spans listed above, you'll see they all begin with "00" as the final two digits and end with "99" as the last two digits. So, you can save some precious "memory space" by not worrying about the "00" and "99"; instead, focus on just the beginning two digits.

The Real Thing: Practice and Exam

Complete the following two practice sets. For Set 1, you can refer back to the boxes. You must answer Set 2 solely from memory. Write your answer next to the question number.

	A	B	C	D	E
	32 Apple 35 Hills 29 Leaf Gray Book	10 Apple 22 Hills 32 Leaf Trace Fish	35 Apple 32 Hills 10 Leaf Arden Paris	22 Apple 29 Hills 35 Leaf Stewart Narrows	29 Apple 10 Hills 22 Leaf Inman Hard

Directions: *Now do the two practice sets. For the first practice exercise, you can refer back to the boxes. The second set must be answered solely from memory. Indicate your answers by writing in your answer next to the question number.*

Set 1

1. 2200–2899 Hills
2. 3500–3599 Leaf
3. Stewart
4. 3200–3499 Apple
5. 3200–3499 Hills
6. 2200–2899 Apple
7. Inman
8. Gray
9. 3500–3599 Hills
10. 2200–2899 Leaf
11. 2900–3199 Leaf
12. Trace
13. Hard
14. Arden
15. 2200–2899 Hills
16. 1000–2199 Hills
17. 1000–2199 Apple
18. Narrows
19. 3200–3499 Leaf
20. Paris
21. 3500–3599 Leaf
22. 3500–3599 Apple

23. 2200–2899 Apple
24. Fish
25. Book
26. 2900–3199 Apple
27. 2900–3199 Hills
28. 1000–2199 Leaf
29. 2200–2899 Hills
30. 3200–3499 Apple
31. Gray
32. Trace
33. Arden
34. 3200–3499 Hills
35. Narrows
36. Hard
37. 2900–3199 Leaf
38. 2200–2899 Hills
39. 3500–3599 Apple
40. 2900–3199 Hills
41. 2200–2899 Leaf
42. Inman
43. Stewart
44. Paris

45. 3500–3599 Hills
46. 1000–2199 Apple
47. Fish
48. Book
49. 3200–3499 Leaf
50. 2200–2899 Apple
51. 3200–3499 Hills
52. 2900–3199 Apple
53. 2200–2899 Leaf
54. Gray
55. Narrows
56. Hard
57. 3200–3499 Apple
58. 1000–2199 Hills
59. 1000–2199 Leaf
60. Inman
61. Book
62. 3500–3599 Hills
63. 2900–3199 Hills
64. 3500–3599 Apple
65. 3500–3599 Leaf
66. Trace

67. Paris
68. 2200–2899 Apple
69. 2900–3199 Leaf
70. Narrows
71. 2900–3199 Apple
72. 1000–2199 Apple
73. Fish
74. Gray

75. 2200–2899 Leaf
76. 3500–3599 Apple
77. 2200–2899 Hills
78. Stewart
79. Hard
80. 3500–3599 Hills
81. 2200–2899 Apple
82. Paris

83. 3500–3599 Leaf
84. 2900–3199 Leaf
85. Gray
86. 2900–3199 Hills
87. Inman
88. 3500–3599 Apple

Set 2

1. 2200–2899 Leaf
2. Narrows
3. 3200–3499 Hills
4. Fish
5. 3200–3499 Apple
6. 2900–3199 Leaf
7. Trace
8. Stewart
9. 2900–3199 Apple
10. 3500–3599 Apple
11. 1000–2199 Leaf
12. Hard
13. 1000–2199 Hills
14. 3500–3599 Leaf
15. 1000–2199 Apple
16. Gray
17. Arden
18. 2200–2899 Hills
19. 3200–3499 Hills
20. Paris
21. Book
22. 3500–3599 Hills
23. 3500–3599 Apple
24. Inman

25. 2200–2899 Apple
26. 2900–3199 Leaf
27. 2900–3199 Apple
28. 3200–3499 Hills
29. Arden
30. Gray
31. 1000–2199 Apple
32. 3500–3599 Leaf
33. 2200–2899 Leaf
34. 3500–3599 Apple
35. Trace
36. Stewart
37. Inman
38. 3500–3599 Hills
39. 2900–3199 Hills
40. 2200–2899 Hills
41. 2200–2899 Apple
42. Hard
43. Fish
44. 3500–3599 Leaf
45. 3200–3499 Hills
46. 3200–3499 Apple
47. 3200–3499 Leaf
48. Narrows

49. Paris
50. 1000–2199 Apple
51. 2900–3199 Hills
52. 3500–3599 Leaf
53. 2200–2899 Apple
54. Book
55. Stewart
56. 3500–3599 Hills
57. 2900–3199 Leaf
58. 1000–2199 Hills
59. 1000–2199 Leaf
60. Fish
61. Hard
62. 3200–3499 Hills
63. 3200–3499 Leaf
64. 2200–2899 Leaf
65. Arden
66. Inman
67. 2900–3199 Apple
68. 1000–2199 Apple
69. 2900–3199 Hills
70. 3500–3599 Hills
71. 2900–3199 Leaf
72. Paris

73. Book

74. Hard

75. Gray

76. 3200–3499 Leaf

77. 3200–3499 Apple

78. 1000–2199 Hills

79. 2200–2899 Hills

80. Stewart

81. Fish

82. 2200–2899 Apple

83. 2900–3199 Leaf

84. 2900–3199 Hills

85. Book

86. Trace

87. 3500–3599 Leaf

88. 2900–3199 Apple

ANSWERS

Set 1

1. B	12. B	23. D	34. C	45. A	56. E	67. C	78. D
2. D	13. E	24. B	35. D	46. B	57. A	68. D	79. E
3. D	14. C	25. A	36. E	47. B	58. E	69. A	80. A
4. A	15. B	26. E	37. A	48. A	59. C	70. D	81. D
5. C	16. E	27. D	38. B	49. B	60. E	71. E	82. C
6. D	17. B	28. C	39. C	50. D	61. A	72. B	83. D
7. E	18. D	29. B	40. D	51. C	62. A	73. B	84. A
8. A	19. B	30. A	41. E	52. E	63. D	74. A	85. A
9. A	20. C	31. A	42. E	53. E	64. C	75. E	86. D
10. E	21. D	32. B	43. D	54. A	65. D	76. C	87. E
11. A	22. C	33. C	44. C	55. D	66. B	77. B	88. C

Set 2

1. E	12. E	23. C	34. C	45. C	56. A	67. E	78. E
2. D	13. E	24. E	35. B	46. A	57. A	68. B	79. B
3. C	14. D	25. D	36. D	47. B	58. E	69. D	80. D
4. B	15. B	26. A	37. E	48. D	59. C	70. A	81. B
5. A	16. A	27. E	38. A	49. C	60. B	71. A	82. D
6. A	17. C	28. C	39. D	50. B	61. E	72. C	83. A
7. B	18. B	29. C	40. B	51. D	62. C	73. A	84. D
8. D	19. C	30. A	41. D	52. D	63. B	74. E	85. A
9. E	20. C	31. B	42. E	53. D	64. E	75. A	86. B
10. C	21. A	32. D	43. B	54. A	65. C	76. B	87. D
11. C	22. A	33. E	44. D	55. D	66. E	77. A	88. E

SCORE HIGHER: STRATEGIES FOR WORKING WITH NUMBER SERIES

Number Series Strategies

Don't worry too much about these types of questions (especially if you don't have very advanced math skills). You're not going to be asked to do algebra, but rather simple addition, subtraction, multiplication, and division. Best of all, you can solve most of these questions quickly, and there is no penalty for guessing.

> Here's a good tip on guessing—if you must guess, make all your guesses the same letter. By the law of averages, this gives you a better chance of hitting the right answer.

Let's get started with the usual practice quiz. The following 10-question test will familiarize you with the question type. The questions are all at varying levels of difficulty—just like they are on the actual test. Again, take your time with this, so you can get used to the type of question that is being asked.

Practice Quiz

Directions: *For each question below, there is at the left a series of numbers that follows some definite order and at the right five sets of two numbers each. You are to look at the numbers in the series at the left and find out what order they follow. Then decide what the next two numbers in the series would be if the same order were continued. Circle the letter of the correct answer.*

1. 21 21 19 17 17 15 13 ....(A) 11 11   (B) 13 11   (C) 11 9   (D) 9 7   (E) 13 13

2. 23 22 20 19 16 15 11 ....(A) 6 5   (B) 10 9   (C) 6 1   (D) 10 6   (E) 10 5

3. 5 6 8 9 11 12 14 ....(A) 15 16   (B) 16 17   (C) 15 17   (D) 16 18   (E) 17 19

4. 7 10 8 13 16 8 19 ....(A) 22 8   (B) 8 22   (C) 20 21   (D) 22 25   (E) 8 25

5. 1 35 2 34 3 33 4 ....(A) 4 5   (B) 32 31   (C) 32 5   (D) 5 32   (E) 31 6

6. 75 75 72 72 69 69 66 ....(A) 66 66   (B) 66 68   (C) 63 63   (D) 66 63   (E) 63 60

7. 12 16 21 27 31 36 42 ....(A) 48 56   (B) 44 48   (C) 48 52   (D) 46 52   (E) 46 51

8. 22 24 12 26 28 12 30 ....(A) 12 32   (B) 32 34   (C) 32 12   (D) 12 12   (E) 32 36

9. 5 70 10 68 15 66 20 ....(A) 25 64   (B) 64 25   (C) 24 63   (D) 25 30   (E) 64 62

10. 13 22 32 43 55 68 82 ....(A) 97 113   (B) 100 115   (C) 96 110   (D) 95 105   (E) 99 112

ANSWERS

Remember, take time to review your answers carefully, and spend a little extra time on any that you missed.

1. **(B)** The pattern of this series is: repeat the number, then subtract 2 and subtract 2 again; repeat the number, then subtract 2 and subtract 2 again, and so on. Following the pattern, the series should continue with (B) 13 11 and then go on 9 9 7 5 5 3 1 1.

2. **(E)** The pattern is: – 1, – 2, – 1, – 3, – 1, – 4, – 1, – 5, and so on. Fitting the pattern to the remaining numbers, it is apparent that (E) is the answer because 11 – 1 = 10 and 10 – 5 = 5.

3. **(C)** The pattern here is: +1, +2; +1, +2; +1, +2 and so on. The answer is (C) because 14 + 1 = 15 and 15 + 2 = 17.

4. **(A)**. You first must notice that the number 8 is repeated after each two numbers. If you disregard the 8s, you can see that the series is increasing by a factor of +3. With this information, you can choose (A) as the correct answer because 19 + 3 = 22, and the two numbers, 19 and 22, are then followed by 8.

5. **(C)** This series is, in reality, two alternating series. One series, beginning with 1, increases at the rate of +1. The other series alternates with the first. It begins with 35 and decreases by – 1. The answer is (C) because the next number in the decreasing series is 32 and the next number in the increasing series is 5.

6. **(D)** The pattern established in this series is: repeat the number, – 3; repeat the number, – 3, and so on. To continue the series, repeat 66, then subtract 3.

7. **(E)** The pattern is: +4, +5, +6; +4, +5, +6; +4, +5, +6. Continuing the series: 42 + 4 = 46 + 5 = 51.

8. **(C)** In this series the basic pattern is +2. The series may be read: 22 24 26 28 30 32. After each two numbers of the series we find the number 12, which serves no function except for repetition. To continue the series, add 2 to 30 to get 32. After 30 and 32, you must put in the number 12.

9. **(B)** In this problem there are two distinct series alternating with one another. The first series is ascending by a factor of +5. It reads: 10 15 20. The alternating series is descending by a factor of – 2. It reads: 70 68 66. At the point where you must continue the series, the next number must be a member of the descending series, so it must be 64. Following that number must come the next number of the ascending series, which is 25.

10. **(A)** The numbers are large but the progression is simple between each number in the series: +9, +10, +11, +12, +13, +14. Continuing the series: 82 + 15 = 97 + 16 = 113.

Strategies for Working with Number Series Questions

Okay, so you're a bit anxious about working with numbers. Well, put your fears aside. Remember, the test isn't going to ask you to break out the calculus (or even a simple calculator, for that matter). You need to work—as usual—with as much speed and efficiency as you can muster. However, if you try to remember the following tips, you might find that this type of question isn't as frightening as you thought!

• **In number series with one pattern, look for the following number arrangements:**

  simple ascending (increasing) or descending (decreasing) numbers where the same number is added to or subtracted from each number in a series alternating ascending or descending numbers where two different numbers are alternately added to or subtracted from each number in a series

simple or alternating multiplication or division

simple repetition where one or more number in the series is repeated immediately before or after addition or subtraction or other arithmetic operation

repetition of a number pattern by itself

unusual pattern

- **In number series with two or more patterns, look for the following kinds of patterns:**

random number (not one of the numbers in the series)

introduced and repeated number in a one-pattern series

two or more alternating series of two or more distinct patterns

two or more alternating series of patterns plus repetitive or random numbers

two or more alternating patterns that include simple multiplication and division

unusual alternating or combination arrangements

- **Solve at a glance** Look for simple number series that "jump out" at you, like 1 2 3 1 2 3. Also, be on the lookout for patterns that are either adding or subtracting to get the next number, such 20 21 22 23 or 35 34 33 32.
- **Vocalize for meaning** With all those numbers flying around, it might easy for your eye (and thus, your brain) to get confused, mistakenly reading a number for something else. That's why it sometimes helps to vocalize (or, say quietly to yourself) what you are reading. You might be able to "hear" a pattern more quickly—and more accurately—than if you had just looked at it.
- **When you spot a difference, mark it down!** By "difference" we mean that you should immediately mark any change in the number series that you find. For example, if you're reading and you notice that the series is increasing by 2 (for example, 2 4 6 8) write down that difference in the numbers of the series (again, in this case 2). Remember, most series are either ascending, descending or a combination of the two. If you can't figure it out with addition and subtraction, try multiplication and division. Number series that use multiplication and division are fairly rare. However, you shouldn't discount this possibility entirely (just remember to try addition and subtraction first).
- **Know how to spot repeating and random numbers** Repeating and random numbers might not be so obvious. Be sure and mark up the question in your test booklet—this helps you spot these types of numbers more easily than if you simply try to "see" them in your brain.

Number Series Practice 1

You should be able to answer the following questions based on your work so far. Take the quiz at your own pace using all of the techniques you learned in this chapter. When you're finished check your answers against the answer key and explanations.

Directions: For each question below, there is at the left a series of numbers that follows some definite order and at the right five sets of two numbers each. You are to look at the numbers in the series at the left and find out what order they follow. Then decide what the next two numbers in the series would be if the same order were continued. Circle the letter of the correct answer.

1. 8 9 10 8 9 10 8 .... (A) 8 9   (B) 9 10   (C) 9 8   (D) 10 8   (E) 8 10

2. 16 16 15 15 14 14 13 .... (A) 12 13   (B) 14 13   (C) 12 11   (D) 12 10   (E) 13 12

3. 2 6 10 2 7 11 15 .... (A) 12 16   (B) 15 19   (C) 15 16   (D) 12 13   (E) 2 19

4. 30 28 27 25 24 22 21 .... (A) 21 20   (B) 19 18   (C) 20 19   (D) 20 18   (E) 21 21

5. 25 25 22 22 19 19 16 .... (A) 18 18   (B) 16 16   (C) 16 13   (D) 15 15   (E) 15 13

6. 9 17 24 30 35 39 42 .... (A) 43 44   (B) 44 46   (C) 44 45   (D) 45 49   (E) 46 50

7. 28 31 34 37 40 43 46 .... (A) 49 52   (B) 47 49   (C) 50 54   (D) 49 53   (E) 51 55

8. 17 17 24 24 31 31 38 .... (A) 38 39   (B) 38 17   (C) 38 45   (D) 38 44   (E) 39 50

9. 87 83 79 75 71 67 63 .... (A) 62 61   (B) 63 59   (C) 60 56   (D) 59 55   (E) 59 54

10. 8 9 11 14 18 23 29 .... (A) 35 45   (B) 32 33   (C) 38 48   (D) 34 40   (E) 36 44

11. 4 8 12 16 20 24 .... (A) 26 28   (B) 28 30   (C) 28 30   (D) 28 32   (E) 28 29

12. 3 4 1 3 4 1 3 .... (A) 4 1   (B) 4 5   (C) 4 3   (D) 1 2   (E) 4 4

ANSWERS

1. B   3. E   5. C   7. A   9. D   10. E   11. D   12. A

2. E   4. B   6. C   8. C

EXPLANATIONS

1. (**B**) The series is simply a repetition of the sequence 8 9 10.
2. (**E**) This series is a simple descending series combined with repetition. Each number is first repeated and then decreased by 1.
3. (**E**) This pattern is +4 then repeat the number 2.
4. (**B**) This pattern is not as easy to spot as the ones in the previous questions. If you write in the direction and degree of change between each number, you can see that this an alternating descending series with the pattern – 2, – 1, – 2, – 1, etc.
5. (**C**) Repeat, – 3, repeat, – 3, repeat, – 3.
6. (**C**) The rule here is: +8, +7, +6, +5, +4, +3, +2.
7. (**A**) A simple +3 rule.
8. (**C**) Each number repeats itself, and then increases by + 7.
9. (**D**) Here the rule is – 4.
10. (**E**) The rule is: +1, +2, +3, +4, +5, +6, +7, +8.
11. (**D**) This is a simple ascending series where each number increases by 4.
12. (**A**) A simple +1 series with the number 1 repeated after each step of the series.

Number Series Practice II

Answer every question to the best of your ability. Write next to each question which technique you used. After you have finished every question, then check your answers against the answer key and explanations that follow.

Directions: *For each question below, there is at the left a series of numbers that follows some definite order and at the right five sets of two numbers each. You are to look at the numbers in the series at the left and find out what order they follow. Then decide what the next two numbers in the series would be if the same order were continued. Circle the letter of the correct answer.*

1. 12 26 15 26 18 26 21 .... (A) 21 24   (B) 24 26   (C) 21 26   (D) 26 24   (E) 26 25

2. 72 67 69 64 66 61 63 .... (A) 58 60   (B) 65 62   (C) 60 58   (D) 65 60   (E) 60 65

3. 81 10 29 81 10 29 81 .... (A) 29 10   (B) 81 29   (C) 10 29   (D) 81 10   (E) 29 81

4. 91 91 90 88 85 81 76 .... (A) 71 66   (B) 70 64   (C) 75 74   (D) 70 65   (E) 70 63

5. 22 44 29 37 36 30 43 .... (A) 50 23   (B) 23 50   (C) 53 40   (D) 40 53   (E) 50 57

6. 0 1 1 0 2 2 0 .... (A) 0 0   (B) 0 3   (C) 3 3   (D) 3 4   (E) 2 3

7. 32 34 36 34 36 38 36 .... (A) 34 32   (B) 36 34   (C) 36 38   (D) 38 40   (E) 38 36

8. 26 36 36 46 46 56 56 .... (A) 66 66   (B) 56 66   (C) 57 57   (D) 46 56   (E) 26 66

9. 64 63 61 58 57 55 52 .... (A) 51 50   (B) 52 49   (C) 50 58   (D) 50 47   (E) 51 49

10. 4 6 8 7 6 8 10 9 8 .... (A) 7 9   (B) 11 12   (C) 12 14   (D) 7 10   (E) 10 12

11. 57 57 52 47 47 42 37 .... (A) 32 32   (B) 37 32   (C) 37 37   (D) 32 27   (E) 27 27

12. 13 26 14 25 16 23 19 .... (A) 20 21   (B) 20 22   (C) 20 23   (D) 20 24   (E) 22 25

13. 15 27 39 51 63 75 87 .... (A) 97 112   (B) 99 111   (C) 88 99   (D) 89 99   (E) 90 99

14. 2 0 2 2 2 4 2 6 2 8 .... (A) 2 2   (B) 2 8   (C) 2 10   (D) 2 12   (E) 2 16

15. 19 18 18 17 17 17 16 .... (A) 16 16   (B) 16 15   (C) 15 15   (D) 15 14   (E) 16 17

16. 55 53 44 51 49 44 47 .... (A) 45 43   (B) 46 45   (C) 46 44   (D) 44 44   (E) 45 44

17. 100 81 64 49 36 25 16 ...... (A) 8 4   (B) 8 2   (C) 9 5   (D) 9 4   (E) 9 3

18. 2 2 4 6 8 18 16 .... (A) 32 64   (B) 32 28   (C) 54 32   (D) 32 54   (E) 54 30

19. 47 43 52 48 57 53 62 .... (A) 58 54   (B) 67 58   (C) 71 67   (D) 58 67   (E) 49 58

20. 38 38 53 48 48 63 58 .... (A) 58 58   (B) 58 73   (C) 73 73   (D) 58 68   (E) 73 83

21. 12 14 16 13 15 17 14 .... (A) 17 15   (B) 15 18   (C) 17 19   (D) 15 16   (E) 16 18

22. 30 30 30 37 37 37 30 .... (A) 30 30   (B) 30 37   (C) 37 37   (D) 37 30   (E) 31 31

23. 75 52 69 56 63 59 57 .... (A) 58 62   (B) 55 65   (C) 51 61   (D) 61 51   (E) 63 55

24. 176 88 88 44 44 22 22 ...... (A) 22 11   (B) 11 11   (C) 11 10   (D) 11 5   (E) 22 10

ANSWERS

1. D	4. E	7. D	10. E	13. B	16. E	19. D	22. A
2. A	5. B	8. A	11. B	14. C	17. D	20. B	23. D
3. C	6. C	9. E	12. C	15. A	18. C	21. E	24. B

EXPLANATIONS

1. **(D)** A + 3 series with the number 26 between terms.

$$12^{+3} \; \boxed{26} \; 15^{+3} \; \boxed{26} \; 18^{+3} \; \boxed{26} \; 21^{+3} \; \boxed{26} \; 24$$

2. **(A)** You may read this as a – 5, +2 series.

$$72^{-5} \; 67^{+2} \; 69^{-5} \; 64^{+2} \; 66^{-5} \; 61^{+2} \; 63^{-5} \; 58^{+2} \; 60$$

or as two alternating – 3 series.

3. **(C)** You should see by inspection that the sequence 81 10 29 repeats itself over and over.

4. **(E)** Write in the numbers for this one.

$$91^{-0} \; 91^{-1} \; 90^{-2} \; 88^{-3} \; 85^{-4} \; 81^{-5} \; 76^{-6} \; 70^{-7} \; 63$$

5. **(B)** Here we have two distinct alternating series.

6. **(C)** The digit 0 intervenes after each repeating number of a simple +1 and repeat series.

7. **(D)** Group the numbers into threes. Each succeeding group of three begins with a number two higher than the first number of the preceding group of three. Within each group the pattern is +2, +2.

8. **(A)** The pattern is + 10, repeat the number, +10, repeat the number.

$$26^{+10} \; 36^{r} \; 36^{+10} 46^{r} \; 46^{+10} \; 56^{r} \; 56^{+10} \; 66^{r} \; 66$$

9. **(E)** The pattern is – 1, – 2, – 3; – 1, – 2, – 3 and so on. If you can't see it, write it in for yourself.

10. **(E)** Here the pattern is +2, +2, – 1, – 1; +2, +2, – 1, – 1.

$$4^{+2} \; 6^{+2} \; 8^{-1} \; 7^{-1} \; 6^{+2} \; 8^{+2} \; 10^{-1} \; 9^{-1} \; 8^{+2} \; 10^{+2} \; 12$$

The series that is given to you is a little bit longer than most to better assist you in establishing this extra long pattern.

11. **(B)** This is a – 5 pattern with every other term repeated.

$$57^{r} \; 57^{-5} \; 52^{-5} \; 47^{r} \; 47^{-5} \; 42^{-5} \; 37^{r} \; 37^{-5} \; 32$$

12. **(C)** This series consists of two alternating series.

13. **(B)** This is a simple +12 series.

14. **(C)** Even with the extra length, you might have trouble with this one. You might have to change your approach a couple of times to figure it out.

$$2^{\times 0} \; 0; \; 2^{\times 1} \; 2; \; 2^{\times 2} \; 4; \; 2^{\times 3} \; 6; \; 2^{\times 4} \; 8; \; 2^{\times 5} \; 10$$

15. **(A)** Each number is repeated one time more than the number before it. Nineteen appears only once, 18 twice, 17 three times and, if the series were extended beyond the question, 16 would appear four times.

16. **(E)** This is a – 2 series with the number 44 appearing after every two numbers of the series. You probably can see this now without writing it out.

17. **(D)** The series consists of the squares of the numbers from 2 to 10 in descending order.

18. **(C)** This is a tricky alternating series question.

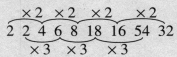

$$2 \quad 2 \quad 4 \quad 6 \quad 8 \quad 18 \quad 16 \quad 54 \quad 32$$

19. **(D)** The progress of this series is – 4, +9; – 4, +9.

20. **(B)** This series is not really difficult, but you might have to write it out to see it.

$$38^r\, 38^{+15}\, 53^{-5}\, 48^r\, 48^{+15}\, 63^{-5}\, 58^r\, 58^{+15}\, 73$$

You might also see this as two alternating +10 series with the numbers ending in 8 repeated.

21. **(E)** Group into groups of three numbers. Each +2 group begins one step up from the previous group.

22. **(A)** By inspection, you can see that this series is nothing more than the number 30 repeated three times and the number 37 repeated three times. Because you have no further clues, you must assume that the series continues with the number 30 repeated three times.

23. **(D)** Here are two alternating series.

$$75 \quad 52 \quad 69 \quad 56 \quad 63 \quad 59 \quad 57 \quad 61 \quad 51$$

24. **(B)** The pattern is +2 and repeat the number, +2 and repeat the number.

$$176^{+2}\, 88^r\, 88^{+2}\, 44^r\, 44^{+2}\, 22^r\, 22^{+2}\, 11^r\, 11$$

SCORE HIGHER: STRATEGIES FOR FOLLOWING ORAL INSTRUCTIONS

Tips for Oral Instruction Questions

It always pays to be a good listener, and oral instruction questions are no exception. Unlike other types of questions you encounter, oral instruction questions require you to focus your attention on another individual (or more precisely, the sound of his or her voice) rather than simply the test booklet. However, like all questions on the exam, you'll score your highest if you concentrate, relax, and are well prepared.

The information in this chapter helps you to do just that.

Use the following tips and techniques to tackle the oral instruction questions:

> Due to the nature of these questions, we're going to dismiss with the "warm-up questions" that have been at the opening of each of these strategy chapters, and start with a list of strategies. Later on in this chapter, you have a chance to try out everything you've learned.

- **Pay attention to the instructions!** We've stressed in previous chapters that concentration is important. Well, with oral instruction questions, attention is paramount! Unlike other questions, if you "space out" during this portion of the exam, you can't simply "re-read" the question in your booklet. Try to stay focused!
- **Mark your answer sheet as instructed.** Unlike other questions, you do not answer the oral instruction questions in sequential order on your answer sheet. In fact, you skip around the page, filing in answers in the order specified. (Actually, you do not use all the answer spaces provided to you!)
- **Work from left to right.** If the instructions say to mark the "fourth letter", it is the fourth letter from the left, no exceptions. Of course, if the instructions tell you differently (for example, if they say, "Please put a circle around the fifth letter from the right"), then you obviously need to make an exception from reading left to right. Again, listen closely!
- **Don't waste time changing answers.** If you are about to enter a choice on your answer sheet, and suddenly realize you've already filled in that choice (for example, you've made that choice from another question), don't make a change. Wait for the next set of instructions, and move on.

> If you find that you've blackened two answer spaces for the same question, erase one of them only if you have time, and if you won't get distracted and fall behind in the instructions.

Practice with Oral Instructions Questions

For this section, you need to find a friend who can read through the instructions to you.

As you work through the sample test, try your best to relax, concentrate, and remember the tips listed previously. Good luck!

TEAR HERE

1. Ⓐ Ⓑ Ⓒ Ⓓ Ⓔ
2. Ⓐ Ⓑ Ⓒ Ⓓ Ⓔ
3. Ⓐ Ⓑ Ⓒ Ⓓ Ⓔ
4. Ⓐ Ⓑ Ⓒ Ⓓ Ⓔ
5. Ⓐ Ⓑ Ⓒ Ⓓ Ⓔ
6. Ⓐ Ⓑ Ⓒ Ⓓ Ⓔ
7. Ⓐ Ⓑ Ⓒ Ⓓ Ⓔ
8. Ⓐ Ⓑ Ⓒ Ⓓ Ⓔ
9. Ⓐ Ⓑ Ⓒ Ⓓ Ⓔ
10. Ⓐ Ⓑ Ⓒ Ⓓ Ⓔ
11. Ⓐ Ⓑ Ⓒ Ⓓ Ⓔ
12. Ⓐ Ⓑ Ⓒ Ⓓ Ⓔ
13. Ⓐ Ⓑ Ⓒ Ⓓ Ⓔ
14. Ⓐ Ⓑ Ⓒ Ⓓ Ⓔ
15. Ⓐ Ⓑ Ⓒ Ⓓ Ⓔ
16. Ⓐ Ⓑ Ⓒ Ⓓ Ⓔ
17. Ⓐ Ⓑ Ⓒ Ⓓ Ⓔ
18. Ⓐ Ⓑ Ⓒ Ⓓ Ⓔ
19. Ⓐ Ⓑ Ⓒ Ⓓ Ⓔ
20. Ⓐ Ⓑ Ⓒ Ⓓ Ⓔ
21. Ⓐ Ⓑ Ⓒ Ⓓ Ⓔ
22. Ⓐ Ⓑ Ⓒ Ⓓ Ⓔ

23. Ⓐ Ⓑ Ⓒ Ⓓ Ⓔ
24. Ⓐ Ⓑ Ⓒ Ⓓ Ⓔ
25. Ⓐ Ⓑ Ⓒ Ⓓ Ⓔ
26. Ⓐ Ⓑ Ⓒ Ⓓ Ⓔ
27. Ⓐ Ⓑ Ⓒ Ⓓ Ⓔ
28. Ⓐ Ⓑ Ⓒ Ⓓ Ⓔ
29. Ⓐ Ⓑ Ⓒ Ⓓ Ⓔ
30. Ⓐ Ⓑ Ⓒ Ⓓ Ⓔ
31. Ⓐ Ⓑ Ⓒ Ⓓ Ⓔ
32. Ⓐ Ⓑ Ⓒ Ⓓ Ⓔ
33. Ⓐ Ⓑ Ⓒ Ⓓ Ⓔ
34. Ⓐ Ⓑ Ⓒ Ⓓ Ⓔ
35. Ⓐ Ⓑ Ⓒ Ⓓ Ⓔ
36. Ⓐ Ⓑ Ⓒ Ⓓ Ⓔ
37. Ⓐ Ⓑ Ⓒ Ⓓ Ⓔ
38. Ⓐ Ⓑ Ⓒ Ⓓ Ⓔ
39. Ⓐ Ⓑ Ⓒ Ⓓ Ⓔ
40. Ⓐ Ⓑ Ⓒ Ⓓ Ⓔ
41. Ⓐ Ⓑ Ⓒ Ⓓ Ⓔ
42. Ⓐ Ⓑ Ⓒ Ⓓ Ⓔ
43. Ⓐ Ⓑ Ⓒ Ⓓ Ⓔ
44. Ⓐ Ⓑ Ⓒ Ⓓ Ⓔ

45. Ⓐ Ⓑ Ⓒ Ⓓ Ⓔ
46. Ⓐ Ⓑ Ⓒ Ⓓ Ⓔ
47. Ⓐ Ⓑ Ⓒ Ⓓ Ⓔ
48. Ⓐ Ⓑ Ⓒ Ⓓ Ⓔ
49. Ⓐ Ⓑ Ⓒ Ⓓ Ⓔ
50. Ⓐ Ⓑ Ⓒ Ⓓ Ⓔ
51. Ⓐ Ⓑ Ⓒ Ⓓ Ⓔ
52. Ⓐ Ⓑ Ⓒ Ⓓ Ⓔ
53. Ⓐ Ⓑ Ⓒ Ⓓ Ⓔ
54. Ⓐ Ⓑ Ⓒ Ⓓ Ⓔ
55. Ⓐ Ⓑ Ⓒ Ⓓ Ⓔ
56. Ⓐ Ⓑ Ⓒ Ⓓ Ⓔ
57. Ⓐ Ⓑ Ⓒ Ⓓ Ⓔ
58. Ⓐ Ⓑ Ⓒ Ⓓ Ⓔ
59. Ⓐ Ⓑ Ⓒ Ⓓ Ⓔ
60. Ⓐ Ⓑ Ⓒ Ⓓ Ⓔ
61. Ⓐ Ⓑ Ⓒ Ⓓ Ⓔ
62. Ⓐ Ⓑ Ⓒ Ⓓ Ⓔ
63. Ⓐ Ⓑ Ⓒ Ⓓ Ⓔ
64. Ⓐ Ⓑ Ⓒ Ⓓ Ⓔ
65. Ⓐ Ⓑ Ⓒ Ⓓ Ⓔ
66. Ⓐ Ⓑ Ⓒ Ⓓ Ⓔ

67. Ⓐ Ⓑ Ⓒ Ⓓ Ⓔ
68. Ⓐ Ⓑ Ⓒ Ⓓ Ⓔ
69. Ⓐ Ⓑ Ⓒ Ⓓ Ⓔ
70. Ⓐ Ⓑ Ⓒ Ⓓ Ⓔ
71. Ⓐ Ⓑ Ⓒ Ⓓ Ⓔ
72. Ⓐ Ⓑ Ⓒ Ⓓ Ⓔ
73. Ⓐ Ⓑ Ⓒ Ⓓ Ⓔ
74. Ⓐ Ⓑ Ⓒ Ⓓ Ⓔ
75. Ⓐ Ⓑ Ⓒ Ⓓ Ⓔ
76. Ⓐ Ⓑ Ⓒ Ⓓ Ⓔ
77. Ⓐ Ⓑ Ⓒ Ⓓ Ⓔ
78. Ⓐ Ⓑ Ⓒ Ⓓ Ⓔ
79. Ⓐ Ⓑ Ⓒ Ⓓ Ⓔ
80. Ⓐ Ⓑ Ⓒ Ⓓ Ⓔ
81. Ⓐ Ⓑ Ⓒ Ⓓ Ⓔ
82. Ⓐ Ⓑ Ⓒ Ⓓ Ⓔ
83. Ⓐ Ⓑ Ⓒ Ⓓ Ⓔ
84. Ⓐ Ⓑ Ⓒ Ⓓ Ⓔ
85. Ⓐ Ⓑ Ⓒ Ⓓ Ⓔ
86. Ⓐ Ⓑ Ⓒ Ⓓ Ⓔ
87. Ⓐ Ⓑ Ⓒ Ⓓ Ⓔ
88. Ⓐ Ⓑ Ⓒ Ⓓ Ⓔ

1.   13   23   2   19   6

2.   E   B   D   E   C   A   B

3. | 30 __ | | 18 __ | | 5 __ | | 14 __ | | 7 __ |

4.   (26 __)   (16 __)   (23 __)   (23 __)   (27 __)

5. | 63 __ | | 16 __ | | 78 __ | | 48 __ |

6.   12 _____   5 _____   22 _____

7.   (14 __)   (1 __)   (36 __)   (7 __)   (19 __)

8.   26 _____   86 _____

9.   57   63   11   78   90   32   45   70   69

10.   16   30   13   25   10   14   23   26   19

11.   (9:12 __ A)   (9:28 __ B)   (9:24 __ C)   (9:11 __ D)   (9:32 __ E)

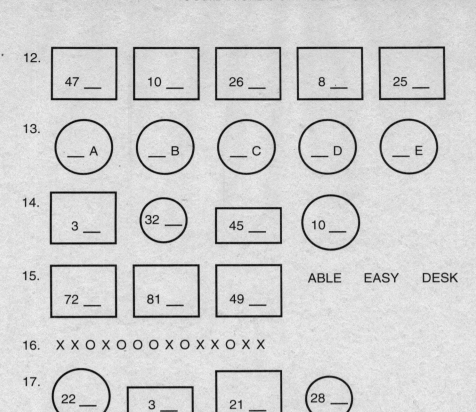

12. 47 __   10 __   26 __   8 __   25 __

13. __ A   __ B   __ C   __ D   __ E

14. 3 __   32 __   45 __   10 __

15. 72 __   81 __   49 __   ABLE   EASY   DESK

16. X X O X O O O X O X X O X X

17. 22 __   3 __   21 __   28 __

18. 21 __   38 __   29 __   31 __

19. __ A   __ C   __ E

TEAR HERE

PRACTICE EXAM 1

*Here are the instructions to be read aloud. Do **not** read aloud the words in parenthesis.*

On the job you will have to listen to directions and then do what you have been told to do. In this test, I will read instructions to you. Try to understand them as I read them; I cannot repeat them. Once we begin, you may not ask any questions until the end of the test.

On the job you won't have to deal with pictures, numbers, and letters like those in the test, but you will have to listen to instructions and follow them. We are using this test to see how well you can follow instructions.

You are to mark your test booklet according to the instructions that I'll read to you. After each set of instructions, I'll give you time to record your answers on the separate answer sheet.

The actual test begins now.

Look at line 1 on the worksheet. (Pause slightly.) Draw a line under the fourth number in the line. (Pause 2 seconds.) Now, on your answer sheet, find the number under which you just drew the line and darken space A for that number. (Pause 5 seconds.)

Look at the letters in line 2 on the worksheet. (Pause slightly.) Draw a line under the fifth letter in the line. Now, on your answer sheet, find number 59 (pause 2 seconds) and darken the space for the letter under which you drew a line. (Pause 5 seconds.)

Look at the letters in line 2 on the worksheet again. (Pause slightly.) Now draw two lines under the third letter in the line. (Pause 2 seconds.) Now, on your answer sheet, find number 65 (pause 2 seconds) and darken the space for the letter under which you drew two lines. (Pause 5 seconds.)

Look at line 3 on the worksheet. (Pause slightly.) Write an E in the last box. (Pause 2 seconds.) Now, on your answer sheet, find the number in that box and darken space E for that number. (Pause 5 seconds.)

Now look at line 3 again. (Pause slightly.) Write an A in the first box. (Pause 2 seconds.) Now, on your answer sheet, find the number in that box and darken space A for that number. (Pause 5 seconds.)

Look at line 4. The number in each circle is the number of packages in a mail sack. In the circle for the sack holding the largest number of packages, write a B as in baker. (Pause 2 seconds.) Now, on your answer sheet, darken the space for the number-letter combination that is in the circle in which you just wrote. (Pause 5 seconds.)

Look at line 4 again. In the circle for the sack holding the smallest number of packages, write an E. (Pause 2 seconds.) Now, on your answer sheet, darken the space for the number-letter combination that is in the circle in which you just wrote. (Pause 5 seconds.)

Look at the drawings on line 5 on the worksheet. The four boxes are trucks for carrying mail. (Pause slightly.) The truck with the highest number is to be loaded first. Write B as in baker on the line beside the highest number. (Pause 2 seconds.) Now, on your answer sheet, darken the space for the number-letter combination that is in the box in which you just wrote. (Pause 5 seconds.)

Look at line 6 on the worksheet. (Pause slightly.) Next to the middle number write the letter D as in dog. (Pause 2 seconds.) Now, on your answer sheet, find the space for the number beside which you wrote and darken space D as in dog. (Pause 5 seconds.)

Look at the five circles in line 7 on the worksheet. Write B as in baker on the blank in the second circle. (Pause 2 seconds.) Now, on your answer sheet, darken the space for the number-letter combination that is in the circle in which you just wrote. (Pause 5 seconds.)

Now take the worksheet again and write C on the blank in the third circle on line 7. (Pause 2 seconds.) Now, on your answer sheet, darken the space for the number-letter combination that is in the circle in which you just wrote. (Pause 5 seconds.)

Now look at line 8 on the worksheet. (Pause slightly.) Write an A on the line next to the right-hand number. (Pause 2 seconds.) Now, on your answer sheet, find the space for the number beside which you wrote and darken box A. (Pause 5 seconds.)

Look at line 9 on the worksheet. (Pause slightly.) Draw a line under every number that is more than 60 but less than 70. (Pause 12 seconds.) Now, on your answer sheet, for each number that you drew a line under, darken space C. (Pause 25 seconds.)

Look at line 10 on the worksheet. (Pause slightly.) Draw a line under every number that is more than 5 and less than 15. (Pause 10 seconds.) Now, on your answer sheet, for each number that you drew a line under, darken space D as in dog. (Pause 25 seconds.)

Look at line 11 on the worksheet. (Pause slightly.) In each circle there is a time when the mail must leave. In the circle for the latest time, write on the line the last two figures of the time. (Pause 5 seconds.) Now, on your answer sheet, darken the space for the number-letter combination that is in the circle in which you just wrote. (Pause 5 seconds.)

Look at the five boxes in line 12 on your worksheet. (Pause slightly.) If 6 is less than 3, put an E in the fourth box. (Pause slightly.) If 6 is not less than 3, put a B as in baker in the first box. (Pause 10 seconds.) Now, on your answer sheet, darken the space for the number-letter combination that is in the box in which you just wrote. (Pause 5 seconds.)

Now look at line 13 on the worksheet. (Pause slightly.) There are five circles. Each circle has a letter. (Pause slightly.) In the second circle, write the answer to this question: Which of the following numbers is smallest: 72, 51, 88, 71, 58? (Pause 10 seconds.) Now, on your answer sheet, darken the space for the number-letter combination that is in the circle you just wrote in. (Pause 5 seconds.) In the third circle on the same line, write 28. (Pause 2 seconds.) Now, on your answer sheet, darken the space for the number-letter combination that is in the circle you just wrote in. (Pause 5 seconds.) In the fourth circle do nothing. In the fifth circle write the answer to this question: How many months are there in a year? (Pause 5 seconds.) Now, on your answer sheet, darken the space for the number-letter combination that is in the circle in which you just wrote. (Pause 5 seconds.)

Look at line 14 on your worksheet. (Pause slightly.) There are two circles and two boxes of different sizes with numbers in them. (Pause slightly.) If 2 is smaller than 4 and if 7 is less than 3, write A in the larger circle. (Pause slightly.) Otherwise, write B as in baker in the smaller box. (Pause 10 seconds.) Now, on your answer sheet, darken the space for the number-letter combination in the box or circle in which you just wrote. (Pause 5 seconds.)

Look at the boxes and words in line 15 on the worksheet. (Pause slightly.) Write the second letter of the first word in the third box. (Pause 5 seconds.) Write the first letter of the second word in the first box. (Pause 5 seconds.) Write the first letter of the third word in the second box. (Pause 5 seconds.) Now, on your answer sheet, darken the spaces for the number-letter combinations that are in the three boxes in which you just wrote. (Pause 15 seconds.)

Look at line 16 on the worksheet. (Pause slightly.) Draw a line under every "0" in the line. (Pause 5 seconds.) Count the number of lines that you have drawn, subtract 2, and write that number at the end of the line. (Pause 5 seconds.) Now, on your answer sheet, find that number and darken space D as in dog for that number. (Pause 5 seconds.)

Look at line 17 on the worksheet. (Pause slightly.) If the number in the left-hand circle is smaller than the number in the right-hand circle, add 2 to the number in the left-hand circle, and change the number in that circle to this number. (Pause 8 seconds.) Then write B as in baker next to the new number. (Pause slightly.) Next, write E beside the number in the smaller box. (Pause 3 seconds.) Then, on your answer sheet, darken the spaces for the number-letter combinations that are in the box and circle in which you just wrote. (Pause 5 seconds.)

Look at line 18 on the worksheet. (Pause slightly.) If in a year, October comes before September, write A in the box with the smallest number. (Pause slightly.) If it does not, write C in the box with the largest number. (Pause 10 seconds.) Now, on your answer sheet, darken the space for the number-letter combination that is in the box in which you just wrote. (Pause 5 seconds.)

Look at line 19 on the worksheet. (Pause slightly.) On the line beside the second letter, write the highest of these numbers: 12, 56, 42, 39, 8. (Pause 2 seconds.) Now, on your answer sheet, darken the space of the number-letter combination you just wrote. (Pause 5 seconds.)

ANSWERS TO PRACTICE EXAM 1

1. A ● C D E
2. A B C D E
3. A B C D ●
4. A B C ● E
5. A B C ● E
6. A B C D E
7. A B C D ●
8. A B C D E
9. A B C D E
10. A B C ● E
11. A B C D E
12. A B C D ●
13. A B C ● E
14. A B C ● E
15. A B C D E
16. A B C D ●
17. A B C D E
18. A B C D E
19. ● B C D E
20. A B C D E
21. A B C D E
22. A B C D E

23. A B C D E
24. A ● C D E
25. A B C D E
26. A B C D E
27. A ● C D E
28. A B ● D E
29. A B C D E
30. ● B C D E
31. A B C D E
32. A B C D ●
33. A B C D E
34. A B C D E
35. A B C D E
36. A B ● D E
37. A B C D E
38. A B ● D E
39. A B C D E
40. A B C D E
41. A B C D E
42. A B C D E
43. A B C D E
44. A B C D E

45. A ● C D E
46. A B C D E
47. A ● C D E
48. A B C D E
49. A ● C D E
50. A B C D E
51. A ● C D E
52. A B C D E
53. A B C D E
54. A B C D E
55. A B C D E
56. A B ● D E
57. A B C D E
58. A B C D E
59. A B ● D E
60. A B C D E
61. A B C D E
62. A B C D E
63. A B ● D E
64. A B C D E
65. A B C ● E
66. A B C D E

67. A B C D E
68. A B C D E
69. A B ● D E
70. A B C D E
71. A B C D E
72. A B C D ●
73. A B C D E
74. A B C D E
75. A B C D E
76. A B C D E
77. A B C D E
78. A ● C D E
79. A B C D E
80. A B C D E
81. A B C ● E
82. A B C D E
83. A B C D E
84. A B C D E
85. A B C D E
86. ● B C D E
87. A B C D E
88. A B C D E

1. 13   23   2   <u>19</u>   6

2. E   B   <u>D</u>   E   <u>C</u>   A   B

3.
| 30 **A** | 18 __ | 5 __ | 14 __ | 7 **E** |

4.
26 __   16 **E**   23 __   23 __   27 **B**

5.
| 63 __ | 16 __ | 78 **B** | 48 __ |

6. 12 ____   5 <u>d</u>   22 ____

7.
14 __   1 <u>B</u>   36 <u>C</u>   7 __   19 __

8. 26 ____   86 <u>A</u>

9. 57   <u>63</u>   11   78   90   32   45   70   <u>69</u>

10. 16   30   <u>13</u>   25   <u>10</u>   <u>14</u>   23   26   19

11.
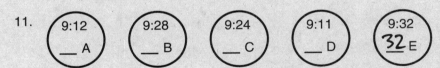

9:12 __ A   9:28 __ B   9:24 __ C   9:11 __ D   9:32 **32** E

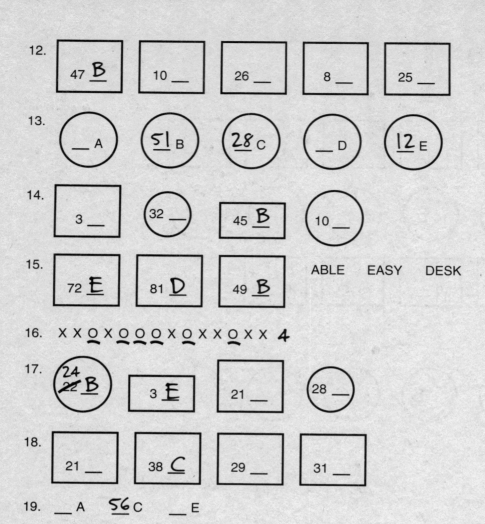

12. 47 B | 10 __ | 26 __ | 8 __ | 25 __

13. __ A | 51 B | 28 C | __ D | 12 E

14. 3 __ | 32 __ | 45 B | 10 __

15. 72 E | 81 D | 49 B | ABLE   EASY   DESK

16. X X O X O O O X O X X O X X 4

17. 24 22 B | 3 E | 21 __ | 28 __

18. 21 __ | 38 C | 29 __ | 31 __

19. __ A   56 C   __ E

PRACTICE EXAM II

How did you do on the first practice exam? Here is another one for you to try.

1. Ⓐ Ⓑ Ⓒ Ⓓ Ⓔ	23. Ⓐ Ⓑ Ⓒ Ⓓ Ⓔ	45. Ⓐ Ⓑ Ⓒ Ⓓ Ⓔ	67. Ⓐ Ⓑ Ⓒ Ⓓ Ⓔ
2. Ⓐ Ⓑ Ⓒ Ⓓ Ⓔ	24. Ⓐ Ⓑ Ⓒ Ⓓ Ⓔ	46. Ⓐ Ⓑ Ⓒ Ⓓ Ⓔ	68. Ⓐ Ⓑ Ⓒ Ⓓ Ⓔ
3. Ⓐ Ⓑ Ⓒ Ⓓ Ⓔ	25. Ⓐ Ⓑ Ⓒ Ⓓ Ⓔ	47. Ⓐ Ⓑ Ⓒ Ⓓ Ⓔ	69. Ⓐ Ⓑ Ⓒ Ⓓ Ⓔ
4. Ⓐ Ⓑ Ⓒ Ⓓ Ⓔ	26. Ⓐ Ⓑ Ⓒ Ⓓ Ⓔ	48. Ⓐ Ⓑ Ⓒ Ⓓ Ⓔ	70. Ⓐ Ⓑ Ⓒ Ⓓ Ⓔ
5. Ⓐ Ⓑ Ⓒ Ⓓ Ⓔ	27. Ⓐ Ⓑ Ⓒ Ⓓ Ⓔ	49. Ⓐ Ⓑ Ⓒ Ⓓ Ⓔ	71. Ⓐ Ⓑ Ⓒ Ⓓ Ⓔ
6. Ⓐ Ⓑ Ⓒ Ⓓ Ⓔ	28. Ⓐ Ⓑ Ⓒ Ⓓ Ⓔ	50. Ⓐ Ⓑ Ⓒ Ⓓ Ⓔ	72. Ⓐ Ⓑ Ⓒ Ⓓ Ⓔ
7. Ⓐ Ⓑ Ⓒ Ⓓ Ⓔ	29. Ⓐ Ⓑ Ⓒ Ⓓ Ⓔ	51. Ⓐ Ⓑ Ⓒ Ⓓ Ⓔ	73. Ⓐ Ⓑ Ⓒ Ⓓ Ⓔ
8. Ⓐ Ⓑ Ⓒ Ⓓ Ⓔ	30. Ⓐ Ⓑ Ⓒ Ⓓ Ⓔ	52. Ⓐ Ⓑ Ⓒ Ⓓ Ⓔ	74. Ⓐ Ⓑ Ⓒ Ⓓ Ⓔ
9. Ⓐ Ⓑ Ⓒ Ⓓ Ⓔ	31. Ⓐ Ⓑ Ⓒ Ⓓ Ⓔ	53. Ⓐ Ⓑ Ⓒ Ⓓ Ⓔ	75. Ⓐ Ⓑ Ⓒ Ⓓ Ⓔ
10. Ⓐ Ⓑ Ⓒ Ⓓ Ⓔ	32. Ⓐ Ⓑ Ⓒ Ⓓ Ⓔ	54. Ⓐ Ⓑ Ⓒ Ⓓ Ⓔ	76. Ⓐ Ⓑ Ⓒ Ⓓ Ⓔ
11. Ⓐ Ⓑ Ⓒ Ⓓ Ⓔ	33. Ⓐ Ⓑ Ⓒ Ⓓ Ⓔ	55. Ⓐ Ⓑ Ⓒ Ⓓ Ⓔ	77. Ⓐ Ⓑ Ⓒ Ⓓ Ⓔ
12. Ⓐ Ⓑ Ⓒ Ⓓ Ⓔ	34. Ⓐ Ⓑ Ⓒ Ⓓ Ⓔ	56. Ⓐ Ⓑ Ⓒ Ⓓ Ⓔ	78. Ⓐ Ⓑ Ⓒ Ⓓ Ⓔ
13. Ⓐ Ⓑ Ⓒ Ⓓ Ⓔ	35. Ⓐ Ⓑ Ⓒ Ⓓ Ⓔ	57. Ⓐ Ⓑ Ⓒ Ⓓ Ⓔ	79. Ⓐ Ⓑ Ⓒ Ⓓ Ⓔ
14. Ⓐ Ⓑ Ⓒ Ⓓ Ⓔ	36. Ⓐ Ⓑ Ⓒ Ⓓ Ⓔ	58. Ⓐ Ⓑ Ⓒ Ⓓ Ⓔ	80. Ⓐ Ⓑ Ⓒ Ⓓ Ⓔ
15. Ⓐ Ⓑ Ⓒ Ⓓ Ⓔ	37. Ⓐ Ⓑ Ⓒ Ⓓ Ⓔ	59. Ⓐ Ⓑ Ⓒ Ⓓ Ⓔ	81. Ⓐ Ⓑ Ⓒ Ⓓ Ⓔ
16. Ⓐ Ⓑ Ⓒ Ⓓ Ⓔ	38. Ⓐ Ⓑ Ⓒ Ⓓ Ⓔ	60. Ⓐ Ⓑ Ⓒ Ⓓ Ⓔ	82. Ⓐ Ⓑ Ⓒ Ⓓ Ⓔ
17. Ⓐ Ⓑ Ⓒ Ⓓ Ⓔ	39. Ⓐ Ⓑ Ⓒ Ⓓ Ⓔ	61. Ⓐ Ⓑ Ⓒ Ⓓ Ⓔ	83. Ⓐ Ⓑ Ⓒ Ⓓ Ⓔ
18. Ⓐ Ⓑ Ⓒ Ⓓ Ⓔ	40. Ⓐ Ⓑ Ⓒ Ⓓ Ⓔ	62. Ⓐ Ⓑ Ⓒ Ⓓ Ⓔ	84. Ⓐ Ⓑ Ⓒ Ⓓ Ⓔ
19. Ⓐ Ⓑ Ⓒ Ⓓ Ⓔ	41. Ⓐ Ⓑ Ⓒ Ⓓ Ⓔ	63. Ⓐ Ⓑ Ⓒ Ⓓ Ⓔ	85. Ⓐ Ⓑ Ⓒ Ⓓ Ⓔ
20. Ⓐ Ⓑ Ⓒ Ⓓ Ⓔ	42. Ⓐ Ⓑ Ⓒ Ⓓ Ⓔ	64. Ⓐ Ⓑ Ⓒ Ⓓ Ⓔ	86. Ⓐ Ⓑ Ⓒ Ⓓ Ⓔ
21. Ⓐ Ⓑ Ⓒ Ⓓ Ⓔ	43. Ⓐ Ⓑ Ⓒ Ⓓ Ⓔ	65. Ⓐ Ⓑ Ⓒ Ⓓ Ⓔ	87. Ⓐ Ⓑ Ⓒ Ⓓ Ⓔ
22. Ⓐ Ⓑ Ⓒ Ⓓ Ⓔ	44. Ⓐ Ⓑ Ⓒ Ⓓ Ⓔ	66. Ⓐ Ⓑ Ⓒ Ⓓ Ⓔ	88. Ⓐ Ⓑ Ⓒ Ⓓ Ⓔ

TEAR HERE

1. A   B   B   D   C   D   E   D

2. 24   12   17   11   14   20

3. [41 __] [62 __] [18 __] (27 __) (73 __) (10 __)

4. ___ B   ___ D   ___ C   ___ E   ___ A

5. 76   14   67   46   11   74

6. (___ A) (___ E) △ ___ B (___ C) (___ D)

7. [9 __] [46 __] [34 __]   LETTER   PARCEL

8. G   G   G   G   G   G   G   G

9. (79 __) (46 __) (32 __)

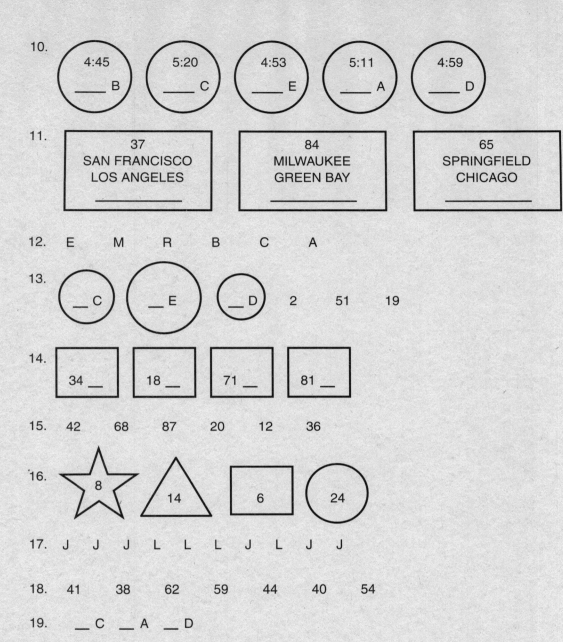

10.

| 4:45 ___ B | 5:20 ___ C | 4:53 ___ E | 5:11 ___ A | 4:59 ___ D |

11.

| 37 SAN FRANCISCO LOS ANGELES _____ | 84 MILWAUKEE GREEN BAY _____ | 65 SPRINGFIELD CHICAGO _____ |

12.   E   M   R   B   C   A

13.   __C   __E   __D   2   51   19

14.   34 __   18 __   71 __   81 __

15.   42   68   87   20   12   36

16.   8   14   6   24

17.   J   J   J   L   L   L   J   L   J   J

18.   41   38   62   59   44   40   54

19.   __ C   __ A   __ D

*Instructions to be read (the words in parentheses should **not** be read aloud).*

On the job you will have to listen to instructions and then do what you have been told to do. In this test, I will read instructions to you. Try to understand them as I read them; I cannot repeat them. Once we begin, you may not ask any questions until the end of the test.

On the job you won't have to deal with pictures, numbers, and letters like those on the test, but you will have to listen to instructions and follow them. We are using this test to see how well you can follow instructions.

You are to mark your worksheet according to the instruction that I'll read to you. After each set of instructions, I'll give you time to record your answers on the separate answer sheet.

The actual test begins now.

Look at line 1 on your worksheet. (Pause slightly.) Circle the seventh letter on line 1. (Pause 5 seconds.) Now, on your answer sheet, find number 83 and for number 83 darken the space for the letter you just circled. (Pause 5 seconds.)

Look at line 2 on your worksheet. (Pause slightly.) Draw a line under all the odd numbers between 12 and 20. (Pause 5 seconds.) Now, on your answer sheet, darken space B as in baker for all the numbers under which you drew a line. (Pause 5 seconds.)

Look at line 2 again. (Pause slightly.) Find the number that is two times another number on line 2 and circle it. (Pause 5 seconds.) Now, on your answer sheet, darken space A for the number you just circled. (Pause 5 seconds.)

Look at line 3 on your worksheet. (Pause slightly.) Write the letter C in the middle box. (Pause 2 seconds.) Now, on your answer sheet, darken the space for the number-letter combination in the figure in which you just wrote. (Pause 5 seconds.)

Look at line 3 again. (Pause slightly.) Write the letter D as in dog in the left-hand circle. (Pause 2 seconds.) Now, on your answer sheet, darken the space for the number-letter combination in the figure in which you just wrote. (Pause 5 seconds.)

Look at line 4 on your worksheet. (Pause slightly.) If first class mail costs more than bulk rate mail, write the number 22 on the third line; if not, write the number 19 on the fourth line. (Pause 5 seconds.) Now, on your answer sheet, darken the space for the number-letter combination on the line on which you just wrote. (Pause 5 seconds.)

Look at line 4 again. (Pause slightly.) Write the number 31 on the second line from the left. (Pause 2 seconds.) Now, on your answer sheet, darken the space for the number-letter combination on the line on which you just wrote. (Pause 5 seconds.)

Look at line 5 on your worksheet. (Pause slightly.) Find the highest number on line 5 and draw a line under the number. (Pause 2 seconds.) Now, on your answer sheet, find the number under which you just drew a line and darken space E for that number. (Pause 5 seconds.)

Look at line 5 again. (Pause slightly.) Find the lowest number on line 5 and draw two lines under the number. (Pause 2 seconds.) Now, on your answer sheet, find the number under which you just drew two lines and darken space A for that number. (Pause 5 seconds.)

Look at line 6 on your worksheet. (Pause slightly.) Write the number 57 in the figure that does not belong on line 6. (Pause 2 seconds.) Now, on your answer sheet, darken the number-letter combination that is in the figure in which you just wrote. (Pause 5 seconds.)

Look at line 7 on your worksheet. (Pause slightly.) Write the second letter of the second word in the first box. (Pause 5 seconds.) Write the fifth letter of the first word in the third box. (Pause 5 seconds.) Write the fourth letter of the second word in the second box. (Pause 5 seconds.) Now, on your answer sheet, darken the number-letter combinations in all three boxes. (Pause 15 seconds.)

Look at line 8 on your worksheet. (Pause slightly.) Count the number of G's on line 8 and divide the number of G's by 2. Write that number at the end of the line. (Pause 5 seconds.) Now, on your answer sheet, darken space D as in dog for the number you wrote at the end of line 8. (Pause 5 seconds.)

Look at line 9 on your worksheet. (Pause slightly.) Write the letter B as in baker in the middle-sized circle. (Pause 2 seconds.) Now, on your answer sheet, darken the space for the number-letter combination in the circle in which you just wrote. (Pause 5 seconds.)

Look at line 10 on your worksheet. (Pause slightly.) The time in each circle represents the last scheduled pickup of the day from a street letterbox. Find the circle with the earliest pickup time and write the last two figures of that time on the line in the circle. (Pause 10 seconds.) Now, on your answer sheet, darken the space for the number-letter combination in the circle in which you just wrote. (Pause 5 seconds.)

Look at line 10 again. (Pause slightly.) Find the circle with the latest pickup time and write the last two figures of that time on the line in the circle. (Pause 10 seconds.) Now, on your answer sheet, darken the space for the number-letter combination in the circle in which you just wrote. (Pause 5 seconds.)

Look at line 11 on your worksheet. (Pause slightly.) Mail directed for San Francisco and Los Angeles is to be placed in box 37; mail for Milwaukee and Green Bay in box 84; mail for Springfield and Chicago in box 65. Find the box for mail being sent to Green Bay and write the letter A in the box. (Pause 2 seconds.) Now, on your answer sheet, darken the number-letter combination for the box in which you just wrote. (Pause 5 seconds.)

Look at line 11 again. (Pause slightly.) Mr. Green lives in Springfield. Find the box in which to put Mr. Green's mail and write E on the line. (Pause 2 seconds.) Now, on your answer sheet, darken the space for the number-letter combination in the box in which you just wrote. (Pause 5 seconds.)

Look at line 12 on your worksheet. (Pause slightly.) Find the letter on line 12 that is not in the word CREAM and draw a line under the letter. (Pause 2 seconds.) Now, on your answer sheet, find number 38 and darken the space for the letter under which you just drew a line. (Pause 5 seconds.)

Look at line 13 on your worksheet. (Pause slightly.) Write the smallest number in the largest circle. (Pause 2 seconds.) Write the largest number in the left-hand circle. (Pause 2 seconds.) Now, on your answer sheet, darken the number-letter combinations that are in the circles in which you just wrote. (Pause 10 seconds.)

Look at line 14 on your worksheet. (Pause slightly.) If there are 36 inches in a foot, write B as in baker in the first box; if not, write D as in dog in the third box. (Pause 5 seconds.) Now, on your answer sheet, darken the number-letter combination that is in the box in which you just wrote. (Pause 5 seconds.)

Look at line 14 again. (Pause slightly.) Find the box that contains a number in the teens and write B as in baker in that box. (Pause 2 seconds.) Now, on your answer sheet, darken the number-letter combination that is in the box in which you just wrote. (Pause 5 seconds.)

Look at line 15 on your worksheet. (Pause slightly.) Circle the only number on line 15 that is not divisible by 2. (Pause 2 seconds.) Now, on your answer sheet, darken space A for the number you circled. (Pause 5 seconds.)

Look at line 16 on your worksheet. (Pause slightly.) If the number in the circle is greater than the number in the box, write the letter E in the box; if not, write the letter E in the circle. (Pause 5 seconds.) Now, on your answer sheet, darken the number-letter combination that is in the figure in which you just wrote. (Pause 5 seconds.)

Look at line 16 again. (Pause slightly.) If the number in the triangle is smaller than the number in the figure directly to its left, write the letter A in the triangle; if not, write the letter C in the triangle. (Pause 5 seconds.) Now, on your answer sheet, darken the number-letter combination that is in the figure in which you just wrote. (Pause 5 seconds.)

Look at line 17 on your worksheet. (Pause slightly.) Count the number of J's on line 17, multiply the number of J's by 5 and write that number at the end of the line. (Pause 5 seconds.) Now, on your answer sheet, find the number you just wrote at the end of the line and darken space C for that number. (Pause 5 seconds.)

Look at line 18 on your worksheet. (Pause slightly.) Draw one line under the number that is at the middle of line 18. (Pause 5 seconds.) Now, on your answer sheet, darken space B as in baker for the number under which you just drew a line. (Pause 5 seconds.)

Look at line 18 again. (Pause slightly.) Draw two lines under each odd number that falls between 35 and 45. (Pause 10 seconds.) Now, on your answer sheet, darken space D as in dog for each number under which you drew two lines. (Pause 5 seconds.)

Look at line 19 on your worksheet. (Pause slightly.) Next to the last letter on line 19, write the first number you hear: 53, 18, 6, 75. (Pause 2 seconds.) Now, on your answer sheet, darken the space for the number-letter combination you just wrote. (Pause 5 seconds.)

ANSWERS TO PRACTICE EXAM II

#	Ans		#	Ans		#	Ans		#	Ans
1.	A B C D E		23.	A B C D E		45.	A **B** C D E		67.	A B C D E
2.	A B C D **E**		24.	**A** B C D E		46.	A B **C** D E		68.	A B C D E
3.	A B C D E		25.	A B C D E		47.	A B C D E		69.	A B C D E
4.	A B C **D** E		26.	A B C D E		48.	A B C D E		70.	A B C D E
5.	A B C D E		27.	A B C **D** E		49.	A B C D E		71.	A B C **D** E
6.	A B C D **E**		28.	A B C D E		50.	A B C D E		72.	A B C D E
7.	A B C D E		29.	A B C D E		51.	A B **C** D E		73.	A B C D E
8.	A B C D E		30.	A B **C** D E		52.	A B C D E		74.	A B C D E
9.	**A** B C D E		31.	A B C **D** E		53.	A B C **D** E		75.	A B C D E
10.	A B C D E		32.	A B C D E		54.	A B C D E		76.	A B C D **E**
11.	**A** B C D E		33.	A B C D E		55.	A B C D E		77.	A B C D E
12.	A B C D E		34.	A B C D **E**		56.	A B C D E		78.	A B C D E
13.	A B C D E		35.	A B C D E		57.	A **B** C D E		79.	A **B** C D E
14.	A B **C** D E		36.	A B C D E		58.	A B C D E		80.	A B C D E
15.	A B C D E		37.	A B C D E		59.	A **B** C D E		81.	A B C D E
16.	A B C D E		38.	A **B** C D E		60.	A B C D E		82.	A B C D E
17.	A **B** C D E		39.	A B C D E		61.	A B C D E		83.	A B C D **E**
18.	A **B** C D E		40.	A B C D E		62.	A B **C** D E		84.	**A** B C D E
19.	A B C D E		41.	A B C **D** E		63.	A B C D E		85.	A B C D E
20.	A B **C** D E		42.	A B C D E		64.	A B C D E		86.	A B C D E
21.	A B C D E		43.	A B C D E		65.	A B C D **E**		87.	**A** B C D E
22.	A B **C** D E		44.	A B C D E		66.	A B C D E		88.	A B C D E

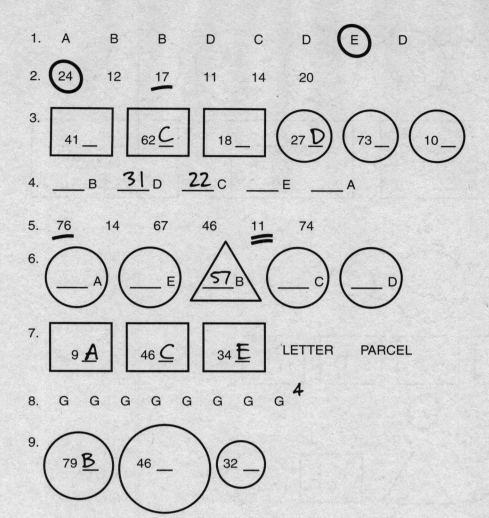

1. A B B D C D (E) D

2. (24) 12 <u>17</u> 11 14 20

3. | 41 __ | 62 C | 18 __ | (27 <u>D</u>) | (73 __) | (10 __) |

4. ___ B <u>31</u> D <u>22</u> C ___ E ___ A

5. <u>76</u> 14 67 46 11 74

6. (___ A) (___ E) △57 B (___ C) (___ D)

7. | 9 <u>A</u> | 46 <u>C</u> | 34 <u>E</u> | LETTER PARCEL

8. G G G G G G G G 4

9. (79 <u>B</u>) (46 __) (32 __)

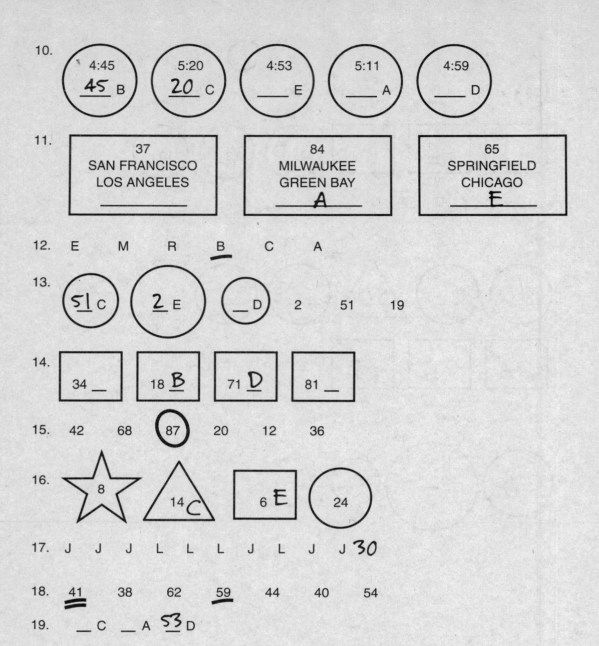

10.
4:45 _45_ B   5:20 _20_ C   4:53 ___ E   5:11 ___ A   4:59 ___ D

11.
| 37 SAN FRANCISCO LOS ANGELES _____ | 84 MILWAUKEE GREEN BAY _A_ | 65 SPRINGFIELD CHICAGO _E_ |

12. E   M   R   B   C   A

13. _51_ C   _2_ E   __ D   2   51   19

14. 34 __   18 _B_   71 _D_   81 __

15. 42   68   (87)   20   12   36

16. 8   14 C   6 E   24

17. J   J   J   L   L   L   J   L   J   J 30

18. _41_   38   62   _59_   44   40   54

19. __ C   __ A   _53_ D

P A R T

THREE
Practice Tests

CONTENTS

Address Checking Practice Tests   123

Memory for Addresses Practice Tests   139

Number Series Practice Tests   151

Following Oral Instructions Practice Tests   159

Full Length Practice Exam: Exam 470 and Exam 460   171

ADDRESS CHECKING PRACTICE TESTS

Taking the Timed Practice Tests

This is your first real chance to answer Address Checking questions under the time constraints of the actual test. To get the most benefits from this practice, proceed as follows:

1. Choose a workspace that is quiet, well lit, clean, and uncluttered.
2. Use a stopwatch or kitchen timer to accurately time each test.
3. Start the first test at a convenient time and stop exactly when your six minutes are up.
4. Give yourself at least a five-minute breather between each test. You can use this non-test time to skim through review material in earlier chapters.
5. After you complete all three tests, check your answers against the answer keys provided. Circle all wrong answers in red so that you can easily locate them.
6. Calculate your raw score for each test as instructed.
7. Check to see where your scores fall on the self-evaluation chart.
8. If you receive less than an excellent score on a test, go back and review the appropriate study chapters in this book.
9. Retake the test to see your improvement.

   Remember not to become discouraged if you cannot answer all 95 questions in 6 minutes. You are not expected to. Work quickly but strive for accuracy using all of the techniques you have learned so far.

Timed Practice Tests

PRACTICE TEST 1

Time: 6 Minutes • 95 Questions.

Directions: *For each question, compare the address in the left column with the address in the right column. If the two addresses are ALIKE in every way, write A next to the question number. If the two addresses are DIFFERENT in any way, write D next to the question number.*

1	...1897 Smicksburg Rd	1897 Smithsburg Rd
2	...3609 E Paseo Aldeano	3909 E Paseo Aldeano
3	...11787 Ornamental Ln	1787 Ornamental Ln
4	...1096 Camino Grande E	1096 Camino Grande E
5	...2544 E Radcliff Ave	2544 E Redcliff Ave
6	...5796 E Narragansett Dr	5796 E Narragasett Dr
7	...12475 Ebbtide Way W	12475 Ebbtide Way W
8	...14396 N Via Armando	14396 S Via Armando
9	...2155 S Del Giorgio Rd	2155 S Del Giorgio Rd
10	...16550 Bainbridge Cir	16505 Bainbridge Cir
11	...1826 Milneburg Rd	1826 Milneburg St
12	...Eureka KS 67045	Eureka KY 67045
13	...4010 Glenaddie Ave	4010 Glenaddie Ave
14	...13501 Stratford Rd	13501 Standford Rd
15	...3296 W 64th St	3296 E 64th St
16	...2201 Tennessee Cir	2201 Tennessee Cir
17	...1502 Avenue M NE	1502 Avenue N NE
18	...1096 SE Longrone Dr	1096 SE Longrone Dr
19	...1267 Darthmouth Ct	1267 Darthmont Ct
20	...825 Ophanage Rd	825 Ophanage Rd
21	...1754 Golden Springs Rd	1754 Golden Springs Road
22	...1015 Tallwoods Ln	1015 Tallwoods Ln
23	...1097 Lambada Dr	1097 Lambadd Dr
24	...Vredenburgh AL 36481	Verdenburgh AL 36481
25	...1800 Monticello Ave	1800 Monticello Ave
26	...1723 Yellowbird Ln	1723 Yellowbird Ct
27	...700 Valca Materials Rd	700 Valca Materials Rd

28	...1569 Ladywood Ln N	1569 Ladywood Ln W
29	...3256 Interurban Dr	3256 Interurban Dr
30	...1507 Haughton Cir	1507 Haughton Ct
31	...8971 Robertson Ave	8971 Robinson Ave
32	...3801 NE 49th Street	3801 NW 49th Street
33	...4102 Chalkville Rd	4102 Chalkview Rd
34	...1709 Ingersoll Cir	1709 Ingersoll Cir
35	...6800 N Nantucket Ln	6800 N Nantucket Ln
36	...12401 Tarrymore Dr	12401 Terrymore Dr
37	...1097 Huntsville Ave	1097 Huntsville Ave
38	...3566 Lornaridge Pl	3566 Lornaridge Pl
39	...2039 Klondike Ave SW	2039 Klondie Ave SW
40	...3267 Mayland Ln	3267 Maryland Ln
41	...12956 Strawberry Ln	12596 Strawberry Ln
42	...De Armanville AL 36257	De Armanville AL 36257
43	...6015 Anniston Dr	6015 Anneston Dr
44	...1525 E 90th St	1525 E 90th St
45	...1299 Chappaque Rd	1266 Chappaque Rd
46	...2156 Juliette Dr	2156 Juliaetta Dr
47	...999 N Hollingsworth St	999 S Hollingsworth St
48	...16901 Odum Crest Ln	19601 Odum Crest Ln
49	...9787 Zellmark Dr	9787 Zealmark Dr
50	...11103 NE Feasell Ave	11103 NE Feasell Ave
51	...51121 N Mattison Rd	51121 S Mattison Rd
52	...8326 Blackjack Ln	8326 Blackjack Blvd
53	...18765 Lagarde Ave	18765 Lagrande Ave
54	...11297 Gallatin Ln	11297 Gallatin Ln
55	...Wormleysburg PA 17043	Wormleysburg PA 17043
56	...22371 N Sprague Ave	22371 S Sprague Ave
57	...15014 Warrior River Rd	15014 Warrior River Rd
58	...45721 Hueytown Plaza	45721 Hueytowne Plaza
59	...8973 Tedescki Dr	8793 Tedescki Dr
60	...12995 Raimond Muscoda Pl	12995 Raimont Muscoda Pl
61	...Phippsburg CO 80469	Phippsburg CA 80469

62 ...52003 W 49th Ave	52003 W 46th Ave
63 ...17201 Zenobia Cir	17210 Zenobia Cir
64 ...4800 Garrison Cir	4800 Garrison Dr
65 ...Los Angeles CA 90070	Los Angeles CA 90076
66 ...14798 W 62nd Ave	14198 W 62nd Ave
67 ...7191 E Eldridge Way	7191 E Eldridge Way
68 ...1279 S Quintard Dr	1279 S Guintard Dr
69 ...21899 Dellwood Ave	21899 Dillwood Ave
70 ...7191 Zenophone Cir	7191 Zenohone Cir
71 ...4301 Los Encinos Way	4301 Los Encinas Way
72 ...19700 Ostronic Dr NW	19700 Ostronic Dr NE
73 ...23291 Van Velsire Dr	23219 Van Velsire Dr
74 ...547 Paradise Valley Rd	547 Paradise Valley Ct
75 ...23167 Saltillo Ave	23167 Santillo Ave
76 ...43001 Mourning Dove Way	43001 Mourning Dove Way
77 ...21183 Declaration Ave	21183 Declaration Ave
78 ...10799 Via Sierra Ramal Ave	10799 Via Sierra Ramel Ave
79 ...16567 Hermosillia Ct	16597 Hermosillia Ct
80 ...Villamont VA 24178	Villamont VA 24178
81 ...18794 Villaboso Ave	18794 Villeboso Ave
82 ...24136 Ranthom Ave	24136 Ranthon Ave
83 ...13489 Golondrina Pl	13489 Golondrina St
84 ...6598 Adamsville Ave	6598 Adamsville Ave
85 ...12641 Indals Pl NE	12641 Indals Pl NW
86 ...19701 SE 2nd Avenue	19701 NE 2nd Avenue
87 ...22754 Cachalote Ln	22754 Cachalott Ln
88 ...12341 Kingfisher Rd	12341 Kingsfisher Rd
89 ...24168 Lorenzana Dr	24168 Lorenzano Dr
90 ...32480 Blackfriar Rd	32480 Blackfriar Rd
91 ...16355 Wheeler Dr	16355 Wheelen Dr
92 ...5100 Magna Carta Rd	5100 Magna Certa Rd
93 ...2341 N Federalist Pl	2341 N Federalist Pl
94 ...22200 Timpangos Rd	22200 Timpangos Rd
95 ...19704 Calderon Rd	19704 Calderon Rd

PRACTICE TEST 2

Time: 6 Minutes • 95 Questions.

Directions: *For each question, compare the address in the left column with the address in the right column. If the two addresses are ALIKE in every way, write A next to the question number. If the two addresses are DIFFERENT in any way, write D next to the question number.*

1	...4623 Grand Concourse	4623 Grand Concourse
2	...6179 Ridgecroft Rd	6719 Ridgecroft Rd
3	...5291 Hanover Cir	5291 Hangover Cir
4	...2333 Palmer Ave	233 Palmer Ave
5	...1859 SE 148th St	1859 SE 148th St
6	...Dowagiac MI 49047	Dowagiac MI 49047
7	...4147 Wykagyl Terr	4147 Wykagyl Terr
8	...1504 N 10th Ave	1504 N 10th St
9	...2967 Montross Ave	2967 Montrose Ave
10	...Chicago IL 60601	Chicago IL 60601
11	...2073 Defoe Ct	2073 Defoe Ct
12	...2433 Westchester Plz	2343 Westchester Plz
13	...6094 Carpenter Ave	6094 Charpenter Ave
14	...5677 Bolman Twrs	5677 Bolman Twrs
15	...Chappaqua NY 10514	Chappaqua NY 10541
16	...3428 Constantine Ave	3248 Constantine Ave
17	...847 S 147th Rd	847 S 147th Rd
18	...6676 Harwood Ct	6676 Hardwood Ct
19	...3486 Mosholu Pky	3486 Mosholu Pkwy
20	...Mindenmines MO 64769	Mindenmines MO 64679
21	...816 Oscawana Lake Rd	816 Ocsawana Lake Rd
22	...9159 Battle Hill Rd	9195 Battle Hill Rd
23	...7558 Winston Ln	7558 Winston Ln
24	...3856 W 385th St	3856 W 386th St
25	...3679 W Alpine Pl	3679 W Alpine Pl
26	...Hartford CT 06115	Hartford CN 06115
27	...6103 Locust Hill Wy	6013 Locust Hill Wy
28	...4941 Annrock Dr	4941 Annrock Dr
29	...2018 N St Andrews Pl	2018 N St Andrews Pl

30 ...8111 Drewville Rd	8111 Drewsville Rd
31 ...463 Peaceable Hill Rd	463 Peaceable Hill Rd
32 ...Biloxi MS 39532	Biloxi MS 39532
33 ...3743 Point Dr S	3734 Point Dr S
34 ...5665 Barnington Rd	5665 Barnington Rd
35 ...2246 E Sheldrake Ave	2246 W Sheldrake Ave
36 ...1443 Bloomingdale Rd	1443 Bloomingdales Rd
37 ...2064 Chalford Ln	2064 Chalford Ln
38 ...McMinnville OR 97128	McMinville OR 97128
39 ...6160 Shadybrook Ln	6160 Shadybrook Ln
40 ...2947 E Lake Blvd	2947 E Lake Blvd
41 ...3907 Evergreen Row	3907 Evergreen Row
42 ...2192 SE Hotel Dr	2192 SE Hotel Dr
43 ...8844 Fremont St	8844 Fremont Rd
44 ...8487 Wolfshead Rd	8487 Wolfshead Rd
45 ...Anamosa IA 52205	Anamoosa IA 52205
46 ...4055 Katonah Ave	4055 Katonah Ave
47 ...1977 Buckingham Apts	1979 Buckingham Apts
48 ...983 W 139th Way	983 W 139th Wy
49 ...7822 Bayliss Ln	7822 Bayliss Ln
50 ...8937 Banksville Rd	8937 Banksville Rd
51 ...4759 Strathmore Rd	4579 Strathmore Rd
52 ...2221 E Main St	221 E Main St
53 ...South Orange NJ 07079	South Orange NJ 07079
54 ...4586 Sylvia Wy	4586 Sylvan Wy
55 ...6335 Soundview Ave	6335 SoundView Ave
56 ...3743 Popham Rd	3743 Poppam Rd
57 ...2845 Brookfield Dr	2485 Brookfield Dr
58 ...3845 Fort Slocum Rd	3845 Fort Slocum St
59 ...9268 Jochum Ave	9268 Jochum Ave
60 ...Bloomington MN 55437	Bloomington MN 54537
61 ...6903 S 184th St	6903 S 184th St
62 ...7486 Rossmor Rd	7486 Rosemor Rd

63 ...4176 Whitlockville Rd	4176 Whitlockville Wy
64 ...4286 Megquire Ln	4286 Megquire Ln
65 ...6270 Tamarock Rd	6270 Tammarock Rd
66 ...3630 Bulkley Mnr	3630 Bulkley Mnr
67 ...7158 Scarswold Apts	7185 Scarswold Apts
68 ...Brooklyn NY 11218	Brooklyn NY 11128
69 ...9598 Prince Edward Rd	9598 Prince Edward Rd
70 ...8439 S 145th St	8439 S 154th St
71 ...9795 Shady Glen Ct	9795 Shady Grove Ct
72 ...7614 Ganung St	7614 Ganung St
73 ...Teaneck NJ 07666	Teaneck NH 07666
74 ...6359 Dempster Rd	6359 Dumpster Rd
75 ...1065 Colchester Hl	1065 Colchester Hl
76 ...5381 Phillipse Pl	5381 Philipse Pl
77 ...6484 Rochester Terr	6484 Rochester Terr
78 ...2956 Quinin St	2956 Quinin St
79 ...Tarzana CA 91356	Tarzana CA 91536
80 ...7558 Winston Ln	7558 Whinston Ln
81 ...1862 W 293rd St	1862 W 393rd St
82 ...8534 S Huntington Ave	8534 N Huntington Ave
83 ...9070 Wild Oaks Vlg	9070 Wild Oakes Vlg
84 ...4860 Smadbeck Ave	4680 Smadbeck Ave
85 ...8596 E Commonwealth Ave	8596 E Commonwealth Ave
86 ...Ridgefield NJ 07657	Ridgefield NJ 07657
87 ...1478 Charter Cir	1478 W Charter Cir
88 ...3963 Priscilla Ave	3963 Pricsilla Ave
89 ...4897 Winding Ln	4897 Winding Ln
90 ...847 Windmill Terr	847 Windmill Terr
91 ...1662 Wixon St W	1662 Wixon St W
92 ...West Hartford CT 06107	West Hartford CT 06107
93 ...6494 Rochelle Terr	9464 Rochelle Terr
94 ...4228 Pocantico Rd	4228 Pocantico Rd
95 ...1783 S 486th Ave	1783 S 486th Ave

PRACTICE TEST 3

Time: 6 Minutes • 95 Questions.

Directions: For each question, compare the address in the left column with the address in the right column. If the two addresses are ALIKE in every way, write A next to the question number. If the two addresses are DIFFERENT in any way, write D next to the question number.

1	...1038 Nutgrove St	1038 Nutgrove St
2	...4830 Schroeder Ave	4380 Schroeder Ave
3	...2343 Martine Ave	2343 Martini Ave
4	...Winkelman AZ 85292	Winkelman AZ 85292
5	...298 Chatterton Pky	298 Chatterton Pky
6	...3798 Hillandale Ave	3798 Hillanddale Ave
7	...7683 Fountain Pl	7863 Fountain Pl
8	...1862 W 164th St	1864 W 164th St
9	...Scarborough NY 10510	Scarbourough NY 10510
10	...1734 N Highland Ave	1734 W Highland Ave
11	...1385 Queens Blvd	1385 Queens Blvd
12	...6742 Mendota Ave	6742 Mendota Ave
13	...8496 E 245th St	8496 E 254th St
14	...2010 Wyndcliff Rd	2010 Wyndecliff Rd
15	...4098 Gramatan Ave	4098 Gramatan Ave
16	...Denver CO 80236	Denver CO 80236
17	...3778 N Broadway	3778 N Broadway
18	...532 Broadhollow Rd	532 Broadhollow Rd
19	...1386 Carriage House Ln	1386 Carriage House Ln
20	...3284 S 10th St	2384 S 10th St
21	...2666 Dunwoodie Rd	266 Dunwoodie Rd
22	...Pontiac MI 48054	Pontiac MI 48054
23	...1080 Nine Acres Ln	1080 Nine Acres Ln
24	...2699 Quaker Church Rd	2669 Quaker Church Rd
25	...7232 S 45th Ave	7232 S 45th Ave
26	...1588 Grand Boulevard	1588 Grand Boulevard
27	...2093 S Waverly Rd	2093 S Waverley Rd
28	...Las Vegas NV 89112	Las Vegas NM 89112

29 ...116 Cottage Pl Gdns	116 Cottage Pl Gdns
30 ...1203 E Lakeview Ave	1203 E Lakeside Ave
31 ...3446 E Westchester Ave	3446 E Westchester Ave
32 ...7482 Horseshoe Hill Rd	7482 Horseshoe Hill Rd
33 ...Waimanalo HI 96795	Waimanale HI 96795
34 ...9138 McGuire Ave	9138 MacGuire Ave
35 ...7438 Meadway	7348 Meadway
36 ...2510 Maryland Ave NW	2510 Maryland Ave NW
37 ...1085 S 83rd Rd	1085 S 83rd Rd
38 ...5232 Maplewood Wy	523 Maplewood Wy
39 ...Kansas City MO 64108	Kansas City MO 61408
40 ...1063 Valentine Ln	1063 Valentine Ln
41 ...1066 Furnace Dock Rd	1606 Furnace Dock Rd
42 ...2121 Rosedale Rd	2121 Rosedale Rd
43 ...1396 Orawapum St	1396 Orawampum St
44 ...3004 Palisade Ave	3004 Palisades Ave
45 ...1776 Independence St	1776 Independence St
46 ...Canton OH 44707	Canton OH 44707
47 ...1515 Geoga Cir	1515 Geogia Cir
48 ...1583 Central Ave	1583 Central Ave
49 ...4096 Valley Terr	4096 Valley Terr
50 ...2075 Boston Post Rd	2075 Boston Post Rd
51 ...1016 Frost Ln	1016 Frost La
52 ...2186 Ashford Ave	2186 Ashford Ave
53 ...Battle Mountain NV 89820	Battle Mountain NV 89820
54 ...6634 Weber Pl	6634 Webber Pl
55 ...6832 Halycon Terr	6832 Halcyon Terr
56 ...198 Gedney Esplnde	198 Gedney Esplnde
57 ...8954 Horsechestnut Rd	8954 Horsechestnut Rd
58 ...1926 S 283rd Wy	1926 S 283rd Wy
59 ...Hartsdale NY 10530	Hartsdale NY 15030
60 ...1569 Ritchy Pl	1569 Ritchy Pl
61 ...423 S Columbia Ave	423 S Colombia Ave

62 ...2466 Linette Ct	2466 Linnette Ct
63 ...2970 Rockledge Ave	2970 Rockridge Ave
64 ...5764 Guion Blvd	5764 Guion Blvd
65 ...6976 SW 5th Ave	6976 SE 5th Ave
66 ...Milwaukie OR 97222	Milwaukee OR 97222
67 ...2243 Hudson View Ests	2234 Hudson View Ests
68 ...7743 S 3rd Ave	7743 S 3rd Ave
69 ...2869 Romaine Ave	2869 Romaine Ave
70 ...2943 Windermere Dr	2943 Windemere Dr
71 ...5117 Balmoral Crsnt	5117 Balmoral Crsnt
72 ...3797 Wappanocca Ave	3797 Wappannocca Ave
73 ...Arkabutla MS 38602	Arkabutla MS 38602
74 ...2275 Greenway Terr	2275 Greenaway Terr
75 ...7153 Taymil Rd	7153 Taymil Rd
76 ...3864 W 248th St	3864 W 284th St
77 ...2032 Central Park S	2023 Central Park S
78 ...1803 Pinewood Rd	1803 Pineywood Rd
79 ...New York NY 10023	New York NY 10023
80 ...1555 E 19th St	1555 E 19th St
81 ...3402 Comer Cir	3402 Comer Ct
82 ...9416 Lakeshore Dr	9416 Lakeshore Dr
83 ...1576 Kimball Ave	1576 Kimbell Ave
84 ...2015 W 51st Ln	2015 W 51st Ln
85 ...Silver Springs NV 89429	Silver Springs NV 89429
86 ...2354 N Washington St	2354 N Washington St
87 ...8528 Convent Pl	8258 Convent Pl
88 ...1911 Downer Ave	1911 Downer Ave
89 ...6108 Woodstock Rd	6108 Woodstock St
90 ...Akron OH 44308	Akron OK 44308
91 ...4548 College Pt Ave	4548 College Pk Ave
92 ...8194 Great Oak Ln	8194 Great Oak Ln
93 ...280 SW Collins Ave	280 SW Collins Ave
94 ...8276 Abbott Mews	8726 Abbott Mews
95 ...4717 Deerfield Blvd	4717 Deerfield Blvd

Practice Test Answers
PRACTICE TEST 1

1. D	13. A	25. A	37. A	49. D	61. D	73. D	85. D
2. D	14. D	26. D	38. A	50. A	62. D	74. D	86. D
3. D	15. D	27. A	39. D	51. D	63. D	75. D	87. D
4. A	16. A	28. D	40. D	52. D	64. D	76. A	88. D
5. D	17. D	29. A	41. D	53. D	65. D	77. A	89. D
6. D	18. A	30. D	42. A	54. A	66. D	78. D	90. A
7. A	19. D	31. D	43. D	55. A	67. A	79. D	91. D
8. D	20. A	32. D	44. A	56. D	68. D	80. A	92. D
9. A	21. D	33. D	45. D	57. A	69. D	81. D	93. A
10. D	22. A	34. A	46. D	58. D	70. D	82. D	94. A
11. D	23. D	35. A	47. D	59. D	71. D	83. D	95. A
12. D	24. D	36. D	48. D	60. D	72. D	84. A	

Determine Your Raw Score

Practice Test 1: Your score on Address Checking is based upon the number of questions you answered correctly minus the number of questions you answered incorrectly:

1. Enter number of right answers _____

2. Enter number of wrong answers _____

3. Subtract number wrong from right _____

   Raw Score = _____

PRACTICE TEST 2

1. A	9. D	17. A	25. A	33. D	41. A	49. A	57. D
2. D	10. A	18. D	26. D	34. A	42. A	50. A	58. D
3. D	11. A	19. D	27. D	35. D	43. D	51. D	59. A
4. D	12. D	20. D	28. A	36. D	44. A	52. D	60. D
5. A	13. D	21. D	29. A	37. A	45. D	53. A	61. A
6. A	14. A	22. D	30. D	38. D	46. A	54. D	62. D
7. A	15. D	23. A	31. A	39. A	47. D	55. D	63. D
8. D	16. D	24. D	32. A	40. A	48. D	56. D	64. A

65. D	69. A	73. D	77. A	81. D	85. A	89. A	93. D
66. A	70. D	74. D	78. A	82. D	86. A	90. A	94. A
67. D	71. D	75. A	79. D	83. D	87. D	91. A	95. A
68. D	72. A	76. D	80. D	84. D	88. D	92. A	

Determine Your Raw Score

Practice Test 2: Your score on Address Checking is based upon the number of questions you answered correctly minus the number of questions you answered incorrectly:

1. Enter number of right answers   _____

2. Enter number of wrong answers   _____

3. Subtract number wrong from right   _____

   Raw Score =   _____

PRACTICE TEST 3

1. A	13. D	25. A	37. A	49. A	61. D	73. A	85. A
2. D	14. D	26. A	38. D	50. A	62. D	74. D	86. A
3. D	15. A	27. D	39. D	51. D	63. D	75. A	87. D
4. A	16. A	28. D	40. A	52. A	64. A	76. D	88. A
5. A	17. A	29. A	41. D	53. A	65. D	77. D	89. D
6. D	18. A	30. D	42. A	54. D	66. D	78. D	90. D
7. D	19. A	31. A	43. D	55. D	67. D	79. A	91. D
8. D	20. D	32. A	44. D	56. A	68. A	80. A	92. A
9. D	21. D	33. D	45. A	57. A	69. A	81. D	93. A
10. D	22. A	34. D	46. A	58. A	70. D	82. A	94. D
11. A	23. A	35. D	47. D	59. D	71. A	83. D	95. A
12. A	24. D	36. A	48. A	60. A	72. D	84. A	

Determine Your Raw Score

Practice Test 3: Your score on Address Checking is based upon the number of questions you answered correctly minus the number of questions you answered incorrectly:

1. Enter number of right answers   _____

2. Enter number of wrong answers   _____

3. Subtract number wrong from right   _____

   Raw Score =   _____

Self-Evaluation Chart

For each practice test, see how your raw score falls on the following scale. You should not be satisfied with less than Excellent. Review all appropriate study material, and then retake the test(s) where you need improvement.

IF your raw score was between	THEN your work was
80–95	Excellent
65–79	Good
50–64	Average
35–49	Fair
1–34	Poor

MEMORY FOR ADDRESSES PRACTICE TESTS

Taking the Timed Test

This is your first real chance to answer Memory for Addresses questions under the time constraints of the actual test. To get the most benefits from this practice, proceed as follows:

1. Choose a workspace that is quiet, well lit, clean, and uncluttered.
2. Use a stopwatch or kitchen timer to accurately time each test.
3. Start the first test at a convenient time and stop exactly when your six minutes are up.
4. Give yourself at least a five-minute breather between each test. You can use this non-test time to skim through review material in earlier chapters.
5. After you complete all three tests, check your answers against the answer keys provided. Circle all wrong answers in red so that you can easily locate them.
6. Calculate your raw score for each test as instructed.
7. Check to see where your scores fall on the self-evaluation chart.
8. If you receive less than an Excellent score on a test, go back and review the appropriate study chapters in this book.
9 Retake the test to see your improvement.

> Do not write down your memorization techniques during the time allowed for memorizing addresses. Do whatever it takes to stay focused. Remember, you must do it all in your head on the actual test.

Remember, you are not expected to answer all the questions. So don't get discouraged if you cannot finish the test. Guess if you can use the process of elimination to weed out one or more incorrect answers.

Timed Test

This exercise is in the same format as the actual test. It includes:
- Sample questions
- Practice I
- Practice II
- Practice III
- Memory for Addresses

SAMPLE QUESTIONS

You will have to memorize the locations (A, B, C, D, and E) of the 25 addresses in the five lettered boxes below. Indicate your answers by writing in your answer (letter) next to the question number.

You now have five minutes to study the locations of the addresses. Then cover the boxes and answer the questions. You may look back at the boxes if you cannot yet mark the address locations from memory.

A	B	C	D	E
2600–3899 Hart	1400–2099 Hart	3900–4199 Hart	4200–5399 Hart	2100–2599 Hart
Linda	Ashley	Farmer	Monroe	Nolan
4200–5399 Dorp	3900–4199 Dorp	2600–3899 Dorp	2100–2599 Dorp	1400–2099 Dorp
Croft	Walton	Brendan	Orton	Gould
2100–2599 Noon	2600–3899 Noon	1400–2099 Noon	3900–4199 Noon	4200–5399 Noon

1. 3900– 4199 Noon
2. 4200– 5399 Dorp
3. Nolan
4. Farmer
5. 1400– 2099 Hart

6. 2100– 2599 Hart
7. 1400– 2099 Noon
8. Monroe
9. Ashley
10. 2100– 2599 Dorp

11. 2600– 3899 Hart
12. 2100– 2599 Noon
13. Orton
14. 2600– 3899 Dorp

ANSWERS

1. D	3. E	5. B	7. C	9. B	11. A	13. D	14. C
2. A	4. C	6. E	8. D	10. D	12. A		

Directions: *The five boxes below are labeled A, B, C, D, and E. In each box are five addresses: three are street addresses with number ranges and two are unnumbered place names. You have three minutes to memorize the box location of each address. The position of an address within a box is not important. You need only remember the letter of the box in which the address is found. You will use these addresses to answer three sets of practice questions that are NOT scored and one actual test that is scored.*

A	B	C	D	E
2600–3899 Hart	1400–2099 Hart	3900–4199 Hart	4200–5399 Hart	2100–2599 Hart
Linda	Ashley	Farmer	Monroe	Nolan
4200–5399 Dorp	3900–4199 Dorp	2600–3899 Dorp	2100–2599 Dorp	1400–2099 Dorp
Croft	Walton	Brendan	Orton	Gould
2100–2599 Noon	2600–3899 Noon	1400–2099 Noon	3900–4199 Noon	4200–5399 Noon

PRACTICE 1

Directions: *You have three minutes to write the letters of the boxes in which each of the following addresses is found. Indicate your answers by writing your answer (letter) next to the question number.*
Try to do this without looking at the boxes. However, if you get stuck, you may refer to the boxes during this practice exercise. If you must look at the boxes, try to memorize as you do so. This test is for practice only. It will not be scored.

1. 4200–5399 Dorp

2. 3900–4199 Hart

3. 4200–5399 Noon

4. Walton

5. Monroe

6. 2100–2599 Noon

7. 1400–2199 Hart

8. Gould

9. 1400–2099 Dorp

10. 2100–2599 Dorp

11. 1400–2099 Noon

12. Linda

13. Croft

14. Brendan

15. 3900–4199 Dorp

16. 2600–3899 Noon

17. 2100–2599 Hart

18. 2600–3899 Hart

19. 1400–2099 Dorp

20. Farmer

21. Ashley

22. 3900–4199 Noon

23. 2100–2599 Dorp

24. 2100–2599 Noon

25. Nolan

26. Croft

27. 4200–5399 Dorp

28. 1400–2099 Noon

29. 4200–5399 Hart

30. Monroe

31. Gould

32. 1400–2099 Hart

33. 2600–3899 Dorp

34. 2600–3899 Noon

35. Linda

36. Walton

37. Orton

38. 3900–4199 Dorp

39. 4200–5399 Noon

40. 3900–4199 Hart

41. Brendan

42. 1400–2099 Dorp

43. 2600–3899 Noon

44. Ashley

45. 4200–5399 Hart

46. 2600–3899 Hart

47. 3900–4199 Dorp

48. Orton

49. Monroe

50. 3900–4199 Noon

51. 2100–2599 Hart

52. 4200–5399 Noon

53. 2100–2599 Noon

54. Walton

55. Farmer

56. 2600–3899 Dorp

57. 3900–4199 Hart

58. 2100–2599 Dorp

59. Gould

60. Brendan

61. 1400–2099 Hart

62. 2600–3899 Noon

63. Ashley

64. 1400–2099 Dorp

65. 4200–5399 Dorp

66. 4200–5399 Hart

67. Linda

68. Croft

69. Nolan

70. 1400–2099 Noon

71. 3900–4199 Hart

72. 2100–2599 Dorp

73. 2600–3899 Noon

74. Walton

75. 2600–3899 Dorp

76. 2600–3899 Hart

77. 4200–5399 Noon

78. Monroe

79. Ashley

80. 2100–2599 Noon

81. 2100–2599 Hart

82. 3900–4199 Hart

83. Brendan

84. Nolan

85. Croft

86. 3900–4199 Dorp

87. 2100–2599 Dorp

88. 1400–2099 Noon

PRACTICE II

Directions: *The next 88 questions are for practice. Indicate your answers by writing your answer (letter) next to the question number. Your time limit is three minutes. This time, however, you must NOT look at the boxes while answering the questions. You must rely on memory in marking the box location of each item. This practice test will not be scored.*

1. 3900–4199 Hart
2. 3900–4199 Dorp
3. 2100–2599 Noon
4. Nolan
5. Orton
6. 4200–5399 Noon
7. 4200–5399 Hart
8. 1400–2099 Noon
9. Croft
10. Ashley
11. 2600–3899 Hart
12. 4200–5399 Dorp
13. 1400–2099 Dorp
14. 1400–2099 Hart
15. Farmer
16. Brendan
17. 2600–3899 Dorp
18. 2100–2599 Dorp
19. 2100–2599 Hart
20. Monroe
21. 4200–5399 Hart
22. Linda
23. 2600–3899 Noon
24. 3900–4199 Noon
25. Walton
26. Monroe
27. Ashley
28. 1400–2099 Dorp
29. 3900–4199 Hart
30. 2100–2599 Noon

31. Brendan
32. Linda
33. 2600–3899 Hart
34. 3900–4199 Dorp
35. 1400–2099 Noon
36. Nolan
37. Farmer
38. 4200–5399 Noon
39. 2100–2599 Dorp
40. 1400–2099 Hart
41. Croft
42. Walton
43. 2100–2599 Hart
44. 2600–3899 Noon
45. 2600–3899 Dorp
46. Gould
47. Orton
48. 3900–4199 Noon
49. 4200–5399 Dorp
50. 4200–5399 Hart
51. 2600–3899 Dorp
52. Linda
53. 2100–2599 Noon
54. Ashley
55. Gould
56. 4200–5399 Noon
57. 3900–4199 Noon
58. 3900–4199 Dorp
59. Nolan
60. Croft

61. 2600–3899 Hart
62. 2100–2599 Dorp
63. 3900–4199 Hart
64. Farmer
65. Orton
66. 4200–5399 Dorp
67. 1400–2099 Dorp
68. 1400–2099 Hart
69. Brendan
70. Linda
71. 1400–2099 Noon
72. 2600–3899 Noon
73. 4200–5399 Hart
74. Walton
75. Monroe
76. 3900–4199 Dorp
77. 2100–2599 Hart
78. 2100–2599 Noon
79. Ashley
80. Gould
81. Orton
82. 2600–3899 Noon
83. 1400–2099 Hart
84. 2600–3899 Dorp
85. 3900–4199 Noon
86. 2600–3899 Hart
87. Brendan
88. Croft

PRACTICE III

Directions: *The same addresses from the previous sets are repeated in the box below. Each address is in the same box as the original set. You now have three minutes to study the locations again. Do your best to memorize the letter of the box in which each address is located. This is your last chance to see the boxes.*

A	B	C	D	E
2600–3899 Hart	1400–2099 Hart	3900–4199 Hart	4200–5399 Hart	2100–2599 Hart
Linda	Ashley	Farmer	Monroe	Nolan
4200–5399 Dorp	3900–4199 Dorp	2600–3899 Dorp	2100–2599 Dorp	1400–2099 Dorp
Croft	Walton	Brendan	Orton	Gould
2100–2599 Noon	2600–3899 Noon	1400–2099 Noon	3900–4199 Noon	4200–5399 Noon

Directions: *This is your last practice set. Mark the location of each of the 88 addresses by writing the answer (letter) next to the question number. Your time limit is five minutes. Do NOT look back at the boxes. This practice test will not be scored.*

1. 2600–3899 Hart
2. 2600–3899 Dorp
3. 2600–3899 Noon
4. Walton
5. Nolan
6. 4200–5399 Noon
7. 2100–2599 Dorp
8. 1400–2099 Noon
9. Gould
10. Monroe
11. 3900–4199 Hart
12. 2100–2599 Hart
13. 3900–4199 Dorp
14. Brendan
15. Ashley
16. 1400–2099 Hart
17. 1400–2099 Dorp
18. 4200–5399 Dorp
19. Farmer
20. Monroe
21. Linda

22. 2100–2599 Noon
23. 3900–4199 Hart
24. 4200–5399 Hart
25. Croft
26. Ashley
27. 3900–4199 Dorp
28. 2600–3899 Noon
29. 2600–3899 Hart
30. Nolan
31. 2100–2599 Dorp
32. 4200–5399 Hart
33. 2600–3899 Noon
34. Monroe
35. Farmer
36. 3900–4199 Noon
37. 3900–4199 Dorp
38. 2600–3899 Hart
39. Nolan
40. Walton
41. 4200–5399 Dorp
42. 4200–5399 Noon

43. 1400–2099 Hart
44. Linda
45. Gould
46. 2100–2599 Hart
47. 3900–4199 Hart
48. 2600–3899 Dorp
49. Ashley
50. Croft
51. 1400–2099 Dorp
52. 1400–2099 Noon
53. 2100–2599 Noon
54. Orton
55. Brendan
56. 2600–3899 Hart
57. 3900–4199 Dorp
58. 4200–5399 Noon
59. 3900–4199 Hart
60. 1400–2099 Noon
61. Ashley
62. Brendan
63. Monroe

64. 1400–2099 Hart

65. 3900–4199 Noon

66. 4200–5399 Hart

67. 3900–4199 Dorp

68. Nolan

69. Walton

70. 4200–5399 Dorp

71. 1400–2099 Dorp

72. 1400–2099 Noon

73. 3900–4199 Hart

74. 2100–2599 Hart

75. Gould

76. Linda

77. Farmer

78. 2600–3899 Hart

79. 2600–3899 Noon

80. 4200–5399 Noon

81. 2600–3899 Dorp

82. 2100–2599 Dorp

83. Croft

84. Orton

85. 2100–2599 Noon

86. 3900–4199 Hart

87. 1400–2099 Dorp

88. 4200–5399 Noon

MEMORY FOR ADDRESSES

Time: 5 Minutes • 88 Questions.

Directions: Indicate the location (A, B, C, D, or E) of each of the 88 addresses below by writing the answer (letter) next to the question number. You are NOT permitted to look at the boxes. Work from memory as quickly and as accurately as you can.

1. Monroe
2. Walton
3. 2600–3899 Dorp
4. 2100–2599 Noon
5. 2100–2599 Hart
6. Linda
7. Gould
8. 4200–5399 Noon
9. 1400–2099 Dorp
10. 2600–3899 Hart
11. Ashley
12. Orton
13. 3900–4199 Hart
14. 1400–2099 Noon
15. 4200–5399 Dorp
16. 4200–5399 Hart
17. 2600–3899 Noon
18. 2100–2599 Dorp
19. Croft
20. Brendan
21. Nolan
22. Farmer
23. 3900–4199 Dorp
24. 3900–4199 Noon
25. 1400–3899 Hart
26. Linda
27. 2100–2599 Hart
28. 3900–4199 Hart
29. Monroe
30. 2600–3899 Dorp

31. 1400–3899 Noon
32. Brendan
33. Ashley
34. 2600–3899 Hart
35. 2100–2599 Noon
36. 1400–2099 Dorp
37. 2100–2599 Dorp
38. 4200–5399 Noon
39. Orton
40. Croft
41. 4200–5399 Hart
42. 2600–3899 Noon
43. 4200–5399 Dorp
44. Gould
45. 3900–4199 Noon
46. 2600–3899 Dorp
47. 1400–2099 Hart
48. Linda
49. Gould
50. 2100–2599 Hart
51. 2100–2599 Dorp
52. 3900–4199 Dorp
53. 2100–2599 Noon
54. Brendan
55. Farmer
56. 2600–3899 Hart
57. 4200–5399 Noon
58. 1400–2099 Dorp
59. Nolan
60. Croft

61. 4200–5399 Dorp
62. 1400–2099 Noon
63. 2600–3899 Noon
64. Monroe
65. Ashley
66. 3900–4199 Hart
67. 4200–5399 Hart
68. Orton
69. Walton
70. 2100–2599 Hart
71. 4200–5399 Dorp
72. 3900–4199 Noon
73. 2100–2599 Noon
74. 2600–3899 Dorp
75. 3900–4199 Hart
76. Croft
77. Farmer
78. 2100–2599 Hart
79. 4200–5399 Noon
80. 4200–5399 Dorp
81. Brendan
82. Monroe
83. 1400–2099 Noon
84. 3900–4199 Dorp
85. 4200–5399 Hart
86. Linda
87. Ashley
88. 1400–2099 Dorp

Answers—Memory for Addresses

PRACTICE I

1. A	12. A	23. D	34. B	45. D	56. C	67. A	78. D
2. C	13. A	24. A	35. A	46. A	57. C	68. A	79. B
3. E	14. C	25. E	36. B	47. B	58. D	69. E	80. A
4. B	15. B	26. A	37. D	48. D	59. E	70. C	81. E
5. D	16. B	27. A	38. B	49. D	60. C	71. C	82. C
6. A	17. E	28. C	39. E	50. D	61. B	72. D	83. C
7. B	18. A	29. D	40. C	51. E	62. B	73. B	84. E
8. E	19. E	30. D	41. C	52. E	63. B	74. B	85. A
9. E	20. C	31. E	42. E	53. A	64. E	75. C	86. B
10. D	21. B	32. B	43. B	54. B	65. A	76. A	87. D
11. C	22. D	33. C	44. B	55. C	66. D	77. E	88. C

PRACTICE II

1. C	12. A	23. B	34. B	45. C	56. E	67. E	78. A
2. B	13. E	24. D	35. C	46. E	57. D	68. B	79. B
3. A	14. B	25. B	36. E	47. D	58. B	69. C	80. E
4. E	15. C	26. D	37. C	48. D	59. E	70. A	81. D
5. D	16. C	27. B	38. E	49. A	60. A	71. C	82. B
6. E	17. C	28. E	39. D	50. D	61. A	72. B	83. B
7. D	18. D	29. C	40. B	51. C	62. D	73. D	84. C
8. C	19. E	30. A	41. A	52. A	63. C	74. B	85. D
9. A	20. D	31. C	42. B	53. A	64. C	75. D	86. A
10. B	21. D	32. A	43. E	54. B	65. D	76. B	87. C
11. A	22. A	33. A	44. B	55. E	66. A	77. E	88. A

PRACTICE III

1. A	12. E	23. C	34. D	45. E	56. A	67. B	78. A
2. C	13. B	24. D	35. C	46. E	57. B	68. E	79. B
3. B	14. C	25. A	36. D	47. C	58. E	69. B	80. E
4. B	15. B	26. B	37. B	48. C	59. C	70. A	81. C
5. E	16. B	27. B	38. A	49. B	60. C	71. E	82. D
6. E	17. E	28. B	39. E	50. A	61. B	72. C	83. A
7. D	18. A	29. A	40. B	51. E	62. C	73. C	84. D
8. C	19. C	30. E	41. A	52. C	63. D	74. E	85. A
9. E	20. D	31. D	42. E	53. A	64. B	75. E	86. C
10. D	21. A	32. D	43. B	54. D	65. D	76. A	87. E
11. C	22. A	33. B	44. A	55. C	66. D	77. C	88. E

MEMORY FOR ADDRESSES

1. D	12. D	23. B	34. A	45. D	56. A	67. D	78. E
2. B	13. C	24. D	35. A	46. C	57. E	68. D	79. E
3. C	14. C	25. B	36. E	47. B	58. E	69. B	80. A
4. A	15. A	26. A	37. D	48. A	59. E	70. E	81. C
5. E	16. D	27. E	38. E	49. E	60. A	71. A	82. D
6. A	17. B	28. C	39. D	50. E	61. A	72. D	83. C
7. E	18. D	29. D	40. A	51. D	62. C	73. A	84. B
8. E	19. A	30. C	41. D	52. B	63. B	74. C	85. D
9. E	20. C	31. C	42. B	53. A	64. D	75. C	86. A
10. A	21. E	32. C	43. A	54. C	65. B	76. A	87. B
11. B	22. C	33. B	44. E	55. C	66. C	77. C	88. E

Determine Your Raw Score

Memory for Addresses—Timed Test: Your score on Memory for Addresses is based on the number of questions you answered correctly minus one-fourth of the questions you answered incorrectly (number wrong divided by four):

1. Number of right answers   _____

2. Number of wrong answers   _____

3. Divide number wrong by 4   _____

4. Subtract answer from number right   _____

   Raw Score =   _____

Self-Evaluation Chart

For the timed test, see how your raw score falls on the following scale. You should not be satisfied with less than Excellent. Review all appropriate study material, then retake the test, if necessary.

IF your raw score was between	THEN your work was
75–88	Excellent
60–74	Good
45–59	Average
30–44	Fair
1–29	Poor

NUMBER SERIES PRACTICE TESTS

Taking the Timed Test

This is your first real chance to answer Number Series questions under the time constraints of the actual test. To get the most benefits from this practice, proceed as follows:

1. Choose a workspace that is quiet, well lit, clean, and uncluttered.
2. Use a stopwatch or kitchen timer to accurately time each test.
3. Start the first test at a convenient time and stop exactly when your six minutes are up.
4. Give yourself at least a five-minute breather between each test. You can use this non-test time to skim through review material in earlier chapters.
5. After you complete all three tests, check your answers against the answer keys provided. Circle all wrong answers in red so that you can easily locate them.
6. Calculate your raw score for each test as instructed.
7. Check to see where your scores fall on the self-evaluation chart.
8. If you receive less than an Excellent score on a test, go back and review the appropriate study chapters in this book.
9. Retake the test to see your improvement.

   Note that there is no guessing penalty on Part C. So remember to guess if you are truly stumped or cannot finish the test in the time allowed.

Practice Test 1

Time: 20 Minutes • 24 Questions.

Directions: *For each question below, there is at the left a series of numbers that follows some definite order and at the right five sets of two numbers each. You are to look at the numbers in the series at the left and find out what order they follow. Then decide what the next two numbers in the series would be if the series were continued. Circle the letter of the correct answer.*

1. 19 18 12 17 16 13 15 ..... (A) 16 12   (B) 14 14   (C) 12 14   (D) 14 12   (E) 12 16

2. 7 15 12 8 16 13 9 .... (A) 17 14   (B) 17 10   (C) 14 10   (D) 14 17   (E) 10 14

3. 18 15 6 16 14 6 14 .... (A) 12 6   (B) 14 13   (C) 6 12   (D) 13 12   (E) 33 6

4. 6 6 5 8 8 7 10 10 .... (A) 8 12   (B) 9 12   (C) 22 12   (D) 12 9   (E) 9 9

5. 17 20 23 26 29 32 35 ..... (A) 37 40   (B) 41 44   (C) 38 41   (D) 38 42   (E) 36 39

6. 15 5 7 16 9 11 17 .... (A) 18 13   (B) 15 17   (C) 12 19   (D) 13 15   (E) 12 13

7. 19 17 16 16 13 15 10 ..... (A) 14 7   (B) 12 9   (C) 14 9   (D) 7 12   (E) 10 14

8. 11 1 16 10 6 21 9 .... (A) 12 26   (B) 26 8   (C) 11 26   (D) 11 8   (E) 8 11

9. 15 22 19 26 23 30 27 ..... (A) 28 34   (B) 27 35   (C) 31 34   (D) 29 33   (E) 34 31

10. 99 9 88 8 77 7 66 .... (A) 55 5   (B) 6 55   (C) 66 5   (D) 55 6   (E) 55 44

11. 25 29 29 33 37 37 41 ..... (A) 41 41   (B) 41 45   (C) 45 49   (D) 45 45   (E) 49 49

12. 81 71 61 52 43 35 27 ..... (A) 27 20   (B) 21 14   (C) 20 14   (D) 21 15   (E) 20 13

13. 12 14 16 48 50 52 156 ... (A) 468 470   (B) 158 316   (C) 158 474   (D) 158 160   (E) 158 158

14. 47 42 38 35 30 26 23 ..... (A) 18 14   (B) 21 19   (C) 23 18   (D) 19 14   (E) 19 13

15. 84 84 91 91 97 97 102 ... (A) 102 102   (B) 102 104   (C) 104 106   (D) 106 106   (E) 102 106

16. 66 13 62 21 58 29 54 ..... (A) 50 48   (B) 62 66   (C) 34 42   (D) 37 50   (E) 58 21

17. 14 12 10 10 20 18 16 16 (A) 32 32   (B) 32 30   (C) 30 28   (D) 16 32   (E) 16 14

18. 25 30 35 30 25 30 35 ..... (A) 30 40   (B) 25 30   (C) 25 20   (D) 35 30   (E) 30 25

19. 19 19 19 57 57 57 171 ... (A) 171 513   (B) 513 513   (C) 171 171   (D) 171 57   (E) 57 18

20. 75 69 63 57 51 45 39 ..... (A) 36 33   (B) 39 36   (C) 39 33   (D) 33 27   (E) 33 33

21. 6 15 23 30 36 41 45 .... (A) 48 50   (B) 49 53   (C) 45 41   (D) 46 47   (E) 47 49

22. 12 58 25 51 38 44 51 ..... (A) 64 37   (B) 37 64   (C) 51 51   (D) 51 64   (E) 51 37

23. 1 2 4 8 16 32 64 .... (A) 64 32   (B) 64 64   (C) 64 128   (D) 128 256   (E) 128 128

24. 5 86 7 81 10 77 14 .... (A) 16 80   (B) 70 25   (C) 79 13   (D) 19 74   (E) 74 19

Practice Test II

Time: 20 Minutes • 24 Questions.

Directions: *For each question below, there is at the left a series of numbers that follows some definite order and at the right five sets of two numbers each. You are to look at the numbers in the series at the left and find out what order they follow. Then decide what the next two numbers in the series would be if the series were continued. Circle the letter of the correct answer.*

1. 5 7 30 9 11 30 13 .... (A) 15 16   (B) 15 17   (C) 14 17   (D) 15 30   (E) 30 17

2. 5 7 11 13 17 19 23 .... (A) 27 29   (B) 25 29   (C) 25 27   (D) 27 31   (E) 29 31

3. 9 15 10 17 12 19 15 21 19 . (A) 23 24   (B) 25 23   (C) 17 23   (D) 23 31   (E) 21 24

4. 34 37 30 33 26 29 22 .... (A) 17 8   (B) 18 11   (C) 25 28   (D) 25 20   (E) 25 18

5. 10 16 12 14 14 12 16 .... (A) 14 12   (B) 10 18   (C) 10 14   (D) 14 18   (E) 14 16

6. 11 12 18 11 13 19 11 14 .... (A) 18 11   (B) 16 11   (C) 20 11   (D) 11 21   (E) 17 11

7. 20 9 8 19 10 9 18 11 10 ..... (A) 19 11   (B) 17 10   (C) 19 12   (D) 17 12   (E) 19 10

8. 28 27 26 31 30 29 34 .... (A) 36 32   (B) 32 31   (C) 33 32   (D) 33 36   (E) 35 36

9. 12 24 15 30 21 42 33 .... (A) 66 57   (B) 44 56   (C) 28 43   (D) 47 69   (E) 24 48

10. 46 76 51 70 56 64 61 .... (A) 61 68   (B) 69 71   (C) 58 65   (D) 66 71   (E) 58 66

11. 37 28 28 19 19 10 10 .... (A) 9 9   (B) 1 1   (C) 10 9   (D) 10 1   (E) 9 1

12. 1 2 3 6 4 5 6 15 7 .... (A) 8 15   (B) 7 8   (C) 8 9   (D) 9 17   (E) 9 24

13. 55 51 12 56 52 12 57 .... (A) 57 12   (B) 12 53   (C) 58 12   (D) 53 12   (E) 12 57

14. 75 75 8 50 50 9 25 .... (A) 25 25   (B) 25 10   (C) 10 25   (D) 25 12   (E) 10 10

15. 1 2 3 4 5 5 4 .... (A) 3 2   (B) 5 4   (C) 4 5   (D) 5 6   (E) 4 4

16. 3 6 9 4 7 10 5 .... (A) 8 9   (B) 9 6   (C) 8 11   (D) 9 12   (E) 11 8

17. 5 7 9 18 20 22 44 .... (A) 60 66   (B) 66 80   (C) 66 68   (D) 88 90   (E) 46 48

18. 94 82 72 64 58 54 .... (A) 52 50   (B) 54 52   (C) 50 46   (D) 52 52   (E) 54 50

19. 85 85 86 85 86 87 85 .... (A) 85 86   (B) 86 87   (C) 87 89   (D) 87 86   (E) 84 83

20. 99 89 79 69 59 49 39 .... (A) 29 19   (B) 39 29   (C) 38 37   (D) 39 38   (E) 19 9

21. 33 42 41 39 48 47 45 .... (A) 42 041   (B) 44 42   (C) 54 53   (D) 54 52   (E) 54 63

22. 85 89 89 84 88 88 83 .... (A) 83 87   (B) 83 83   (C) 87 87   (D) 87 82   (E) 87 83

23. 1 2 3 3 4 5 5 6 7 .... (A) 7 7   (B) 8 8   (C) 8 9   (D) 7 6   (E) 7 8

24. 5 10 15 15 20 15 25 .... (A) 30 35   (B) 15 30   (C) 15 15   (D) 30 15   (E) 30 30

Answers—Practice Test I

1. B	4. B	7. A	10. B	13. D	16. D	19. C	22. B
2. A	5. C	8. C	11. D	14. A	17. B	20. D	23. D
3. E	6. D	9. E	12. E	15. E	18. E	21. A	24. E

EXPLANATIONS

1. **(B)** There are two series. The first series descends one number at a time, beginning with 19. The second series enters between each two numbers of the first series. The second series increases by +1. Thus, the series are: 19 18 17 16 15 14 and 12 13 14.

2. **(A)** The repeating pattern is $+8, -3, -5$.

3. **(E)** This is a difficult problem. The first series begins with 18 and decreases by 2: 18 16 14, and so forth. The second series begins with 15 and descends by 1: 15 14 13, and so forth. The number 6 separates each pair of descending numbers.

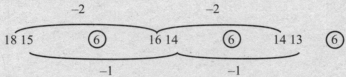

4. **(B)** The even numbers repeat themselves as they increase; the odd numbers simply increase by 2, alternating with the evens.

5. **(C)** Just add three to each number to get the next number.

6. **(D)** One series increases by 1: 15 16 17 18. The other series, which intervenes with two numbers to the first series's one, increases by 2: 5 7 9 11 13.

7. **(A)** The rule for the first series is -3. The rule for the alternating series is -1.

8. **(C)** There are two series here. The first reads 11 10 9. The second series starts at 1 and follows the rule $+15, -10, +15, -10$. The second series takes two steps to the first series's one. The solution to this problem is best seen by diagramming.

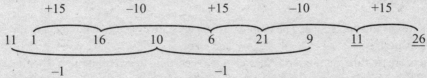

9. **(E)** The pattern is: $+7, -3; +7, -3$; and so on. Or, you might see alternating series, both increasing by $+4$.

10. **(B)** You might see two series. One series decreases at the rate of 11; the other decreases at the rate of 1. Or, you might see a series of the multiples of 11 each divided by 11.

11. **(D)** The pattern is +4, repeat the number, +4; +4, repeat the number, +4; +4, repeat the number, +4, and so on.

12. **(E)** The pattern is: $-10, -10, -9, -9, -8, -8, -7, -7, -6$, and so on.

13. **(D)** The pattern is: $+2, +2, \times 3; +2, +2, \times 3$, and so on.

14. **(A)** The pattern is: $-5, -4, -3; -5, -4, -3; -5$, and so on.

15. **(E)** The pattern is: repeat the number, +7, repeat the number, +6, repeat the number, +5, repeat the number, +4, and so on.

16. **(D)** There are two alternating series. The first series descends at the rate of 4. The alternating series ascends at the rate of 8.

17. **(B)** The pattern is: $-2, -2$, repeat the number, $\times 2; -2, -2$, repeat the number, $\times 2; -2$, and so on.

18. **(E)** The pattern is: +5, +5, − 5, − 5; +5, +5, − 5, − 5; and so on. Or you might see the repeat of the four numbers 25, 30, 35, 30.

19. **(C)** The pattern is: repeat the number three times, ×3; repeat the number three times, ×3; repeat the number three times, ×3.

20. **(D)** The pattern is simply: − 6, − 6, − 6, and so on.

21. **(A)** The pattern is: +9, +8, +7, +6, +5, +4, +3, +2, +1.

22. **(B)** There are two alternating series. The first series increases at the rate of +13. The alternating series decreases at the rate of − 7.

23. **(D)** The pattern is: ×2, ×2, ×2, and so on.

24. **(E)** There are two alternating series. The pattern of the first series is: +2, +3, +4, +5. The pattern of the alternating series is: − 5, − 4, − 3, − 2.

DETERMINE YOUR RAW SCORE

Practice Test 1: Your score is based on the number of questions answered correctly:

Enter number right   _____

Raw Score =   _____

Answers—Practice Test II

1. D	4. E	7. D	10. E	13. D	16. C	19. B	22. C
2. B	5. B	8. C	11. B	14. B	17. E	20. A	23. E
3. A	6. C	9. A	12. C	15. A	18. D	21. C	24. D

EXPLANATIONS

1. **(D)** The series increases by 2. The number 30 appears after each two numbers in the series.

2. **(B)** The pattern is: +2, +4; +2, +4; +2, +4; and so on.

3. **(A)** There are two alternating series that advance according to different rules. The first series begins with 9. The rule for this series is +1, +2, +3, +4, +5. The alternating series begins with 15 and advances in steady increments of 2.

4. **(E)** There are two alternating series, one series beginning with 34 and the other with 37. Both series decrease by subtracting 4 each time.

5. **(B)** The two series are moving in opposite directions. The first series begins with 10 and increases by 2. The alternating series begins with 16 and decreases by 2.

6. **(C)** You might be able to figure this one by reading it rhythmically. If not, consider that there are two series, one beginning with 12, the other with 18. Both series advance by 1. The number 11 separates each progression of the two series.

7. **(D)** There are two series alternating at the rate of 1 to 2. The first series decreases by 1: 20 19 18 17. The other series goes one step backward and two steps forward, or − 1, +2. Read: 9^{-1} 8^{+2} 10^{-1} 9^{+2} 11^{-1} 10^{+2} 12.

8. **(C)** The pattern is − 1, − 1, +5, and repeat; − 1, − 1, +5, and repeat again.

9. **(A)** The pattern is: ×2, − 9; ×2, − 9; and so on.

10. **(E)** There are two alternating series. The first series increases by 5. The alternating series decreases at the rate of 6.

11. **(B)** The pattern is – 9 and repeat the number; – 9 and repeat the number; – 9 and repeat the number.

12. **(C)** The series is: 1 2 3 4 5 6 7 8, and so on. After each three numbers in the series we find the sum of those three numbers. So: $1 + 2 + 3 = 6$; $4 + 5 + 6 = 15$; $7 + 8 + 9 = 24$; 10, and so on.

13. **(D)** The pattern is – 4, +5, and the number 12; – 4, +5, and the number 12 and so on.

14. **(B)** There are two series. One series proceeds: repeat the number, – 25; repeat the number, – 25. The other series simply advances by 1.

15. **(A)** The series proceeds upward from 1 to 5, and then turns around and descends, one number at a time.

16. **(C)** There are two interpretations for this series. You may see +3, +3, – 5; +3, +3, – 5, and so on. Or, you might see a series of +3, +3 mini-series, each mini-series beginning at a number one higher than the beginning number of the previous mini-series.

17. **(E)** The pattern is: +2, +2, ×2; +2, +2, ×2, and so on.

18. **(D)** The pattern is: – 12, – 10, – 8, – 6, – 4, – 2, – 0, and so on.

19. **(B)** Each mini-series begins with 85. With each cycle the series progresses to one more number: 85; 85 86; 85 86 87; 85 86 87 88, and so on.

20. **(A)** This is a simple – 10 series.

21. **(C)** The pattern is: +9, – 1, – 2; +9, – 1, – 2, and so on.

22. **(C)** The pattern is +4, repeat the number, – 5; +4, repeat the number, – 5; +4, and so on. You might instead have seen two descending series, one beginning with 85 and descending by 1, the other beginning with 89 and repeating itself before each descent.

23. **(E)** This is a deceptive series. Actually, the series consists of a series of mini-series, each beginning with the last number of the previous mini-series. If you group the numbers, you can see: 1 2 3; 3 4 5; 5 6 7; 7 8, and so on.

24. **(D)** The series is a +5 series with the number 15 interposing after each two numbers of the series. If you substitute X for the interposing 15, you can see that the series reads: 5 10 X 15 20 X 25 30 X.

DETERMINE YOUR RAW SCORE

Practice Test 2: Your score is based on the number of questions answered correctly:

Enter number right _____

Raw Score = _____

Self—Evaluation Chart

For each practice test, see how your raw score falls on the following scale. You should not be satisfied with less than Excellent. Review all appropriate study material, and then retake the test(s) where you need improvement.

IF your raw score was between	THEN your work was
25–24	Excellent
18–20	Good
14–17	Average
11–13	Fair
1–10	Poor

FOLLOWING ORAL INSTRUCTIONS PRACTICE TESTS

Taking the Timed Test

Because of the nature of this question type, you're going to need someone to help you practice with Oral Instructions questions. However, you can still simulate the actual conditions of the real test, if you follow these steps:

1. Before starting the test, give your reader (the person who is helping you practice for this question type) at least 10 to 15 minutes to practice reading the oral instructions (preferably, in a separate room), so he or she can get comfortable with the material.
2. Choose a workspace that is quiet, well-lit, and uncluttered. Make sure that you have a comfortable sitting or standing place for your reader, too!
3. Given that you are depending on the assistance of another person for this question type, be sure to schedule a time when the both of you are not rushed, so you can relax and concentrate on the task at hand.
4. Proceed through the entire test without repeating any instructions!
5. After finishing the test, check your answers against the correctly completed answer grid and worksheet. Circle any incorrect answers and mistakes on your worksheet.

If you really want to be fully prepared for this question type, you might also arrange to have someone read and record the instructions on tape. Depending on where you take the test, you might have a live reader, or you might have to take this section of the test by listening to a pre-recorded tape.

The Timed Test

The answer sheet, worksheet, and oral instructions for this practice test are on the following pages. **You will have 25 minutes to complete the test.**

ANSWER SHEET

TEAR HERE

1. Ⓐ Ⓑ Ⓒ Ⓓ Ⓔ	23. Ⓐ Ⓑ Ⓒ Ⓓ Ⓔ	45. Ⓐ Ⓑ Ⓒ Ⓓ Ⓔ	67. Ⓐ Ⓑ Ⓒ Ⓓ Ⓔ
2. Ⓐ Ⓑ Ⓒ Ⓓ Ⓔ	24. Ⓐ Ⓑ Ⓒ Ⓓ Ⓔ	46. Ⓐ Ⓑ Ⓒ Ⓓ Ⓔ	68. Ⓐ Ⓑ Ⓒ Ⓓ Ⓔ
3. Ⓐ Ⓑ Ⓒ Ⓓ Ⓔ	25. Ⓐ Ⓑ Ⓒ Ⓓ Ⓔ	47. Ⓐ Ⓑ Ⓒ Ⓓ Ⓔ	69. Ⓐ Ⓑ Ⓒ Ⓓ Ⓔ
4. Ⓐ Ⓑ Ⓒ Ⓓ Ⓔ	26. Ⓐ Ⓑ Ⓒ Ⓓ Ⓔ	48. Ⓐ Ⓑ Ⓒ Ⓓ Ⓔ	70. Ⓐ Ⓑ Ⓒ Ⓓ Ⓔ
5. Ⓐ Ⓑ Ⓒ Ⓓ Ⓔ	27. Ⓐ Ⓑ Ⓒ Ⓓ Ⓔ	49. Ⓐ Ⓑ Ⓒ Ⓓ Ⓔ	71. Ⓐ Ⓑ Ⓒ Ⓓ Ⓔ
6. Ⓐ Ⓑ Ⓒ Ⓓ Ⓔ	28. Ⓐ Ⓑ Ⓒ Ⓓ Ⓔ	50. Ⓐ Ⓑ Ⓒ Ⓓ Ⓔ	72. Ⓐ Ⓑ Ⓒ Ⓓ Ⓔ
7. Ⓐ Ⓑ Ⓒ Ⓓ Ⓔ	29. Ⓐ Ⓑ Ⓒ Ⓓ Ⓔ	51. Ⓐ Ⓑ Ⓒ Ⓓ Ⓔ	73. Ⓐ Ⓑ Ⓒ Ⓓ Ⓔ
8. Ⓐ Ⓑ Ⓒ Ⓓ Ⓔ	30. Ⓐ Ⓑ Ⓒ Ⓓ Ⓔ	52. Ⓐ Ⓑ Ⓒ Ⓓ Ⓔ	74. Ⓐ Ⓑ Ⓒ Ⓓ Ⓔ
9. Ⓐ Ⓑ Ⓒ Ⓓ Ⓔ	31. Ⓐ Ⓑ Ⓒ Ⓓ Ⓔ	53. Ⓐ Ⓑ Ⓒ Ⓓ Ⓔ	75. Ⓐ Ⓑ Ⓒ Ⓓ Ⓔ
10. Ⓐ Ⓑ Ⓒ Ⓓ Ⓔ	32. Ⓐ Ⓑ Ⓒ Ⓓ Ⓔ	54. Ⓐ Ⓑ Ⓒ Ⓓ Ⓔ	76. Ⓐ Ⓑ Ⓒ Ⓓ Ⓔ
11. Ⓐ Ⓑ Ⓒ Ⓓ Ⓔ	33. Ⓐ Ⓑ Ⓒ Ⓓ Ⓔ	55. Ⓐ Ⓑ Ⓒ Ⓓ Ⓔ	77. Ⓐ Ⓑ Ⓒ Ⓓ Ⓔ
12. Ⓐ Ⓑ Ⓒ Ⓓ Ⓔ	34. Ⓐ Ⓑ Ⓒ Ⓓ Ⓔ	56. Ⓐ Ⓑ Ⓒ Ⓓ Ⓔ	78. Ⓐ Ⓑ Ⓒ Ⓓ Ⓔ
13. Ⓐ Ⓑ Ⓒ Ⓓ Ⓔ	35. Ⓐ Ⓑ Ⓒ Ⓓ Ⓔ	57. Ⓐ Ⓑ Ⓒ Ⓓ Ⓔ	79. Ⓐ Ⓑ Ⓒ Ⓓ Ⓔ
14. Ⓐ Ⓑ Ⓒ Ⓓ Ⓔ	36. Ⓐ Ⓑ Ⓒ Ⓓ Ⓔ	58. Ⓐ Ⓑ Ⓒ Ⓓ Ⓔ	80. Ⓐ Ⓑ Ⓒ Ⓓ Ⓔ
15. Ⓐ Ⓑ Ⓒ Ⓓ Ⓔ	37. Ⓐ Ⓑ Ⓒ Ⓓ Ⓔ	59. Ⓐ Ⓑ Ⓒ Ⓓ Ⓔ	81. Ⓐ Ⓑ Ⓒ Ⓓ Ⓔ
16. Ⓐ Ⓑ Ⓒ Ⓓ Ⓔ	38. Ⓐ Ⓑ Ⓒ Ⓓ Ⓔ	60. Ⓐ Ⓑ Ⓒ Ⓓ Ⓔ	82. Ⓐ Ⓑ Ⓒ Ⓓ Ⓔ
17. Ⓐ Ⓑ Ⓒ Ⓓ Ⓔ	39. Ⓐ Ⓑ Ⓒ Ⓓ Ⓔ	61. Ⓐ Ⓑ Ⓒ Ⓓ Ⓔ	83. Ⓐ Ⓑ Ⓒ Ⓓ Ⓔ
18. Ⓐ Ⓑ Ⓒ Ⓓ Ⓔ	40. Ⓐ Ⓑ Ⓒ Ⓓ Ⓔ	62. Ⓐ Ⓑ Ⓒ Ⓓ Ⓔ	84. Ⓐ Ⓑ Ⓒ Ⓓ Ⓔ
19. Ⓐ Ⓑ Ⓒ Ⓓ Ⓔ	41. Ⓐ Ⓑ Ⓒ Ⓓ Ⓔ	63. Ⓐ Ⓑ Ⓒ Ⓓ Ⓔ	85. Ⓐ Ⓑ Ⓒ Ⓓ Ⓔ
20. Ⓐ Ⓑ Ⓒ Ⓓ Ⓔ	42. Ⓐ Ⓑ Ⓒ Ⓓ Ⓔ	64. Ⓐ Ⓑ Ⓒ Ⓓ Ⓔ	86. Ⓐ Ⓑ Ⓒ Ⓓ Ⓔ
21. Ⓐ Ⓑ Ⓒ Ⓓ Ⓔ	43. Ⓐ Ⓑ Ⓒ Ⓓ Ⓔ	65. Ⓐ Ⓑ Ⓒ Ⓓ Ⓔ	87. Ⓐ Ⓑ Ⓒ Ⓓ Ⓔ
22. Ⓐ Ⓑ Ⓒ Ⓓ Ⓔ	44. Ⓐ Ⓑ Ⓒ Ⓓ Ⓔ	66. Ⓐ Ⓑ Ⓒ Ⓓ Ⓔ	88. Ⓐ Ⓑ Ⓒ Ⓓ Ⓔ

WORKSHEET

Directions: *Listen carefully to the instructions read to you, and mark each item on this worksheet as directed. Then, complete each question by marking the answer sheet as directed. For each answer, you will darken the answer sheet for a number-letter combination.*

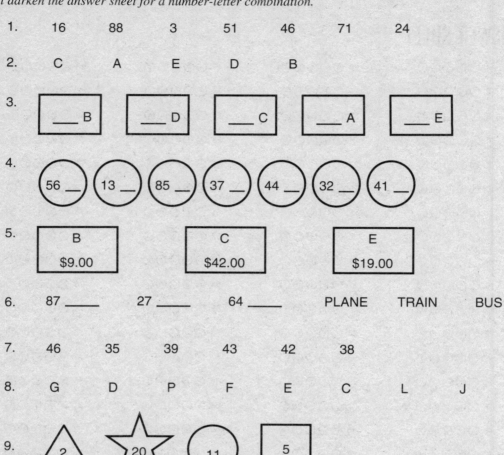

1. 16 88 3 51 46 71 24

2. C A E D B

3. [__ B] [__ D] [__ C] [__ A] [__ E]

4. (56 __) (13 __) (85 __) (37 __) (44 __) (32 __) (41 __)

5. [B $9.00] [C $42.00] [E $19.00]

6. 87 ____ 27 ____ 64 ____ PLANE TRAIN BUS

7. 46 35 39 43 42 38

8. G D P F E C L J

9. △2 ☆20 ◯11 ☐5

10.　74　　21　　53　　57　　42　　51

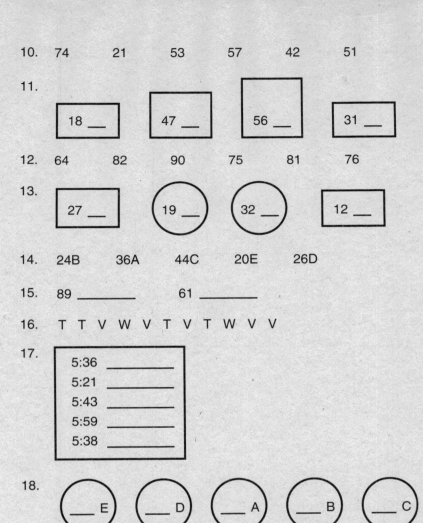

11.

18 ___   47 ___   56 ___   31 ___

12.　64　　82　　90　　75　　81　　76

13.

27 ___   19 ___   32 ___   12 ___

14.　24B　　36A　　44C　　20E　　26D

15.　89 _____   61 _____

16.　T　T　V　W　V　T　V　T　W　V　V

17.

5:36 _____
5:21 _____
5:43 _____
5:59 _____
5:38 _____

18.

___ E   ___ D   ___ A   ___ B   ___ C

19.

___ C   ___ A   ___ B   ___ E

ORAL INSTRUCTIONS

*Instructions to be read (the words in parentheses should **not** be read aloud).*

On the job you will have to listen to directions and then do what you have been told to do. In this test, I will read instructions to you. Try to understand them as I read them; I cannot repeat them. Once we begin, you may not ask any questions until the end of the test.

On the job you won't have to deal with pictures, numbers, and letters like those in the test, but you will have to listen to instructions and follow them. We are using this test to see how well you can follow instructions.

You are to mark your test booklet according to the instructions that I'll read to you. After each set of instructions, I'll give you time to record your answers on the separate answer sheet.

The actual test begins now.

Look at line 1 on your worksheet. (Pause slightly.) Draw a line under the sixth number in line 1. (Pause 2 seconds.) Now, on your answer sheet, darken space E for the number under which you just drew a line. (Pause 5 seconds.)

Look at line 1 again. (Pause slightly.) Draw two lines under the third number on the line. (Pause 2 seconds.) Now, on your answer sheet, darken space B as in baker for the number under which you drew two lines. (Pause 5 seconds.)

Look at line 2 on your worksheet. (Pause slightly.) Find the letter that is fifth in the alphabet and circle it. (Pause 2 seconds.) Now darken that letter for number 77 on your answer sheet. (Pause 5 seconds.)

Look at line 3 on your worksheet. (Pause slightly.) Write the number 17 in the third box. (Pause 2 seconds.) Now, on your answer sheet, darken the number-letter combination that is in the box in which you just wrote. (Pause 5 seconds.)

Look at line 3 again. (Pause slightly.) In the fourth box, write the number of hours in a day. (Pause 2 seconds.) Now, on your answer sheet, darken the number-letter combination that is in the box in which you just wrote. (Pause 5 seconds.)

Look at line 4 on your worksheet. (Pause slightly.) Write D as in dog in the circle right next to the second-lowest number. (Pause 5 seconds.) Now, on your answer sheet, darken the space for the number-letter combination in the circle in which you just wrote. (Pause 5 seconds.)

Look at line 4 again. (Pause slightly.) Write the letter C on the line in the middle circle. (Pause 2 seconds.) Now, on your answer sheet, darken the space for the number-letter combination in the circle in which you just wrote. (Pause 5 seconds.)

Look at line 5 on your worksheet. Each box represents a letter carrier and the amount of money that he or she collected on the route in one day. (Pause slightly.) Find the carrier who collected the smallest amount of money that day and circle his or her letter. (Pause 2 seconds.) On your answer sheet, darken the number-letter combination in the box in which you circled a letter. (Pause 5 seconds.)

Look at line 6 on your worksheet. (Pause slightly.) Write the first letter of the third means of transportation on the second line. (Pause 8 seconds.) Write the last letter of the first means of transportation on the first line. (Pause 8 seconds.) Write the middle letter of the middle means of transportation on the last line. (Pause 8 seconds.) Now, on your answer sheet, darken the number-letter combinations on the three lines. (Pause 15 seconds.)

Look at line 7 on your worksheet. (Pause slightly.) Reading right to left, find the first number that is higher than the number 39 and draw a box around the number. (Pause 5 seconds.) Now, on your answer sheet, darken D as in dog for the number around which you just drew a box. (Pause 5 seconds.)

Look at line 8 on your worksheet. (Pause slightly.) Find, on line 8, the letter that appears first in the alphabet and underline that letter. (Pause 5 seconds.) Now, on your answer sheet, darken that letter for space number 1. (Pause 5 seconds.)

Look at line 9 on your worksheet. (Pause slightly.) In the figure with the least number of points, write the letter A. (Pause 2 seconds.) In the figure with the greatest number of points, write the letter E. (Pause 2 seconds.) Now, on your answer sheet, darken the number-letter combinations in the two figures in which you just wrote. (Pause 10 seconds.)

Look at line 10 on your worksheet. (Pause slightly.) If the third number in line 10 should, in normal counting, appear before the fourth number in line 10, write the letter B as in baker above the third number; if not, write the letter A above the fourth number. (Pause 5 seconds.) Now, on your answer sheet, darken the number-letter combination of the number you just wrote. (Pause 5 seconds.)

Look at line 11 on your worksheet. (Pause slightly.) Write the letter A in the second box. (Pause 2 seconds.) Now, on your answer sheet, darken the number-letter combination in the box in which you just wrote. (Pause 5 seconds.)

Look at line 11 again. (Pause slightly.) If the number in the smallest box is greater than the number in the first box, write the letter C in the largest box (pause 5 seconds); if not, write the letter D as in dog in the largest box. (Pause 2 seconds.) Now, on your answer sheet, darken the number-letter combination in the box in which you just wrote. (Pause 5 seconds.)

Look at line 12 on your worksheet. (Pause slightly.) Draw one line under each number that falls between 75 and 90 and is even. (Pause 8 seconds.) Now, on your answer sheet, blacken space D as in dog for each number under which you drew one line. (Pause 10 seconds.)

Look at line 12 again. (Pause slightly.) Draw two lines under each number that falls between 75 and 90 and is odd. (Pause 8 seconds.) Now, on your answer sheet, darken space E for each number under which you drew two lines. (Pause 5 seconds.)

Look at line 13 on your worksheet. (Pause slightly.) Write the letter A in the left-hand circle. (Pause 2 seconds.) Now, on your answer sheet, darken the space for the number-letter combination in the figure in which you just wrote. (Pause 5 seconds.)

Look at line 13 again. (Pause slightly.) Write the letter B as in baker in the right-hand square. (Pause 2 seconds.) Now, on your answer sheet, darken the space for the number-letter combination in the figure in which you just wrote. (Pause 5 seconds.)

Look at line 14 on your worksheet. (Pause slightly.) Write the answer to this question at the end of line 14: $22 \times 2 =$. (Pause 2 seconds.) Find the answer that you wrote among the numbers on line 14 (pause 2 seconds) and darken that number-letter combination on your answer sheet. (Pause 5 seconds.)

Look at line 15 on your worksheet. (Pause slightly.) If 3 is less than 5 and more than 7, write the letter E next to number 89 (pause 5 seconds); if not, write the letter E next to number 61. (Pause 2 seconds.) Now, on your answer sheet, darken the number-letter combination of the line on which you just wrote. (Pause 5 seconds.)

Look at line 16 on your worksheet. (Pause slightly.) Count the number of V's on line 16 and write the number at the end of the line. (Pause 2 seconds.) Now, add 11 to that number and, on your answer sheet, darken space D as in dog for the number of V's plus 11. (Pause 10 seconds.)

Look at line 17 on your worksheet. (Pause slightly.) Each time represents the scheduled arrival time of a mail truck. Write the letter A on the line beside the earliest scheduled time. (Pause 2 seconds.) Write the letter C next to the latest scheduled time. (Pause 2 seconds.) Now, on your answer sheet, darken the number-letter combinations of the last two digits of the times beside which you wrote letters. (Pause 10 seconds.)

Look at line 18 on your worksheet. (Pause slightly.) If in one day there are more hours before noon than after noon, write the number 47 in the second circle (pause 2 seconds); if not, write the number 38 in the first circle. (Pause 2 seconds.) Now, on your answer sheet, blacken the space for the number-letter combination in the circle in which you just wrote. (Pause 5 seconds.)

Look at line 18 again. (Pause slightly.) Write the number 69 in the second circle from the right. (Pause 2 seconds.) Now, on your answer sheet, darken the space for the number-letter combination in the circle in which you just wrote. (Pause 5 seconds.)

Look at line 19 on your worksheet. (Pause slightly.) Write the smallest of these numbers in the first box: 84, 35, 73. (Pause 5 seconds.) Now, on your answer sheet, darken the space for the number-letter combination in the figure in which you just wrote. (Pause 5 seconds.)

TIMED TEST ANSWERS

#	Answer	#	Answer	#	Answer	#	Answer
1.	C	23.	—	45.	—	67.	—
2.	—	24.	A	46.	—	68.	—
3.	B	25.	—	47.	A	69.	B
4.	—	26.	—	48.	—	70.	—
5.	—	27.	B	49.	—	71.	E
6.	—	28.	—	50.	—	72.	—
7.	—	29.	—	51.	—	73.	—
8.	—	30.	—	52.	—	74.	—
9.	B	31.	—	53.	B	75.	—
10.	—	32.	D	54.	—	76.	D
11.	A	33.	—	55.	—	77.	E
12.	B	34.	—	56.	C	78.	—
13.	—	35.	A	57.	—	79.	—
14.	—	36.	—	58.	—	80.	—
15.	—	37.	C	59.	C	81.	E
16.	D	38.	E	60.	—	82.	D
17.	C	39.	—	61.	E	83.	—
18.	—	40.	—	62.	—	84.	—
19.	A	41.	—	63.	—	85.	—
20.	E	42.	D	64.	A	86.	—
21.	A	43.	—	65.	—	87.	E
22.	—	44.	C	66.	—	88.	—

CORRECTLY FILLED WORKSHEET

1.   16   88   <u>3</u>   51   46   <u>71</u>   24

2.   C   A   (E)   D   B

3.
| ___ B | ___ D | 17 C | 24 A | ___ E |

4.
(56 __) (13 __) (85 __) (37 C) (44 __) (32 D) (41 __)

5.
| (B) $9.00 | C $42.00 | E $19.00 |

6.   87 <u>E</u>   27 <u>B</u>   64 <u>A</u>   PLANE   TRAIN   BUS

7.   46   35   39   43   [42]   38

8.   G   D   P   F   E   <u>C</u>   L   J

9.   △ 2   ★ E 20   (A 11)   □ 5

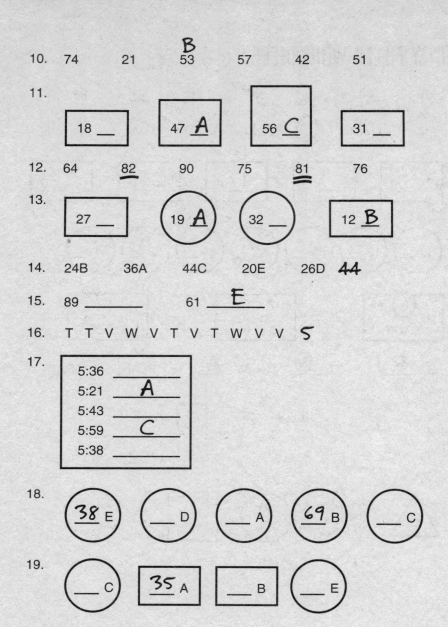

10. 74   21   B
                        53   57   42   51

11.

    [18 __]   [47 **A**]   [56 **C**]   [31 __]

12. 64   82   90   75   81   76

13.

    [27 __]   (19 **A**)   (32 __)   [12 **B**]

14. 24B   36A   44C   20E   26D   **44**

15. 89 _____   61 ___**E**___

16. T T V W V T V T W V V **S**

17.

    5:36 _____
    5:21 ___**A**___
    5:43 _____
    5:59 ___**C**___
    5:38 _____

18. (**38** E)   (__ D)   (__ A)   (**69** B)   (__ C)

19. (__ C)   [**35** A]   [__ B]   (__ E)

FULL LENGTH PRACTICE EXAM: EXAM 470 AND EXAM 460

Model Examination 1

ANSWER SHEET

Exam 470

Clerk

City Carrier

Distribution Clerk, Machine (Letter-Sorting Machine Operator)

Flat Sorting Machine Operator

Mail Handler

Mail Processor

Mark-up Clerk, Automated

Exam 460

Rural Carrier

Part A—Address Checking

1. Ⓐ Ⓓ	20. Ⓐ Ⓓ	39. Ⓐ Ⓓ	58. Ⓐ Ⓓ	77. Ⓐ Ⓓ
2. Ⓐ Ⓓ	21. Ⓐ Ⓓ	40. Ⓐ Ⓓ	59. Ⓐ Ⓓ	78. Ⓐ Ⓓ
3. Ⓐ Ⓓ	22. Ⓐ Ⓓ	41. Ⓐ Ⓓ	60. Ⓐ Ⓓ	79. Ⓐ Ⓓ
4. Ⓐ Ⓓ	23. Ⓐ Ⓓ	42. Ⓐ Ⓓ	61. Ⓐ Ⓓ	80. Ⓐ Ⓓ
5. Ⓐ Ⓓ	24. Ⓐ Ⓓ	43. Ⓐ Ⓓ	62. Ⓐ Ⓓ	81. Ⓐ Ⓓ
6. Ⓐ Ⓓ	25. Ⓐ Ⓓ	44. Ⓐ Ⓓ	63. Ⓐ Ⓓ	82. Ⓐ Ⓓ
7. Ⓐ Ⓓ	26. Ⓐ Ⓓ	45. Ⓐ Ⓓ	64. Ⓐ Ⓓ	83. Ⓐ Ⓓ
8. Ⓐ Ⓓ	27. Ⓐ Ⓓ	46. Ⓐ Ⓓ	65. Ⓐ Ⓓ	84. Ⓐ Ⓓ
9. Ⓐ Ⓓ	28. Ⓐ Ⓓ	47. Ⓐ Ⓓ	66. Ⓐ Ⓓ	85. Ⓐ Ⓓ
10. Ⓐ Ⓓ	29. Ⓐ Ⓓ	48. Ⓐ Ⓓ	67. Ⓐ Ⓓ	86. Ⓐ Ⓓ
11. Ⓐ Ⓓ	30. Ⓐ Ⓓ	49. Ⓐ Ⓓ	68. Ⓐ Ⓓ	87. Ⓐ Ⓓ
12. Ⓐ Ⓓ	31. Ⓐ Ⓓ	50. Ⓐ Ⓓ	69. Ⓐ Ⓓ	88. Ⓐ Ⓓ
13. Ⓐ Ⓓ	32. Ⓐ Ⓓ	51. Ⓐ Ⓓ	70. Ⓐ Ⓓ	89. Ⓐ Ⓓ
14. Ⓐ Ⓓ	33. Ⓐ Ⓓ	52. Ⓐ Ⓓ	71. Ⓐ Ⓓ	90. Ⓐ Ⓓ
15. Ⓐ Ⓓ	34. Ⓐ Ⓓ	53. Ⓐ Ⓓ	72. Ⓐ Ⓓ	91. Ⓐ Ⓓ
16. Ⓐ Ⓓ	35. Ⓐ Ⓓ	54. Ⓐ Ⓓ	73. Ⓐ Ⓓ	92. Ⓐ Ⓓ
17. Ⓐ Ⓓ	36. Ⓐ Ⓓ	55. Ⓐ Ⓓ	74. Ⓐ Ⓓ	93. Ⓐ Ⓓ
18. Ⓐ Ⓓ	37. Ⓐ Ⓓ	56. Ⓐ Ⓓ	75. Ⓐ Ⓓ	94. Ⓐ Ⓓ
19. Ⓐ Ⓓ	38. Ⓐ Ⓓ	57. Ⓐ Ⓓ	76. Ⓐ Ⓓ	95. Ⓐ Ⓓ

TEAR HERE

Part B—Memory for Addresses
PRACTICE I ANSWER SHEET

1 Ⓐ Ⓑ Ⓒ Ⓓ Ⓔ	23 Ⓐ Ⓑ Ⓒ Ⓓ Ⓔ	45 Ⓐ Ⓑ Ⓒ Ⓓ Ⓔ	67 Ⓐ Ⓑ Ⓒ Ⓓ Ⓔ
2 Ⓐ Ⓑ Ⓒ Ⓓ Ⓔ	24 Ⓐ Ⓑ Ⓒ Ⓓ Ⓔ	46 Ⓐ Ⓑ Ⓒ Ⓓ Ⓔ	68 Ⓐ Ⓑ Ⓒ Ⓓ Ⓔ
3 Ⓐ Ⓑ Ⓒ Ⓓ Ⓔ	25 Ⓐ Ⓑ Ⓒ Ⓓ Ⓔ	47 Ⓐ Ⓑ Ⓒ Ⓓ Ⓔ	69 Ⓐ Ⓑ Ⓒ Ⓓ Ⓔ
4 Ⓐ Ⓑ Ⓒ Ⓓ Ⓔ	26 Ⓐ Ⓑ Ⓒ Ⓓ Ⓔ	48 Ⓐ Ⓑ Ⓒ Ⓓ Ⓔ	70 Ⓐ Ⓑ Ⓒ Ⓓ Ⓔ
5 Ⓐ Ⓑ Ⓒ Ⓓ Ⓔ	27 Ⓐ Ⓑ Ⓒ Ⓓ Ⓔ	49 Ⓐ Ⓑ Ⓒ Ⓓ Ⓔ	71 Ⓐ Ⓑ Ⓒ Ⓓ Ⓔ
6 Ⓐ Ⓑ Ⓒ Ⓓ Ⓔ	28 Ⓐ Ⓑ Ⓒ Ⓓ Ⓔ	50 Ⓐ Ⓑ Ⓒ Ⓓ Ⓔ	72 Ⓐ Ⓑ Ⓒ Ⓓ Ⓔ
7 Ⓐ Ⓑ Ⓒ Ⓓ Ⓔ	29 Ⓐ Ⓑ Ⓒ Ⓓ Ⓔ	51 Ⓐ Ⓑ Ⓒ Ⓓ Ⓔ	73 Ⓐ Ⓑ Ⓒ Ⓓ Ⓔ
8 Ⓐ Ⓑ Ⓒ Ⓓ Ⓔ	30 Ⓐ Ⓑ Ⓒ Ⓓ Ⓔ	52 Ⓐ Ⓑ Ⓒ Ⓓ Ⓔ	74 Ⓐ Ⓑ Ⓒ Ⓓ Ⓔ
9 Ⓐ Ⓑ Ⓒ Ⓓ Ⓔ	31 Ⓐ Ⓑ Ⓒ Ⓓ Ⓔ	53 Ⓐ Ⓑ Ⓒ Ⓓ Ⓔ	75 Ⓐ Ⓑ Ⓒ Ⓓ Ⓔ
10 Ⓐ Ⓑ Ⓒ Ⓓ Ⓔ	32 Ⓐ Ⓑ Ⓒ Ⓓ Ⓔ	54 Ⓐ Ⓑ Ⓒ Ⓓ Ⓔ	76 Ⓐ Ⓑ Ⓒ Ⓓ Ⓔ
11 Ⓐ Ⓑ Ⓒ Ⓓ Ⓔ	33 Ⓐ Ⓑ Ⓒ Ⓓ Ⓔ	55 Ⓐ Ⓑ Ⓒ Ⓓ Ⓔ	77 Ⓐ Ⓑ Ⓒ Ⓓ Ⓔ
12 Ⓐ Ⓑ Ⓒ Ⓓ Ⓔ	34 Ⓐ Ⓑ Ⓒ Ⓓ Ⓔ	56 Ⓐ Ⓑ Ⓒ Ⓓ Ⓔ	78 Ⓐ Ⓑ Ⓒ Ⓓ Ⓔ
13 Ⓐ Ⓑ Ⓒ Ⓓ Ⓔ	35 Ⓐ Ⓑ Ⓒ Ⓓ Ⓔ	57 Ⓐ Ⓑ Ⓒ Ⓓ Ⓔ	79 Ⓐ Ⓑ Ⓒ Ⓓ Ⓔ
14 Ⓐ Ⓑ Ⓒ Ⓓ Ⓔ	36 Ⓐ Ⓑ Ⓒ Ⓓ Ⓔ	58 Ⓐ Ⓑ Ⓒ Ⓓ Ⓔ	80 Ⓐ Ⓑ Ⓒ Ⓓ Ⓔ
15 Ⓐ Ⓑ Ⓒ Ⓓ Ⓔ	37 Ⓐ Ⓑ Ⓒ Ⓓ Ⓔ	59 Ⓐ Ⓑ Ⓒ Ⓓ Ⓔ	81 Ⓐ Ⓑ Ⓒ Ⓓ Ⓔ
16 Ⓐ Ⓑ Ⓒ Ⓓ Ⓔ	38 Ⓐ Ⓑ Ⓒ Ⓓ Ⓔ	60 Ⓐ Ⓑ Ⓒ Ⓓ Ⓔ	82 Ⓐ Ⓑ Ⓒ Ⓓ Ⓔ
17 Ⓐ Ⓑ Ⓒ Ⓓ Ⓔ	39 Ⓐ Ⓑ Ⓒ Ⓓ Ⓔ	61 Ⓐ Ⓑ Ⓒ Ⓓ Ⓔ	83 Ⓐ Ⓑ Ⓒ Ⓓ Ⓔ
18 Ⓐ Ⓑ Ⓒ Ⓓ Ⓔ	40 Ⓐ Ⓑ Ⓒ Ⓓ Ⓔ	62 Ⓐ Ⓑ Ⓒ Ⓓ Ⓔ	84 Ⓐ Ⓑ Ⓒ Ⓓ Ⓔ
19 Ⓐ Ⓑ Ⓒ Ⓓ Ⓔ	41 Ⓐ Ⓑ Ⓒ Ⓓ Ⓔ	63 Ⓐ Ⓑ Ⓒ Ⓓ Ⓔ	85 Ⓐ Ⓑ Ⓒ Ⓓ Ⓔ
20 Ⓐ Ⓑ Ⓒ Ⓓ Ⓔ	42 Ⓐ Ⓑ Ⓒ Ⓓ Ⓔ	64 Ⓐ Ⓑ Ⓒ Ⓓ Ⓔ	86 Ⓐ Ⓑ Ⓒ Ⓓ Ⓔ
21 Ⓐ Ⓑ Ⓒ Ⓓ Ⓔ	43 Ⓐ Ⓑ Ⓒ Ⓓ Ⓔ	65 Ⓐ Ⓑ Ⓒ Ⓓ Ⓔ	87 Ⓐ Ⓑ Ⓒ Ⓓ Ⓔ
22 Ⓐ Ⓑ Ⓒ Ⓓ Ⓔ	44 Ⓐ Ⓑ Ⓒ Ⓓ Ⓔ	66 Ⓐ Ⓑ Ⓒ Ⓓ Ⓔ	88 Ⓐ Ⓑ Ⓒ Ⓓ Ⓔ

PRACTICE II ANSWER SHEET

1 Ⓐ Ⓑ Ⓒ Ⓓ Ⓔ   23 Ⓐ Ⓑ Ⓒ Ⓓ Ⓔ   45 Ⓐ Ⓑ Ⓒ Ⓓ Ⓔ   67 Ⓐ Ⓑ Ⓒ Ⓓ Ⓔ

2 Ⓐ Ⓑ Ⓒ Ⓓ Ⓔ   24 Ⓐ Ⓑ Ⓒ Ⓓ Ⓔ   46 Ⓐ Ⓑ Ⓒ Ⓓ Ⓔ   68 Ⓐ Ⓑ Ⓒ Ⓓ Ⓔ

3 Ⓐ Ⓑ Ⓒ Ⓓ Ⓔ   25 Ⓐ Ⓑ Ⓒ Ⓓ Ⓔ   47 Ⓐ Ⓑ Ⓒ Ⓓ Ⓔ   69 Ⓐ Ⓑ Ⓒ Ⓓ Ⓔ

4 Ⓐ Ⓑ Ⓒ Ⓓ Ⓔ   26 Ⓐ Ⓑ Ⓒ Ⓓ Ⓔ   48 Ⓐ Ⓑ Ⓒ Ⓓ Ⓔ   70 Ⓐ Ⓑ Ⓒ Ⓓ Ⓔ

5 Ⓐ Ⓑ Ⓒ Ⓓ Ⓔ   27 Ⓐ Ⓑ Ⓒ Ⓓ Ⓔ   49 Ⓐ Ⓑ Ⓒ Ⓓ Ⓔ   71 Ⓐ Ⓑ Ⓒ Ⓓ Ⓔ

6 Ⓐ Ⓑ Ⓒ Ⓓ Ⓔ   28 Ⓐ Ⓑ Ⓒ Ⓓ Ⓔ   50 Ⓐ Ⓑ Ⓒ Ⓓ Ⓔ   72 Ⓐ Ⓑ Ⓒ Ⓓ Ⓔ

7 Ⓐ Ⓑ Ⓒ Ⓓ Ⓔ   29 Ⓐ Ⓑ Ⓒ Ⓓ Ⓔ   51 Ⓐ Ⓑ Ⓒ Ⓓ Ⓔ   73 Ⓐ Ⓑ Ⓒ Ⓓ Ⓔ

8 Ⓐ Ⓑ Ⓒ Ⓓ Ⓔ   30 Ⓐ Ⓑ Ⓒ Ⓓ Ⓔ   52 Ⓐ Ⓑ Ⓒ Ⓓ Ⓔ   74 Ⓐ Ⓑ Ⓒ Ⓓ Ⓔ

9 Ⓐ Ⓑ Ⓒ Ⓓ Ⓔ   31 Ⓐ Ⓑ Ⓒ Ⓓ Ⓔ   53 Ⓐ Ⓑ Ⓒ Ⓓ Ⓔ   75 Ⓐ Ⓑ Ⓒ Ⓓ Ⓔ

10 Ⓐ Ⓑ Ⓒ Ⓓ Ⓔ   32 Ⓐ Ⓑ Ⓒ Ⓓ Ⓔ   54 Ⓐ Ⓑ Ⓒ Ⓓ Ⓔ   76 Ⓐ Ⓑ Ⓒ Ⓓ Ⓔ

11 Ⓐ Ⓑ Ⓒ Ⓓ Ⓔ   33 Ⓐ Ⓑ Ⓒ Ⓓ Ⓔ   55 Ⓐ Ⓑ Ⓒ Ⓓ Ⓔ   77 Ⓐ Ⓑ Ⓒ Ⓓ Ⓔ

12 Ⓐ Ⓑ Ⓒ Ⓓ Ⓔ   34 Ⓐ Ⓑ Ⓒ Ⓓ Ⓔ   56 Ⓐ Ⓑ Ⓒ Ⓓ Ⓔ   78 Ⓐ Ⓑ Ⓒ Ⓓ Ⓔ

13 Ⓐ Ⓑ Ⓒ Ⓓ Ⓔ   35 Ⓐ Ⓑ Ⓒ Ⓓ Ⓔ   57 Ⓐ Ⓑ Ⓒ Ⓓ Ⓔ   79 Ⓐ Ⓑ Ⓒ Ⓓ Ⓔ

14 Ⓐ Ⓑ Ⓒ Ⓓ Ⓔ   36 Ⓐ Ⓑ Ⓒ Ⓓ Ⓔ   58 Ⓐ Ⓑ Ⓒ Ⓓ Ⓔ   80 Ⓐ Ⓑ Ⓒ Ⓓ Ⓔ

15 Ⓐ Ⓑ Ⓒ Ⓓ Ⓔ   37 Ⓐ Ⓑ Ⓒ Ⓓ Ⓔ   59 Ⓐ Ⓑ Ⓒ Ⓓ Ⓔ   81 Ⓐ Ⓑ Ⓒ Ⓓ Ⓔ

16 Ⓐ Ⓑ Ⓒ Ⓓ Ⓔ   38 Ⓐ Ⓑ Ⓒ Ⓓ Ⓔ   60 Ⓐ Ⓑ Ⓒ Ⓓ Ⓔ   82 Ⓐ Ⓑ Ⓒ Ⓓ Ⓔ

17 Ⓐ Ⓑ Ⓒ Ⓓ Ⓔ   39 Ⓐ Ⓑ Ⓒ Ⓓ Ⓔ   61 Ⓐ Ⓑ Ⓒ Ⓓ Ⓔ   83 Ⓐ Ⓑ Ⓒ Ⓓ Ⓔ

18 Ⓐ Ⓑ Ⓒ Ⓓ Ⓔ   40 Ⓐ Ⓑ Ⓒ Ⓓ Ⓔ   62 Ⓐ Ⓑ Ⓒ Ⓓ Ⓔ   84 Ⓐ Ⓑ Ⓒ Ⓓ Ⓔ

19 Ⓐ Ⓑ Ⓒ Ⓓ Ⓔ   41 Ⓐ Ⓑ Ⓒ Ⓓ Ⓔ   63 Ⓐ Ⓑ Ⓒ Ⓓ Ⓔ   85 Ⓐ Ⓑ Ⓒ Ⓓ Ⓔ

20 Ⓐ Ⓑ Ⓒ Ⓓ Ⓔ   42 Ⓐ Ⓑ Ⓒ Ⓓ Ⓔ   64 Ⓐ Ⓑ Ⓒ Ⓓ Ⓔ   86 Ⓐ Ⓑ Ⓒ Ⓓ Ⓔ

21 Ⓐ Ⓑ Ⓒ Ⓓ Ⓔ   43 Ⓐ Ⓑ Ⓒ Ⓓ Ⓔ   65 Ⓐ Ⓑ Ⓒ Ⓓ Ⓔ   87 Ⓐ Ⓑ Ⓒ Ⓓ Ⓔ

22 Ⓐ Ⓑ Ⓒ Ⓓ Ⓔ   44 Ⓐ Ⓑ Ⓒ Ⓓ Ⓔ   66 Ⓐ Ⓑ Ⓒ Ⓓ Ⓔ   88 Ⓐ Ⓑ Ⓒ Ⓓ Ⓔ

TEAR HERE

PRACTICE III ANSWER SHEET

1 Ⓐ Ⓑ Ⓒ Ⓓ Ⓔ   23 Ⓐ Ⓑ Ⓒ Ⓓ Ⓔ   45 Ⓐ Ⓑ Ⓒ Ⓓ Ⓔ   67 Ⓐ Ⓑ Ⓒ Ⓓ Ⓔ

2 Ⓐ Ⓑ Ⓒ Ⓓ Ⓔ   24 Ⓐ Ⓑ Ⓒ Ⓓ Ⓔ   46 Ⓐ Ⓑ Ⓒ Ⓓ Ⓔ   68 Ⓐ Ⓑ Ⓒ Ⓓ Ⓔ

3 Ⓐ Ⓑ Ⓒ Ⓓ Ⓔ   25 Ⓐ Ⓑ Ⓒ Ⓓ Ⓔ   47 Ⓐ Ⓑ Ⓒ Ⓓ Ⓔ   69 Ⓐ Ⓑ Ⓒ Ⓓ Ⓔ

4 Ⓐ Ⓑ Ⓒ Ⓓ Ⓔ   26 Ⓐ Ⓑ Ⓒ Ⓓ Ⓔ   48 Ⓐ Ⓑ Ⓒ Ⓓ Ⓔ   70 Ⓐ Ⓑ Ⓒ Ⓓ Ⓔ

5 Ⓐ Ⓑ Ⓒ Ⓓ Ⓔ   27 Ⓐ Ⓑ Ⓒ Ⓓ Ⓔ   49 Ⓐ Ⓑ Ⓒ Ⓓ Ⓔ   71 Ⓐ Ⓑ Ⓒ Ⓓ Ⓔ

6 Ⓐ Ⓑ Ⓒ Ⓓ Ⓔ   28 Ⓐ Ⓑ Ⓒ Ⓓ Ⓔ   50 Ⓐ Ⓑ Ⓒ Ⓓ Ⓔ   72 Ⓐ Ⓑ Ⓒ Ⓓ Ⓔ

7 Ⓐ Ⓑ Ⓒ Ⓓ Ⓔ   29 Ⓐ Ⓑ Ⓒ Ⓓ Ⓔ   51 Ⓐ Ⓑ Ⓒ Ⓓ Ⓔ   73 Ⓐ Ⓑ Ⓒ Ⓓ Ⓔ

8 Ⓐ Ⓑ Ⓒ Ⓓ Ⓔ   30 Ⓐ Ⓑ Ⓒ Ⓓ Ⓔ   52 Ⓐ Ⓑ Ⓒ Ⓓ Ⓔ   74 Ⓐ Ⓑ Ⓒ Ⓓ Ⓔ

9 Ⓐ Ⓑ Ⓒ Ⓓ Ⓔ   31 Ⓐ Ⓑ Ⓒ Ⓓ Ⓔ   53 Ⓐ Ⓑ Ⓒ Ⓓ Ⓔ   75 Ⓐ Ⓑ Ⓒ Ⓓ Ⓔ

10 Ⓐ Ⓑ Ⓒ Ⓓ Ⓔ   32 Ⓐ Ⓑ Ⓒ Ⓓ Ⓔ   54 Ⓐ Ⓑ Ⓒ Ⓓ Ⓔ   76 Ⓐ Ⓑ Ⓒ Ⓓ Ⓔ

11 Ⓐ Ⓑ Ⓒ Ⓓ Ⓔ   33 Ⓐ Ⓑ Ⓒ Ⓓ Ⓔ   55 Ⓐ Ⓑ Ⓒ Ⓓ Ⓔ   77 Ⓐ Ⓑ Ⓒ Ⓓ Ⓔ

12 Ⓐ Ⓑ Ⓒ Ⓓ Ⓔ   34 Ⓐ Ⓑ Ⓒ Ⓓ Ⓔ   56 Ⓐ Ⓑ Ⓒ Ⓓ Ⓔ   78 Ⓐ Ⓑ Ⓒ Ⓓ Ⓔ

13 Ⓐ Ⓑ Ⓒ Ⓓ Ⓔ   35 Ⓐ Ⓑ Ⓒ Ⓓ Ⓔ   57 Ⓐ Ⓑ Ⓒ Ⓓ Ⓔ   79 Ⓐ Ⓑ Ⓒ Ⓓ Ⓔ

14 Ⓐ Ⓑ Ⓒ Ⓓ Ⓔ   36 Ⓐ Ⓑ Ⓒ Ⓓ Ⓔ   58 Ⓐ Ⓑ Ⓒ Ⓓ Ⓔ   80 Ⓐ Ⓑ Ⓒ Ⓓ Ⓔ

15 Ⓐ Ⓑ Ⓒ Ⓓ Ⓔ   37 Ⓐ Ⓑ Ⓒ Ⓓ Ⓔ   59 Ⓐ Ⓑ Ⓒ Ⓓ Ⓔ   81 Ⓐ Ⓑ Ⓒ Ⓓ Ⓔ

16 Ⓐ Ⓑ Ⓒ Ⓓ Ⓔ   38 Ⓐ Ⓑ Ⓒ Ⓓ Ⓔ   60 Ⓐ Ⓑ Ⓒ Ⓓ Ⓔ   82 Ⓐ Ⓑ Ⓒ Ⓓ Ⓔ

17 Ⓐ Ⓑ Ⓒ Ⓓ Ⓔ   39 Ⓐ Ⓑ Ⓒ Ⓓ Ⓔ   61 Ⓐ Ⓑ Ⓒ Ⓓ Ⓔ   83 Ⓐ Ⓑ Ⓒ Ⓓ Ⓔ

18 Ⓐ Ⓑ Ⓒ Ⓓ Ⓔ   40 Ⓐ Ⓑ Ⓒ Ⓓ Ⓔ   62 Ⓐ Ⓑ Ⓒ Ⓓ Ⓔ   84 Ⓐ Ⓑ Ⓒ Ⓓ Ⓔ

19 Ⓐ Ⓑ Ⓒ Ⓓ Ⓔ   41 Ⓐ Ⓑ Ⓒ Ⓓ Ⓔ   63 Ⓐ Ⓑ Ⓒ Ⓓ Ⓔ   85 Ⓐ Ⓑ Ⓒ Ⓓ Ⓔ

20 Ⓐ Ⓑ Ⓒ Ⓓ Ⓔ   42 Ⓐ Ⓑ Ⓒ Ⓓ Ⓔ   64 Ⓐ Ⓑ Ⓒ Ⓓ Ⓔ   86 Ⓐ Ⓑ Ⓒ Ⓓ Ⓔ

21 Ⓐ Ⓑ Ⓒ Ⓓ Ⓔ   43 Ⓐ Ⓑ Ⓒ Ⓓ Ⓔ   65 Ⓐ Ⓑ Ⓒ Ⓓ Ⓔ   87 Ⓐ Ⓑ Ⓒ Ⓓ Ⓔ

22 Ⓐ Ⓑ Ⓒ Ⓓ Ⓔ   44 Ⓐ Ⓑ Ⓒ Ⓓ Ⓔ   66 Ⓐ Ⓑ Ⓒ Ⓓ Ⓔ   88 Ⓐ Ⓑ Ⓒ Ⓓ Ⓔ

MEMORY FOR ADDRESSES

1 Ⓐ Ⓑ Ⓒ Ⓓ Ⓔ   23 Ⓐ Ⓑ Ⓒ Ⓓ Ⓔ   45 Ⓐ Ⓑ Ⓒ Ⓓ Ⓔ   67 Ⓐ Ⓑ Ⓒ Ⓓ Ⓔ

2 Ⓐ Ⓑ Ⓒ Ⓓ Ⓔ   24 Ⓐ Ⓑ Ⓒ Ⓓ Ⓔ   46 Ⓐ Ⓑ Ⓒ Ⓓ Ⓔ   68 Ⓐ Ⓑ Ⓒ Ⓓ Ⓔ

3 Ⓐ Ⓑ Ⓒ Ⓓ Ⓔ   25 Ⓐ Ⓑ Ⓒ Ⓓ Ⓔ   47 Ⓐ Ⓑ Ⓒ Ⓓ Ⓔ   69 Ⓐ Ⓑ Ⓒ Ⓓ Ⓔ

4 Ⓐ Ⓑ Ⓒ Ⓓ Ⓔ   26 Ⓐ Ⓑ Ⓒ Ⓓ Ⓔ   48 Ⓐ Ⓑ Ⓒ Ⓓ Ⓔ   70 Ⓐ Ⓑ Ⓒ Ⓓ Ⓔ

5 Ⓐ Ⓑ Ⓒ Ⓓ Ⓔ   27 Ⓐ Ⓑ Ⓒ Ⓓ Ⓔ   49 Ⓐ Ⓑ Ⓒ Ⓓ Ⓔ   71 Ⓐ Ⓑ Ⓒ Ⓓ Ⓔ

6 Ⓐ Ⓑ Ⓒ Ⓓ Ⓔ   28 Ⓐ Ⓑ Ⓒ Ⓓ Ⓔ   50 Ⓐ Ⓑ Ⓒ Ⓓ Ⓔ   72 Ⓐ Ⓑ Ⓒ Ⓓ Ⓔ

7 Ⓐ Ⓑ Ⓒ Ⓓ Ⓔ   29 Ⓐ Ⓑ Ⓒ Ⓓ Ⓔ   51 Ⓐ Ⓑ Ⓒ Ⓓ Ⓔ   73 Ⓐ Ⓑ Ⓒ Ⓓ Ⓔ

8 Ⓐ Ⓑ Ⓒ Ⓓ Ⓔ   30 Ⓐ Ⓑ Ⓒ Ⓓ Ⓔ   52 Ⓐ Ⓑ Ⓒ Ⓓ Ⓔ   74 Ⓐ Ⓑ Ⓒ Ⓓ Ⓔ

9 Ⓐ Ⓑ Ⓒ Ⓓ Ⓔ   31 Ⓐ Ⓑ Ⓒ Ⓓ Ⓔ   53 Ⓐ Ⓑ Ⓒ Ⓓ Ⓔ   75 Ⓐ Ⓑ Ⓒ Ⓓ Ⓔ

10 Ⓐ Ⓑ Ⓒ Ⓓ Ⓔ   32 Ⓐ Ⓑ Ⓒ Ⓓ Ⓔ   54 Ⓐ Ⓑ Ⓒ Ⓓ Ⓔ   76 Ⓐ Ⓑ Ⓒ Ⓓ Ⓔ

11 Ⓐ Ⓑ Ⓒ Ⓓ Ⓔ   33 Ⓐ Ⓑ Ⓒ Ⓓ Ⓔ   55 Ⓐ Ⓑ Ⓒ Ⓓ Ⓔ   77 Ⓐ Ⓑ Ⓒ Ⓓ Ⓔ

12 Ⓐ Ⓑ Ⓒ Ⓓ Ⓔ   34 Ⓐ Ⓑ Ⓒ Ⓓ Ⓔ   56 Ⓐ Ⓑ Ⓒ Ⓓ Ⓔ   78 Ⓐ Ⓑ Ⓒ Ⓓ Ⓔ

13 Ⓐ Ⓑ Ⓒ Ⓓ Ⓔ   35 Ⓐ Ⓑ Ⓒ Ⓓ Ⓔ   57 Ⓐ Ⓑ Ⓒ Ⓓ Ⓔ   79 Ⓐ Ⓑ Ⓒ Ⓓ Ⓔ

14 Ⓐ Ⓑ Ⓒ Ⓓ Ⓔ   36 Ⓐ Ⓑ Ⓒ Ⓓ Ⓔ   58 Ⓐ Ⓑ Ⓒ Ⓓ Ⓔ   80 Ⓐ Ⓑ Ⓒ Ⓓ Ⓔ

15 Ⓐ Ⓑ Ⓒ Ⓓ Ⓔ   37 Ⓐ Ⓑ Ⓒ Ⓓ Ⓔ   59 Ⓐ Ⓑ Ⓒ Ⓓ Ⓔ   81 Ⓐ Ⓑ Ⓒ Ⓓ Ⓔ

16 Ⓐ Ⓑ Ⓒ Ⓓ Ⓔ   38 Ⓐ Ⓑ Ⓒ Ⓓ Ⓔ   60 Ⓐ Ⓑ Ⓒ Ⓓ Ⓔ   82 Ⓐ Ⓑ Ⓒ Ⓓ Ⓔ

17 Ⓐ Ⓑ Ⓒ Ⓓ Ⓔ   39 Ⓐ Ⓑ Ⓒ Ⓓ Ⓔ   61 Ⓐ Ⓑ Ⓒ Ⓓ Ⓔ   83 Ⓐ Ⓑ Ⓒ Ⓓ Ⓔ

18 Ⓐ Ⓑ Ⓒ Ⓓ Ⓔ   40 Ⓐ Ⓑ Ⓒ Ⓓ Ⓔ   62 Ⓐ Ⓑ Ⓒ Ⓓ Ⓔ   84 Ⓐ Ⓑ Ⓒ Ⓓ Ⓔ

19 Ⓐ Ⓑ Ⓒ Ⓓ Ⓔ   41 Ⓐ Ⓑ Ⓒ Ⓓ Ⓔ   63 Ⓐ Ⓑ Ⓒ Ⓓ Ⓔ   85 Ⓐ Ⓑ Ⓒ Ⓓ Ⓔ

20 Ⓐ Ⓑ Ⓒ Ⓓ Ⓔ   42 Ⓐ Ⓑ Ⓒ Ⓓ Ⓔ   64 Ⓐ Ⓑ Ⓒ Ⓓ Ⓔ   86 Ⓐ Ⓑ Ⓒ Ⓓ Ⓔ

21 Ⓐ Ⓑ Ⓒ Ⓓ Ⓔ   43 Ⓐ Ⓑ Ⓒ Ⓓ Ⓔ   65 Ⓐ Ⓑ Ⓒ Ⓓ Ⓔ   87 Ⓐ Ⓑ Ⓒ Ⓓ Ⓔ

22 Ⓐ Ⓑ Ⓒ Ⓓ Ⓔ   44 Ⓐ Ⓑ Ⓒ Ⓓ Ⓔ   66 Ⓐ Ⓑ Ⓒ Ⓓ Ⓔ   88 Ⓐ Ⓑ Ⓒ Ⓓ Ⓔ

Part C—Number Series

1. Ⓐ Ⓑ Ⓒ Ⓓ Ⓔ   7. Ⓐ Ⓑ Ⓒ Ⓓ Ⓔ   13. Ⓐ Ⓑ Ⓒ Ⓓ Ⓔ   19. Ⓐ Ⓑ Ⓒ Ⓓ Ⓔ

2. Ⓐ Ⓑ Ⓒ Ⓓ Ⓔ   8. Ⓐ Ⓑ Ⓒ Ⓓ Ⓔ   14. Ⓐ Ⓑ Ⓒ Ⓓ Ⓔ   20. Ⓐ Ⓑ Ⓒ Ⓓ Ⓔ

3. Ⓐ Ⓑ Ⓒ Ⓓ Ⓔ   9. Ⓐ Ⓑ Ⓒ Ⓓ Ⓔ   15. Ⓐ Ⓑ Ⓒ Ⓓ Ⓔ   21. Ⓐ Ⓑ Ⓒ Ⓓ Ⓔ

4. Ⓐ Ⓑ Ⓒ Ⓓ Ⓔ   10. Ⓐ Ⓑ Ⓒ Ⓓ Ⓔ   16. Ⓐ Ⓑ Ⓒ Ⓓ Ⓔ   22. Ⓐ Ⓑ Ⓒ Ⓓ Ⓔ

5. Ⓐ Ⓑ Ⓒ Ⓓ Ⓔ   11. Ⓐ Ⓑ Ⓒ Ⓓ Ⓔ   17. Ⓐ Ⓑ Ⓒ Ⓓ Ⓔ   23. Ⓐ Ⓑ Ⓒ Ⓓ Ⓔ

6. Ⓐ Ⓑ Ⓒ Ⓓ Ⓔ   12. Ⓐ Ⓑ Ⓒ Ⓓ Ⓔ   18. Ⓐ Ⓑ Ⓒ Ⓓ Ⓔ   24. Ⓐ Ⓑ Ⓒ Ⓓ Ⓔ

TEAR HERE

Part D—Following Oral Instructions

1 Ⓐ Ⓑ Ⓒ Ⓓ Ⓔ   23 Ⓐ Ⓑ Ⓒ Ⓓ Ⓔ   45 Ⓐ Ⓑ Ⓒ Ⓓ Ⓔ   67 Ⓐ Ⓑ Ⓒ Ⓓ Ⓔ

2 Ⓐ Ⓑ Ⓒ Ⓓ Ⓔ   24 Ⓐ Ⓑ Ⓒ Ⓓ Ⓔ   46 Ⓐ Ⓑ Ⓒ Ⓓ Ⓔ   68 Ⓐ Ⓑ Ⓒ Ⓓ Ⓔ

3 Ⓐ Ⓑ Ⓒ Ⓓ Ⓔ   25 Ⓐ Ⓑ Ⓒ Ⓓ Ⓔ   47 Ⓐ Ⓑ Ⓒ Ⓓ Ⓔ   69 Ⓐ Ⓑ Ⓒ Ⓓ Ⓔ

4 Ⓐ Ⓑ Ⓒ Ⓓ Ⓔ   26 Ⓐ Ⓑ Ⓒ Ⓓ Ⓔ   48 Ⓐ Ⓑ Ⓒ Ⓓ Ⓔ   70 Ⓐ Ⓑ Ⓒ Ⓓ Ⓔ

5 Ⓐ Ⓑ Ⓒ Ⓓ Ⓔ   27 Ⓐ Ⓑ Ⓒ Ⓓ Ⓔ   49 Ⓐ Ⓑ Ⓒ Ⓓ Ⓔ   71 Ⓐ Ⓑ Ⓒ Ⓓ Ⓔ

6 Ⓐ Ⓑ Ⓒ Ⓓ Ⓔ   28 Ⓐ Ⓑ Ⓒ Ⓓ Ⓔ   50 Ⓐ Ⓑ Ⓒ Ⓓ Ⓔ   72 Ⓐ Ⓑ Ⓒ Ⓓ Ⓔ

7 Ⓐ Ⓑ Ⓒ Ⓓ Ⓔ   29 Ⓐ Ⓑ Ⓒ Ⓓ Ⓔ   51 Ⓐ Ⓑ Ⓒ Ⓓ Ⓔ   73 Ⓐ Ⓑ Ⓒ Ⓓ Ⓔ

8 Ⓐ Ⓑ Ⓒ Ⓓ Ⓔ   30 Ⓐ Ⓑ Ⓒ Ⓓ Ⓔ   52 Ⓐ Ⓑ Ⓒ Ⓓ Ⓔ   74 Ⓐ Ⓑ Ⓒ Ⓓ Ⓔ

9 Ⓐ Ⓑ Ⓒ Ⓓ Ⓔ   31 Ⓐ Ⓑ Ⓒ Ⓓ Ⓔ   53 Ⓐ Ⓑ Ⓒ Ⓓ Ⓔ   75 Ⓐ Ⓑ Ⓒ Ⓓ Ⓔ

10 Ⓐ Ⓑ Ⓒ Ⓓ Ⓔ   32 Ⓐ Ⓑ Ⓒ Ⓓ Ⓔ   54 Ⓐ Ⓑ Ⓒ Ⓓ Ⓔ   76 Ⓐ Ⓑ Ⓒ Ⓓ Ⓔ

11 Ⓐ Ⓑ Ⓒ Ⓓ Ⓔ   33 Ⓐ Ⓑ Ⓒ Ⓓ Ⓔ   55 Ⓐ Ⓑ Ⓒ Ⓓ Ⓔ   77 Ⓐ Ⓑ Ⓒ Ⓓ Ⓔ

12 Ⓐ Ⓑ Ⓒ Ⓓ Ⓔ   34 Ⓐ Ⓑ Ⓒ Ⓓ Ⓔ   56 Ⓐ Ⓑ Ⓒ Ⓓ Ⓔ   78 Ⓐ Ⓑ Ⓒ Ⓓ Ⓔ

13 Ⓐ Ⓑ Ⓒ Ⓓ Ⓔ   35 Ⓐ Ⓑ Ⓒ Ⓓ Ⓔ   57 Ⓐ Ⓑ Ⓒ Ⓓ Ⓔ   79 Ⓐ Ⓑ Ⓒ Ⓓ Ⓔ

14 Ⓐ Ⓑ Ⓒ Ⓓ Ⓔ   36 Ⓐ Ⓑ Ⓒ Ⓓ Ⓔ   58 Ⓐ Ⓑ Ⓒ Ⓓ Ⓔ   80 Ⓐ Ⓑ Ⓒ Ⓓ Ⓔ

15 Ⓐ Ⓑ Ⓒ Ⓓ Ⓔ   37 Ⓐ Ⓑ Ⓒ Ⓓ Ⓔ   59 Ⓐ Ⓑ Ⓒ Ⓓ Ⓔ   81 Ⓐ Ⓑ Ⓒ Ⓓ Ⓔ

16 Ⓐ Ⓑ Ⓒ Ⓓ Ⓔ   38 Ⓐ Ⓑ Ⓒ Ⓓ Ⓔ   60 Ⓐ Ⓑ Ⓒ Ⓓ Ⓔ   82 Ⓐ Ⓑ Ⓒ Ⓓ Ⓔ

17 Ⓐ Ⓑ Ⓒ Ⓓ Ⓔ   39 Ⓐ Ⓑ Ⓒ Ⓓ Ⓔ   61 Ⓐ Ⓑ Ⓒ Ⓓ Ⓔ   83 Ⓐ Ⓑ Ⓒ Ⓓ Ⓔ

18 Ⓐ Ⓑ Ⓒ Ⓓ Ⓔ   40 Ⓐ Ⓑ Ⓒ Ⓓ Ⓔ   62 Ⓐ Ⓑ Ⓒ Ⓓ Ⓔ   84 Ⓐ Ⓑ Ⓒ Ⓓ Ⓔ

19 Ⓐ Ⓑ Ⓒ Ⓓ Ⓔ   41 Ⓐ Ⓑ Ⓒ Ⓓ Ⓔ   63 Ⓐ Ⓑ Ⓒ Ⓓ Ⓔ   85 Ⓐ Ⓑ Ⓒ Ⓓ Ⓔ

20 Ⓐ Ⓑ Ⓒ Ⓓ Ⓔ   42 Ⓐ Ⓑ Ⓒ Ⓓ Ⓔ   64 Ⓐ Ⓑ Ⓒ Ⓓ Ⓔ   86 Ⓐ Ⓑ Ⓒ Ⓓ Ⓔ

21 Ⓐ Ⓑ Ⓒ Ⓓ Ⓔ   43 Ⓐ Ⓑ Ⓒ Ⓓ Ⓔ   65 Ⓐ Ⓑ Ⓒ Ⓓ Ⓔ   87 Ⓐ Ⓑ Ⓒ Ⓓ Ⓔ

22 Ⓐ Ⓑ Ⓒ Ⓓ Ⓔ   44 Ⓐ Ⓑ Ⓒ Ⓓ Ⓔ   66 Ⓐ Ⓑ Ⓒ Ⓓ Ⓔ   88 Ⓐ Ⓑ Ⓒ Ⓓ Ⓔ

Part A—Address Checking

SAMPLE QUESTIONS

You will be allowed three minutes to read the directions and answer the five sample questions that follow. On the actual test, however, you will have only 6 minutes to answer 95 questions, so see how quickly you can compare addresses and still get the correct answer.

Directions: Each question consists of two addresses. If the two addresses are alike in EVERY way, mark A on your answer sheet. If the two addresses are different in ANY way, mark D on your answer sheet.

1 ... 4836 Mineola Blvd	4386 Mineola Blvd
2 ... 3062 W 197th St	3062 W 197th Rd
3 ... Columbus OH 43210	Columbus OH 43210
4 ... 9413 Alcan Hwy So	9413 Alcan Hwy So
5 ... 4186 Carrier Ln	4186 Carreer Ln

```
┌─────────────────────────────┐        ┌─────────────────────────────┐
│     SAMPLE ANSWER SHEET      │        │       CORRECT ANSWERS        │
│                              │        │                              │
│  1. Ⓐ Ⓓ      4. Ⓐ Ⓓ        │        │  1. Ⓐ ●      4. ● Ⓓ         │
│  2. Ⓐ Ⓓ      5. Ⓐ Ⓓ        │        │  2. Ⓐ ●      5. Ⓐ ●         │
│  3. Ⓐ Ⓓ                     │        │  3. ● Ⓓ                     │
└─────────────────────────────┘        └─────────────────────────────┘
```

ADDRESS CHECKING

Time: 6 Minutes • 95 Questions.

Directions: For each question, compare the address in the left column with the address in the right column. If the two addresses are ALIKE IN EVERY WAY, blacken space A on your answer sheet. If the two addresses are DIFFERENT IN ANY WAY, blacken space D on your answer sheet. Correct answers for this test are on page 201.

1 ...	462 Midland Ave	462 Midland Ave
2 ...	2319 Sherry Dr	3219 Sherry Dr
3 ...	1015 Kimball Ave	1015 Kimball Av
4 ...	Wappinger Falls NY 12590	Wappinger Falls NY 12590
5 ...	1255 North Ave	1225 North Ave
6 ...	1826 Tibbets Rd	1826 Tibetts Rd
7 ...	603 N Division St	603 N Division St
8 ...	2304 Manhattan Ave	2034 Manhattan Ave
9 ...	Worcester MA 01610	Worcester ME 01610
10 ...	1186 Vernon Drive	1186 Vernon Drive
11 ...	209 Peter Bont Rd	209 Peter Bent Rd
12 ...	Miami Beach FL 33139	Miami Beach FL 33193
13 ...	1100 West Ave	1100 East Ave
14 ...	2063 Winyah Ter	2036 Winyah Ter
15 ...	3483 Suncrest Ave	3483 Suncrest Dr
16 ...	234 Rochambeau Rd	234 Roshambeau Rd
17 ...	306 N Terrace Blvd	306 N Terrace Blvd
18 ...	1632 Paine St	1632 Pain St
19 ...	Palm Springs CA 92262	Palm Spring CA 92262
20 ...	286 Marietta Ave	286 Marrietta Ave
21 ...	2445 Pigott Rd	2445 Pigott Rd
22 ...	2204 PineBrook Blvd	2204 Pinebrook Blvd
23 ...	Buffalo NY 42113	Buffulo NY 42113
24 ...	487 Warburton Ave	487 Warburton Ave
25 ...	9386 North St	9386 North Ave
26 ...	2272 Glandale Rd	2772 Glandale Rd
27 ...	9236 Puritan Dr	9236 Puritan Pl
28 ...	Watertown MA 02172	Watertown MA 02172

29 ... 7803 Kimball Ave	7803 Kimbal Ave
30 ... 1362 Colonial Pkwy	1362 Colonial Pkwy
31 ... 115 Rolling Hills Rd	115 Rolling Hills Rd
32 ... 218 Rockledge Rd	2181 Rockledge Rd
33 ... 8346 N Broadway	8346 W Broadway
34 ... West Chester PA 19380	West Chester PA 19830
35 ... 9224 Highland Way	9244 Highland Way
36 ... 8383 Mamaroneck Ave	8383 Mamaroneck Ave
37 ... 276 Furnace Dock Rd	276 Furnace Dock Rd
38 ... 4137 Loockerman St	4137 Lockerman St
39 ... 532 Broadhollow Rd	532 Broadhollow Rd
40 ... Sunrise FL 33313	Sunrise FL 33133
41 ... 148 Cortlandt Rd	148 Cortland Rd
42 ... 5951 W Hartsdale Rd	5951 W Hartsdale Ave
43 ... 5231 Alta Vista Cir	5321 Alta Vista Cir
44 ... 6459 Chippewa Rd	6459 Chippewa Rd
45 ... 1171 S Highland Rd	1771 S Highland Rd
46 ... Dover DE 19901	Dover DL 19901
47 ... 2363 Old Farm Ln	2363 Old Farm Ln
48 ... 1001 Hemingway Dr	1001 Hemmingway Dr
49 ... 1555 Morningside Ave	1555 Morningslide Ave
50 ... Purchase NY 10577	Purchase NY 10577
51 ... 1189 E 9th St	1189 E 9th St
52 ... 168 Old Lyme Rd	186 Old Lyme Rd
53 ... 106 Notingham Rd	106 Nottingham Rd
54 ... 1428 Midland Ave	1428 Midland Ave
55 ... Elmhurst NY 11373	Elmherst NY 11373
56 ... 1450 West Chester Pike	1450 West Chester Pike
57 ... 3357 NW Main St	3357 NE Main St
58 ... 5062 Marietta Ave	5062 Marrietta Ave
59 ... 1890 NE 3rd Ct	1980 NE 3rd Ct
60 ... Wilmington DE 19810	Wilmington DE 19810
61 ... 1075 Central Park Av	1075 Central Park W
62 ... 672 Bacon Hill Rd	672 Beacon Hill Rd

63 ... 1725 W 17th St		1725 W 17th St
64 ... Bronxville NY 10708		Bronxville NJ 10708
65 ... 2066 Old Wilmot Rd		2066 Old Wilmont Rd
66 ... 3333 S State St		3333 S State St
67 ... 1483 Meritoria Dr		1438 Meritoria Dr
68 ... 2327 E 23rd St		2327 E 27th St
69 ... Baltimore MD 21215		Baltimore MD 21215
70 ... 137 Clarence Rd		137 Claremont Rd
71 ... 3516 N Ely Ave		3516 N Ely Ave
72 ... 111 Beechwood St		1111 Beechwood St
73 ... 143 N Highland Ave		143 N Highland Ave
74 ... Miami Beach FL 33179		Miami FL 33179
75 ... 6430 Spring Mill Rd		6340 Spring Mill Rd
76 ... 1416 87th Ave		1416 78th Ave
77 ... 4204 S Lexington Ave		4204 Lexington Ave
78 ... 3601 Clarks Lane		3601 Clark Lane
79 ... Indianapolis IN 46260		Indianapolis IN 46260
80 ... 4256 Fairfield Ave		4256 Fairfield Ave
81 ... Jamaica NY 11435		Jamiaca NY 11435
82 ... 1809 83rd St		1809 83rd St
83 ... 3288 Page Ct		3288 Paige Ct
84 ... 2436 S Broadway		2436 S Broadway
85 ... 6309 The Green		6309 The Green
86 ... Kew Gardens NY 11415		Kew Garden NY 11415
87 ... 4370 W 158th St		4370 W 158th St
88 ... 4263 3rd Ave		4623 3rd Ave
89 ... 1737 Fisher Ave		1737 Fischer Ave
90 ... Bronx NY 10475		Bronx NY 10475
91 ... 5148 West End Ave		5184 West End Ave
92 ... 1011 Ocean Ave		1011 Ocean Ave
93 ... 1593 Webster Dr		1593 Webster Dr
94 ... Darien CT 06820		Darien CT 06820
95 ... 1626 E 115th St		1662 E 115th St

END OF ADDRESS CHECKING

Part B—Memory for Addresses

SAMPLE QUESTIONS

The sample questions for this part are based on the addresses in the five boxes below. Your task is to mark on your answer sheet the letter of the box in which each address belongs. You will have five minutes now to study the locations of the addresses. Then cover the boxes and try to mark the location of the sample questions. You may look back at the boxes if you cannot yet mark the address locations from memory.

The exam itself provides three practice sessions before the question set that really counts. Practice I and Practice III supply you with the boxes and permit you to refer to them if necessary. Practice II and the Memory for Addresses Test itself do not permit you to look at the boxes. The test itself is based on memory.

A	B	C	D	E
4100–4199 Plum	1000–1399 Plum	4200–4599 Plum	1400–4099 Plum	4600–5299 Plum
Bardack	Greenhouse	Flynn	Pepper	Cedar
4200–4599 Ash	4600–5299 Ash	1400–4099 Ash	1000–1399 Ash	4100–4199 Ash
Lemon	Dalby	Race	Clown	Hawk
1000–1399 Neff	4100–4199 Neff	4600–5299 Neff	4200–4599 Neff	1400–4099 Neff

1. 1400–4099 Plum

2. 1000–1399 Neff

3. Lemon

4. Flynn

5. 4200–4599 Ash

6. 4600–5299 Ash

7. Cedar

8. Pepper

9. 4100–4199 Plum

10. 4600–5299 Neff

11. 1000–1399 Plum

12. Clown

13. Greenhouse

14. 4100–4199 Ash

SAMPLE ANSWER SHEET

1. Ⓐ Ⓑ Ⓒ Ⓓ Ⓔ   8. Ⓐ Ⓑ Ⓒ Ⓓ Ⓔ
2. Ⓐ Ⓑ Ⓒ Ⓓ Ⓔ   9. Ⓐ Ⓑ Ⓒ Ⓓ Ⓔ
3. Ⓐ Ⓑ Ⓒ Ⓓ Ⓔ   10. Ⓐ Ⓑ Ⓒ Ⓓ Ⓔ
4. Ⓐ Ⓑ Ⓒ Ⓓ Ⓔ   11. Ⓐ Ⓑ Ⓒ Ⓓ Ⓔ
5. Ⓐ Ⓑ Ⓒ Ⓓ Ⓔ   12. Ⓐ Ⓑ Ⓒ Ⓓ Ⓔ
6. Ⓐ Ⓑ Ⓒ Ⓓ Ⓔ   13. Ⓐ Ⓑ Ⓒ Ⓓ Ⓔ
7. Ⓐ Ⓑ Ⓒ Ⓓ Ⓔ   14. Ⓐ Ⓑ Ⓒ Ⓓ Ⓔ

CORRECT ANSWERS

1. Ⓐ Ⓑ Ⓒ ● Ⓔ   8. Ⓐ Ⓑ Ⓒ ● Ⓔ
2. ● Ⓑ Ⓒ Ⓓ Ⓔ   9. ● Ⓑ Ⓒ Ⓓ Ⓔ
3. ● Ⓑ Ⓒ Ⓓ Ⓔ   10. Ⓐ Ⓑ ● Ⓓ Ⓔ
4. Ⓐ Ⓑ ● Ⓓ Ⓔ   11. Ⓐ ● Ⓒ Ⓓ Ⓔ
5. ● Ⓑ Ⓒ Ⓓ Ⓔ   12. Ⓐ Ⓑ Ⓒ ● Ⓔ
6. Ⓐ ● Ⓒ Ⓓ Ⓔ   13. Ⓐ ● Ⓒ Ⓓ Ⓔ
7. Ⓐ Ⓑ Ⓒ Ⓓ ●   14. Ⓐ Ⓑ Ⓒ Ⓓ ●

PRACTICE FOR MEMORY FOR ADDRESSES

Directions: The five boxes below are labeled A, B, C, D, and E. In each box are three sets of number spans with names and two names that are not associated with numbers. In the next THREE MINUTES, you must try to memorize the box location of each name and number span. The position of a name or number span within its box is not important. You need only remember the letter of the box in which the item is to be found. You will use these names and numbers to answer three sets of practice questions that are NOT scored and one actual test that is scored. Correct answers are on pages 202 and 203.

A	B	C	D	E
4100–4199 Plum	1000–1399 Plum	4200–4599 Plum	1400–4099 Plum	4600–5299 Plum
Bardack	Greenhouse	Flynn	Pepper	Cedar
4200–4599 Ash	4600–5299 Ash	1400–4099 Ash	1000–1399 Ash	4100–4199 Ash
Lemon	Dalby	Race	Clown	Hawk
1000–1399 Neff	4100–4199 Neff	4600–5299 Neff	4200–4599 Neff	1400–4099 Neff

Practice I

Directions: Use the next THREE MINUTES to mark on your answer sheet the letter of the box in which each item that follows is to be found. Try to mark each item without looking back at the boxes. If, however, you get stuck, you may refer to the boxes during this practice exercise. If you find that you must look at the boxes, try to memorize as you do so. This test is for practice only. It will not be scored.

1. 4600–5299 Ash
2. 4600–5299 Neff
3. 1400–4099 Plum
4. Cedar
5. Bardack
6. 1400–4099 Neff
7. 1400–4099 Ash
8. 1000–1399 Plum
9. Greenhouse
10. Lemon
11. 4600–5299 Plum
12. 4200–4599 Ash
13. 4600–5299 Neff
14. Dalby
15. Hawk
16. 4100–4199 Plum
17. 4200–4599 Plum
18. 4600–5299 Ash
19. 4200–4599 Neff

20. Race
21. Pepper
22. 4100–4199 Ash
23. 1000–1399 Neff
24. 1000–1399 Plum
25. Cedar
26. Dalby
27. 4600–5299 Plum
28. 1400–4099 Plum
29. Bardack
30. 4200–4599 Ash
31. 1400–4099 Neff
32. 4600–5299 Neff
33. 1400–4099 Ash
34. Flynn
35. Lemon
36. Clown
37. 4100–4199 Plum
38. 1000–1399 Ash

39. 4100–4199 Neff
40. Greenhouse
41. Hawk
42. 4600–5299 Plum
43. 1000–1399 Neff
44. 1400–4099 Ash
45. 4600–5299 Ash
46. Cedar
47. Greenhouse
48. 1400–4099 Plum
49. 4200–4599 Neff
50. 1000–1399 Ash
51. Race
52. Flynn
53. 4600–5299 Ash
54. 4600–5299 Plum
55. 4600–5299 Neff
56. Pepper
57. Lemon

58. 1000–1399 Plum

59. 4100–4199 Plum

60. 1000–1399 Neff

61. 4100–4199 Ash

62. Bardack

63. Dalby

64. Clown

65. 4200–4599 Ash

66. 1400–4099 Ash

67. 4200–4599 Plum

68. Hawk

69. 4100–4199 Neff

70. 1400–4099 Neff

71. 1000–1399 Plum

72. Pepper

73. 1000–1399 Neff

74. 4100–4199 Ash

75. Dalby

76. Cedar

77. 4100–4199 Plum

78. 1400–4099 Ash

79. 1400–4099 Plum

80. 1400–4099 Neff

81. Pepper

82. Hawk

83. 4600–5299 Ash

84. 4600–5299 Plum

85. 1000–1399 Ash

86. 1000–1399 Neff

87. Cedar

88. Greenhouse

Practice II

Directions: *The next 88 questions constitute another practice exercise. Again, you should mark your answers on your answer sheet. Again, the time limit is THREE MINUTES. This time, however, you must NOT look at the boxes while answering the questions. You must rely on your memory in marking the box location of each item. This practice test will not be scored.*

1. 4100–4199 Plum

2. 1400–4099 Neff

3. 1400–4099 Ash

4. Clown

5. Greenhouse

6. 4100–4199 Neff

7. 1000–1399 Ash

8. 4100–4199 Ash

9. Race

10. Flynn

11. 4600–5299 Plum

12. 1000–1399 Neff

13. 4200–4599 Ash

14. 1000–1399 Plum

15. Cedar

16. Dalby

17. Pepper

18. 4600–5299 Neff

19. 4200–4599 Neff

20. 1400–4099 Plum

21. Bardack

22. Lemon

23. Hawk

24. 4200–4599 Plum

25. 4600–5299 Ash

26. 4200–4599 Plum

27. 4600–5299 Neff

28. 1400–4099 Ash

29. Lemon

30. Pepper

31. 4100–4199 Neff

32. 1400–4099 Plum

33. 4200–4599 Neff

34. Dalby

35. Flynn

36. 4200–4599 Ash

37. 4600–5299 Plum

38. 4100–4199 Plum

39. Bardack

40. Hawk

41. 1000–1399 Plum

42. 1000–1399 Neff

43. 1000–1399 Ash

44. Greenhouse

45. Clown

46. 4600–5299 Ash

47. 4100–4199 Ash

48. 1400–4099 Neff

49. Race

50. Cedar

51. Flynn

52. Hawk

53. 4100–4199 Neff

54. 1000–1399 Ash

55. 4100–4199 Plum

56. 1400–4099 Plum

57. 4200–4599 Plum

58. Bardack

59. 4600–5299 Neff

60. 4200–4599 Neff

61. 4200–4599 Ash

62. Pepper

63. Clown

64. 4600–5299 Ash

65. 1000–1399 Neff

66. 1000–1399 Plum

67. Race

68. Dalby

69. 1400–4099 Ash

70. 4100–4199 Ash

71. 4600–5299 Plum

72. 4600–5299 Neff

73. Cedar

74. 1400–4099 Neff

75. Greenhouse

76. 4100–4199 Plum

77. 4200–4599 Neff

78. 4200–4599 Ash

79. Clown

80. Dalby

81. 4200–4599 Plum

82. 1400–4099 Ash

83. 1000–1399 Neff

84. Pepper

85. Bardack

86. 4100–4199 Plum

87. 1400–4099 Neff

88. 4100–4199 Ash

Practice III

Directions: *The names and address are repeated for you in the boxes below. Each name and each number span is in the same box in which you found it in the original set. You will now be allowed FIVE MINUTES to study the locations again. Do your best to memorize the letter of the box in which each item is located. This is your last chance to see the boxes.*

A	B	C	D	E
4100–4199 Plum	1000–1399 Plum	4200–4599 Plum	1400–4099 Plum	4600–5299 Plum
Bardack	Greenhouse	Flynn	Pepper	Cedar
4200–4599 Ash	4600–5299 Ash	1400–4099 Ash	1000–1399 Ash	4100–4199 Ash
Lemon	Dalby	Race	Clown	Hawk
1000–1399 Neff	4100–4199 Neff	4600–5299 Neff	4200–4599 Neff	1400–4099 Neff

Directions: *This is your last practice test. Mark the location of each of the 88 items on your answer sheet. You will have FIVE MINUTES to answer these questions. Do NOT look back at the boxes. This practice test will not be scored.*

1. 1400–4099 Ash

2. 4600–5299 Plum

3. 1000–1399 Neff

4. Pepper

5. Greenhouse

6. 4100–4199 Plum

7. 1400–4099 Neff

8. 4600–5299 Ash

9. 1000–1399 Ash

10. Bardack

11. Lemon

12. Hawk

13. 1000–1399 Plum

14. 4200–4599 Neff

15. 4200–4599 Ash

16. 4100–4199 Neff

17. 1400–4099 Plum

18. 4100–4199 Ash

19. Clown

20. Flynn

21. 4600–5299 Ash

22. 1000–1399 Plum

23. 4200–4599 Ash

24. Lemon

25. Race

26. 4600–5299 Neff

27. 4600–5299 Plum

28. Dalby

29. Cedar

30. 4200–4599 Neff

31. 1000–1399 Plum

32. 1400–4099 Ash

33. 4200–4599 Neff

34. 1400–4099 Plum

35. 4100–4199 Neff

36. Ceda

37. Clown

38. Dalby

39. 4200–4599 Ash

40. 4100–4199 Ash

41. 4600–5299 Plum

42. 1000–1399 Neff

43. Greenhouse

44. Pepper

45. 4100–4199 Plum

46. 1400–4099 Neff

47. 4600–5299 Ash

48. 1000–1399 Ash

49. Clown

50. Bardack

51. Lemon

52. 4200–4599 Plum

53. 4600–5299 Neff

54. Hawk

55. Flynn

56. Race

57. 1400–4099 Plum

58. 1000–1399 Neff

59. 4100–4199 Ash

60. 1400–4099 Ash

61. 1400–4099 Plum

62. 4100–4199 Neff

63. 1400–4099 Neff

64. Hawk

65. Lemon

66. 1000–1399 Plum

67. 4100–4199 Neff

68. 4600–5299 Ash

69. Pepper

70. Dalby

71. 1000–1399 Neff

72. 4600–5299 Plum

73. 4100–4199 Ash

74. Greenhouse

75. Race

76. 4200–4599 Neff

77. 1000–1399 Ash

78. 4200–4599 Plum

79. Bardack

80. Cedar

81. 4200–4599 Ash

82. 4100–4199 Plum

83. 4600–5299 Neff

84. Flynn

85. Clown

86. 1400–4099 Ash

87. 4600–5299 Plum

88. 4100–4199 Plum

MEMORY FOR ADDRESSES

Time: 5 Minutes • 88 Questions.

Directions: Mark your answers on the answer sheet in the section headed "MEMORY FOR AD-DRESSES." This test will be scored. You are NOT permitted to look at the boxes. Work from memory, as quickly and as accurately as you can. Correct answers are on page 203.

1. 1400–4099 Neff
2. 4100–4199 Plum
3. 1400–4099 Ash
4. Pepper
5. Dalby
6. 4200–4599 Plum
7. 4600–5299 Neff
8. 4100–4199 Ash
9. 4200–4599 Ash
10. Bardack
11. Hawk
12. 4600–5299 Plum
13. 1000–1399 Neff
14. 1000–1399 Ash
15. Clown
16. Flynn
17. 4600–5299 Ash
18. 1400–4099 Plum
19. 1000–1399 Plum
20. Cedar
21. Race
22. Lemon
23. 4100–4199 Neff
24. Greenhouse
25. 4200–4599 Neff
26. 1000–1399 Plum
27. 1400–4099 Neff
28. 4200–4599 Ash
29. Hawk
30. Flynn

31. 4100–4199 Plum
32. 4200–4599 Neff
33. 1400–4099 Ash
34. Clown
35. Dalby
36. 4100–4199 Ash
37. 4100–4199 Neff
38. 1400–4099 Plum
39. Cedar
40. Bardack
41. 1000–1399 Plum
42. 4600–5299 Neff
43. 1400–4099 Plum
44. Lemon
45. Cedar
46. 4200–4599 Ash
47. 4100–4199 Ash
48. 4100–4199 Plum
49. 1000–1399 Neff
50. 4100–4199 Neff
51. Hawk
52. Greenhouse
53. Dalby
54. 1400–4099 Ash
55. 4600–5299 Ash
56. 4200–4599 Plum
57. Clown
58. Race
59. 1000–1399 Ash
60. 4600–5299 Plum

61. Bardack
62. 4200–4599 Neff
63. Flynn
64. Pepper
65. 1400–4099 Neff
66. 4100–4199 Ash
67. 4600–5299 Neff
68. 1000–1399 Plum
69. 4100–4199 Plum
70. 4600–5299 Ash
71. 4600–5299 Neff
72. Lemon
73. Pepper
74. Cedar
75. 1400–4099 Ash
76. 1400–4099 Neff
77. 4100–4199 Ash
78. 4600–5299 Plum
79. Greenhouse
80. Dalby
81. 1000–1399 Plum
82. 1000–1399 Ash
83. 4100–4199 Neff
84. 4200–4599 Plum
85. Flynn
86. Clown
87. 4200–4599 Ash
88. 4100–4199 Ash

END OF MEMORY FOR ADDRESSES

Part C—Number Series

SAMPLE QUESTIONS

The following sample questions show you the type of question that will be used in Part C. You will have three minutes to answer the sample questions below and to study the explanations.

Directions: Each number series question consists of a series of numbers that follows some definite order. The numbers progress from left to right according to some rule. One pair of numbers to the right of the series comprises the next two numbers in the series. Study each series to try to find a pattern to the series and to figure out the rule that governs the progression. Choose the answer pair that continues the series according to the pattern established and mark its letter on your answer sheet.

1. 23 25 27 29 31 33 35 ...... (A) 35 36   (B) 35 37   (C) 36 37   (D) 37 38   (E) 37 39

The answer (**E**) should be easy to see. This series progresses by adding 2. 35 + 2 = 37 + 2 = 39.

2. 3 3 6 6 12 12 24 .... (A) 24 36   (B) 36 36   (C) 24 24   (D) 24 48   (E) 48 48

The answer is (**D**) because the series requires you to repeat a number, then multiply it by 2.

3. 11 13 16 20 25 31 38 ...... (A) 46 55   (B) 45 55   (C) 40 42   (D) 47 58   (E) 42 46

The easiest way to solve this problem is to write the degree and direction of change between the numbers. By doing this, you see that the pattern is +2, +3, +4, +5, +6, +7. Continue the series by continuing the pattern: 38 + 8 = 46 + 9 = 55. The answer is (**A**).

4. 76 72 72 68 64 64 60 ...... (A) 60 56   (B) 60 60   (C) 56 56   (D) 56 52   (E) 56 54

Here the pattern is: −4, repeat the number, −4; −4, repeat the number, −4. To find that (**C**) is the answer you must realize that you are at the beginning of the pattern. 60 − 4 = 56, then repeat the number 56.

5. 92 94 96 92 94 96 92 ...... (A) 92 94   (B) 94 96   (C) 96 92   (D) 96 94   (E) 96 98

The series consists of the sequence 92 94 96 repeated over and over again. (**B**) is the answer because 94 96 continues the sequence after 92.

SAMPLE ANSWER SHEET	CORRECT ANSWERS
1. Ⓐ Ⓑ Ⓒ Ⓓ Ⓔ	1. Ⓐ Ⓑ Ⓒ Ⓓ ●
2. Ⓐ Ⓑ Ⓒ Ⓓ Ⓔ	2. Ⓐ Ⓑ Ⓒ ● Ⓔ
3. Ⓐ Ⓑ Ⓒ Ⓓ Ⓔ	3. ● Ⓑ Ⓒ Ⓓ Ⓔ
4. Ⓐ Ⓑ Ⓒ Ⓓ Ⓔ	4. Ⓐ Ⓑ ● Ⓓ Ⓔ
5. Ⓐ Ⓑ Ⓒ Ⓓ Ⓔ	5. Ⓐ ● Ⓒ Ⓓ Ⓔ

NUMBER SERIES

Time: 20 Minutes • 24 Questions.

Directions: *Each number series question consists of a series of numbers that follows some definite order. The numbers progress from left to right according to some rule. One lettered pair of numbers comprises the next two numbers in the series. Study each series to try to find a pattern to the series and to figure out the rule that governs the progression. Choose the answer pair that continues the series according to the pattern established and mark its letter on your answer sheet. Correct answers are on page 203 and 204.*

1. 8 9 9 8 10 10 8 .... (A) 11 8   (B) 8 13   (C) 8 11   (D) 11 11   (E) 8 8

2. 10 10 11 11 12 12 13 .... (A) 15 15   (B) 13 13   (C) 14 14   (D) 13 14   (E) 14 15

3. 6 6 10 6 6 12 6 .... (A) 6 14   (B) 13 6   (C) 14 6   (D) 6 13   (E) 6 6

4. 17 11 5 16 10 4 15 .... (A) 13 9   (B) 13 11   (C) 8 5   (D) 9 5   (E) 9 3

5. 1 3 2 4 3 5 4 .... (A) 6 8   (B) 5 6   (C) 6 5   (D) 3 4   (E) 3 5

6. 11 11 10 12 12 11 13 .... (A) 12 14   (B) 14 12   (C) 14 14   (D) 13 14   (E) 13 12

7. 18 5 6 18 7 8 18 .... (A) 9 9   (B) 9 10   (C) 18 9   (D) 8 9   (E) 18 7

8. 8 1 9 3 10 5 11 .... (A) 7 12   (B) 6 12   (C) 12 6   (D) 7 8   (E) 6 7

9. 14 12 10 20 18 16 32 30 .. (A) 60 18   (B) 32 64   (C) 30 28   (D) 28 56   (E) 28 28

10. 67 59 52 44 37 29 22 .... (A) 15 7   (B) 14 8   (C) 14 7   (D) 15 8   (E) 16 11

11. 17 79 20 74 23 69 26 .... (A) 64 29   (B) 65 30   (C) 29 64   (D) 23 75   (E) 26 64

12. 3 5 10 8 4 6 12 10 5 .... (A) 8 16   (B) 7 14   (C) 10 20   (D) 10 5   (E) 7 9

13. 58 52 52 46 46 40 40 .... (A) 34 28   (B) 28 28   (C) 40 34   (D) 35 35   (E) 34 34

14. 32 37 33 33 38 34 34 .... (A) 38 43   (B) 34 39   (C) 39 35   (D) 39 39   (E) 34 40

15. 15 17 19 16 18 20 17 .... (A) 14 16   (B) 19 21   (C) 17 19   (D) 16 18   (E) 19 16

16. 5 15 7 21 13 39 31 .... (A) 93 85   (B) 62 69   (C) 39 117   (D) 93 87   (E) 31 93

17. 84 76 70 62 56 48 42 .... (A) 42 36   (B) 34 26   (C) 36 28   (D) 36 24   (E) 34 28

18. 47 23 43 27 39 31 35 .... (A) 31 27   (B) 39 43   (C) 39 35   (D) 35 31   (E) 31 35

19. 14 23 31 38 44 49 53 .... (A) 55 57   (B) 57 61   (C) 56 58   (D) 57 59   (E) 58 62

20. 5 6 8 8 9 11 11 12 .... (A) 12 13   (B) 14 14   (C) 14 15   (D) 14 16   (E) 12 14

21. 9 18 41 41 36 72 41 .... (A) 108 108   (B) 41 108   (C) 41 144   (D) 144 144   (E) 72 41

22. 13 15 17 13 15 17 13 .... (A) 17 15   (B) 13 15   (C) 17 13   (D) 15 13   (E) 15 17

23. 13 92 17 89 21 86 25 .... (A) 83 29   (B) 24 89   (C) 29 83   (D) 25 83   (E) 89 21

24. 10 20 23 13 26 29 19 .... (A) 9 12   (B) 38 41   (C) 22 44   (D) 44 33   (E) 36 39

END OF NUMBER SERIES

Part D—Following Oral Instructions

DIRECTIONS AND SAMPLE QUESTIONS

Listening to Instructions

When you are ready to try these sample questions, give the following instructions to a friend and have the friend read them aloud to you at the rate of 80 words per minute. Do not read them to yourself. Your friend will need a watch with a second hand. Listen carefully and do exactly what your friend tells you to do with the worksheet and answer sheet. Your friend will tell you some things to do with each item on the worksheet. After each set of instructions, your friend will give you time to mark your answer by darkening a circle on the sample answer sheet. Because B and D sound very much alike, your friend will say "B as in baker" when he or she means B and "D as in dog" when he or she means D.

> **Before proceeding further, tear out the worksheet on page 193. Then hand this book to your friend.**

TO THE PERSON WHO IS TO READ THE INSTRUCTIONS: The instructions are to be read at the rate of 80 words per minute. Do not read aloud the material that is in parentheses. Do not repeat any instructions.

Read Aloud to the Candidate

Look at line 1 on your worksheet. (Pause slightly.) Draw two lines under the middle number on line 1. (Pause 2 seconds.) Now, on your answer sheet, find the number under which you just drew two lines and darken space D as in dog for that number. (Pause 5 seconds.)

Look at line 2 on your worksheet. (Pause slightly.) Write the letter A in the left-hand circle. (Pause 2 seconds.) Now, on your answer sheet, darken the space for the number-letter combination in the circle in which you just wrote. (Pause 5 seconds.)

Look at line 3 on your worksheet. (Pause slightly.) Count the number of times the letter E appears on line 3 and write the number at the end of the line. (Pause 2 seconds.) Now, on your answer sheet, darken space C for the number you just wrote. (Pause 5 seconds.)

Look at line 4 on your worksheet. (Pause slightly.) If an hour is longer than a day, write the letter B as in baker on the line next to the first number on line 4; if not, write the letter E on the line next to the third number. (Pause 5 seconds.) Now, on your answer sheet, darken the space for the number-letter combination you just wrote. (Pause 5 seconds.)

Look at line 4 again. (Pause slightly.) Write the second letter of the alphabet on the line next to the middle number. (Pause 2 seconds.) Now, on your answer sheet, darken the space for the number-letter combination you just wrote. (Pause 5 seconds.)

Sample Worksheet

Directions: *Listening carefully to each set of instructions, mark each item on this worksheet as directed. Then complete each question by marking the sample answer sheet below as directed. For each answer you will darken the answer for a number-letter combination. Should you fall behind and miss an instruction, don't become excited. Let that one go and listen for the next one. If, when you start to darken a space for a number, and you find that you have already darkened another space for that number, either erase the first mark and darken the space for the new combination or let the first mark stay and do not darken a space for the new combination. Write with a pencil that has a clean eraser. When you finish, you should have no more than one space darkened for each number.*

1.   9   7   12 . 14   1

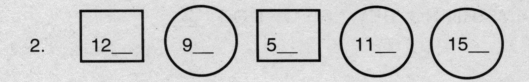

2.   12__   9__   5__   11__   15__

3.   WARNING. BEWARE OF DOG. __

4.   4___   13___   6___

SAMPLE ANSWER SHEET

1. Ⓐ Ⓑ Ⓒ Ⓓ Ⓔ	6. Ⓐ Ⓑ Ⓒ Ⓓ Ⓔ	11. Ⓐ Ⓑ Ⓒ Ⓓ Ⓔ
2. Ⓐ Ⓑ Ⓒ Ⓓ Ⓔ	7. Ⓐ Ⓑ Ⓒ Ⓓ Ⓔ	12. Ⓐ Ⓑ Ⓒ Ⓓ Ⓔ
3. Ⓐ Ⓑ Ⓒ Ⓓ Ⓔ	8. Ⓐ Ⓑ Ⓒ Ⓓ Ⓔ	13. Ⓐ Ⓑ Ⓒ Ⓓ Ⓔ
4. Ⓐ Ⓑ Ⓒ Ⓓ Ⓔ	9. Ⓐ Ⓑ Ⓒ Ⓓ Ⓔ	14. Ⓐ Ⓑ Ⓒ Ⓓ Ⓔ
5. Ⓐ Ⓑ Ⓒ Ⓓ Ⓔ	10. Ⓐ Ⓑ Ⓒ Ⓓ Ⓔ	15. Ⓐ Ⓑ Ⓒ Ⓓ Ⓔ

CORRECT ANSWERS TO SAMPLE QUESTIONS

1. Ⓐ Ⓑ Ⓒ Ⓓ Ⓔ	6. Ⓐ Ⓑ Ⓒ Ⓓ ●	11. Ⓐ Ⓑ Ⓒ Ⓓ Ⓔ
2. Ⓐ Ⓑ ● Ⓓ Ⓔ	7. Ⓐ Ⓑ Ⓒ Ⓓ Ⓔ	12. Ⓐ Ⓑ Ⓒ ● Ⓔ
3. Ⓐ Ⓑ Ⓒ Ⓓ Ⓔ	8. Ⓐ Ⓑ Ⓒ Ⓓ Ⓔ	13. Ⓐ ● Ⓒ Ⓓ Ⓔ
4. Ⓐ Ⓑ Ⓒ Ⓓ Ⓔ	9. ● Ⓑ Ⓒ Ⓓ Ⓔ	14. Ⓐ Ⓑ Ⓒ Ⓓ Ⓔ
5. Ⓐ Ⓑ Ⓒ Ⓓ Ⓔ	10. Ⓐ Ⓑ Ⓒ Ⓓ Ⓔ	15. Ⓐ Ⓑ Ⓒ Ⓓ Ⓔ

Correctly Filled Worksheet

1.   9   7   <u>12</u>   14   1

2.   [12__]   (9**A**)   [5__]   (11__)   (15__)

3.   WARNING. BEWARE OF DOG. <u>**2**</u>

4.   4___   13 <u>**B**</u>   6 <u>**E**</u>

FOLLOWING ORAL INSTRUCTIONS

Time: 25 Minutes.

Listening to Instructions

Directions: *When you are ready to try this test of the Model Exam, give the following instructions to a friend and have the friend read them aloud to you at the rate of 80 words per minute. Do NOT read them to yourself. Your friend will need a watch with a second hand. Listen carefully and do exactly what your friend tells you to do with the worksheet and with the answer sheet. Your friend will tell you some things to do with each item on the worksheet. After each set of instructions, your friend will give you time to mark your answer by darkening a circle on the answer sheet. Because B and D sound very much alike, your friend will say "B as in baker" when he or she means B, and "D as in dog" when he or she means D.*

> **Before proceeding further, tear out the worksheet on page 199 and 200. Then hand this book to your friend.**

TO THE PERSON WHO IS TO READ THE INSTRUCTIONS: The instructions are to be read at the rate of 80 words per minute. Do not read aloud the material that is in parentheses. Once you have begun the test itself do not repeat any instructions. The next three paragraphs consist of approximately 120 words. Read these three paragraphs aloud to the candidate in about $1\frac{1}{2}$ minutes. You may reread these paragraphs as often as necessary to establish an 80 words-per-minute reading speed.

Read Aloud to the Candidate

On the job you will have to listen to directions and then do what you have been told to do. In this test, I will read instructions to you. Try to understand them as I read them; I cannot repeat them. After we begin, you may not ask any questions until the end of the test.

On the job you won't have to deal with pictures, numbers, and letters like those in the test, but you will have to listen to instructions and follow them. We are using this test to see how well you can follow instructions.

You are to mark your test booklet according to the instructions that I'll read to you. After each set of instructions, I'll give you time to record your answers on the separate answer sheet.

The actual test begins now.

Look at line 1 on your worksheet. (Pause slightly.) Draw one line under the first number on line 1. (Pause 2 seconds.) Now, on your answer sheet, darken space E for the number under which you just drew one line. (Pause 5 seconds.)

Look at line 1 again. (Pause slightly.) Draw two lines under the lowest number on line 1. (Pause 2 seconds.) Now, on your answer sheet, darken space B as in baker for the number under which you just drew two lines. (Pause 5 seconds.)

Look at line 2 on your worksheet. (Pause slightly.) Write the number 38 in front of the letter that comes second in the alphabet. (Pause 2 seconds.) Now, on your answer sheet, darken the space for the number-letter combination you just wrote. (Pause 5 seconds.)

Look at line 3 on your worksheet. The numbers represent afternoon pickup times at corner mailboxes. (Pause slightly.) Draw a line under the latest pickup time. (Pause 2 seconds.) Now, on your answer sheet, darken the letter A for the last two digits, the minutes, of the time under which you just drew a line. (Pause 5 seconds.)

Look at line 3 again. (Pause slightly.) Find the earliest pickup time and add together all the digits of that time. Write the sum of the digits on the line at the end of line 3. (Pause 8 seconds.) Now, on your answer sheet, darken letter D as in dog for the number you just wrote. (Pause 5 seconds.)

Look at line 4 on your worksheet. (Pause slightly.) In the first circle, write the answer to this question: How many hours are there in a day? (Pause 2 seconds.) In the third circle write the answer to this question: How many working hours are there in a 5-day, 8-hours-per-day workweek? (Pause 5 seconds.) Now, on your answer sheet, darken the number-letter combinations that appear in both circles that you wrote in. (Pause 10 seconds.)

Look at line 5 on your worksheet. (Pause slightly.) If a yard is longer than 10 inches, write the letter C in the triangle. If not, write E. (Pause 2 seconds.) Now, on your answer sheet, darken the space for the number-letter combination in the triangle. (Pause 5 seconds.)

Look at line 5 again. (Pause slightly.) If you are older than 36 months, write the letter A in the rectangle. If not, write the letter B as in baker in the square. (Pause 5 seconds.) Now, on your answer sheet, darken the space for the number-letter combination in the figure you just wrote in. (Pause 5 seconds.)

Look at line 6 on your worksheet. (Pause slightly.) Write the letter E beside the number that is second from the last on line 6. (Pause 2 seconds.) Now, on your answer sheet, darken the space for the number-letter combination you just wrote. (Pause 5 seconds.)

Look at line 7 on your worksheet. The numbers on line 7 represent a bar code. (Pause slightly.) Draw a line under each 0 in the bar code. (Pause 5 seconds.) Count the number of lines you have drawn, add 50, and write that number at the end of line 7. (Pause 5 seconds.) Now, on your answer sheet, darken space E for the number you just wrote. (Pause 5 seconds.)

Look at line 8 on your worksheet. The numbers in the mailsacks represent the weight of the mailsacks in pounds. (Pause slightly.) Write the letter D as in dog in the heaviest mailsack. (Pause 2 seconds.) Now, on your answer sheet, darken the space for the number-letter combination in the mailsack in which you just wrote. (Pause 5 seconds.)

Look at line 9 on your worksheet. (Pause slightly.) Mark an X through the second number on line 9 and an X through every other number thereafter on line 9. (Pause 5 seconds.) Now, on your answer sheet, darken space A for the first number you drew an X through. (Pause 5 seconds.)

Look at line 9 again. (Pause slightly.) For all other numbers through which you drew an X, mark C on your answer sheet. (Pause 15 seconds.)

Look at line 10 on your worksheet. (Pause slightly.) Write the number 1 in the second figure in line 10. (Pause 2 seconds.) Now, on your answer sheet, darken the space for the number-letter combination in the figure in which you just wrote. (Pause 5 seconds.)

Look at line 10 again. (Pause slightly.) Write the number 12 in the first circle on line 10. (Pause 2 seconds.) Now, on your answer sheet, darken the space for the number-letter combination in the figure in which you just wrote. (Pause 5 seconds.)

Look at line 11 on your worksheet. (Pause slightly.) Write the letter A in the figure with fewer sides. (Pause 2 seconds.) Now, on your answer sheet, darken the space for the number-letter combination in the figure in which you just wrote. (Pause 5 seconds.)

Look at line 12 on your worksheet. (Pause slightly.) If 3 is less than 5 and 10 is more than 2, write the number 79 in the first box. (Pause 5 seconds.) If not, write the number 76 in the second box. (Pause 5 seconds.) Now, on your answer sheet, darken the space for the number-letter combination in the box in which you just wrote. (Pause 5 seconds.)

Look at line 13 on your worksheet. (Pause slightly.) Write the first letter of the third word in the second box. (Pause 5 seconds.) Write the third letter of the second word in the first box. (Pause 5 seconds.) Write the second letter of the first word in the third box. (Pause 5 seconds.) Now, on your answer sheet, darken the spaces for the number-letter combinations in the three boxes. (Pause 15 seconds.)

Look at line 14 on your worksheet. (Pause slightly.) If it is possible to purchase two 29 cent stamps for 55 cents, write the number 72 on the second line. (Pause 5 seconds.) If not, write the number 19 on the first line. (Pause 5 seconds.) Now, on your answer sheet, darken the space for the number-letter combination you just wrote. (Pause 5 seconds.)

Look at line 15 on your worksheet. (Pause slightly.) Write the larger of these two numbers, 65 and 46, in the smaller box. (Pause 2 seconds.) Now, on your answer sheet, darken the space for the number-letter combination in the figure in which you just wrote. (Pause 5 seconds.)

Look at line 15 again. (Pause slightly.) Write the sum of 10 plus 20 in the first box. (Pause 2 seconds.) Now, on your answer sheet, darken the space for the number-letter combination in the figure in which you just wrote. (Pause 5 seconds.)

Look at line 16 on your worksheet. (Pause slightly.) Circle the fourth number on line 16. (Pause 2 seconds.) Now, on your answer sheet, darken the space for letter C for the number you just circled. (Pause 5 seconds.)

Look at line 17 on your worksheet. (Pause slightly.) If the number in the oval is greater than the number in the square, write the letter A in the circle. (Pause 5 seconds.) If not, write the letter B as in baker in the square. (Pause 5 seconds.) Now, on your answer sheet, darken the space for the number-letter combination in the figure in which you just wrote. (Pause 5 seconds.)

Look at line 17 again. (Pause slightly.) If the number in the triangle is less than 25, write the letter D as in dog in the triangle. (Pause 2 seconds.) If not, write the letter C in the oval. (Pause 2 seconds.) Now, on your answer sheet, darken the space for the number-letter combination in the figure you just wrote in. (Pause 5 seconds.)

Look at line 18 on your worksheet. (Pause slightly.) Find the letter on line 18 that does not appear in the word GRADE and circle that letter. (Pause 2 seconds.) Now, on your answer sheet, find the number 44 and darken the space for the letter you just circled. (Pause 5 seconds.)

Look at line 19 on your worksheet. (Pause slightly.) Listen to the following numbers and write the smallest number beside the second letter: 59, 62, 49, 54, 87. (Pause 5 seconds.) Now, on your answer sheet, darken the number-letter combination you just wrote. (Pause 5 seconds.)

FOLLOWING ORAL INSTRUCTIONS

Worksheet

Directions: Listening carefully to each set of instructions, mark each item on this worksheet as directed. Then complete each question by marking the answer sheet as directed. For each answer you will darken the answer for a number-letter combination. Should you fall behind and miss an instruction, don't become excited. Let that one go and listen for the next one. If when you start to darken a space for a number, you find that you have already darkened another space for that number, either erase the first mark and darken the space for the new combination or let the first mark stay and do not darken a space for the new combination. Write with a pencil that has a clean eraser. When you finish, you should have no more than one space darkened for each number. Correct answers are on page 205–207.

1. 75   14   9   27   54   12

2. ___ B   ___ D   ___C   ___A   ___E

3. 5:43   4:32   3:58   6:27

4.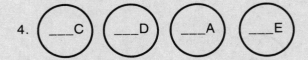
  ___C   ___D   ___A   ___E

5.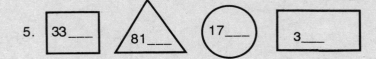
  33___   81___   17___   3___

6. 35___   16 ___   10 ___   52 ___   6 ___   80___

7. 7 1 0 5 0 3 3 0 6 8 0 4 0

8.
  61__   39__   45__   58__   47__

9. 17   51   37   46   76   87   12   5

TEAR HERE

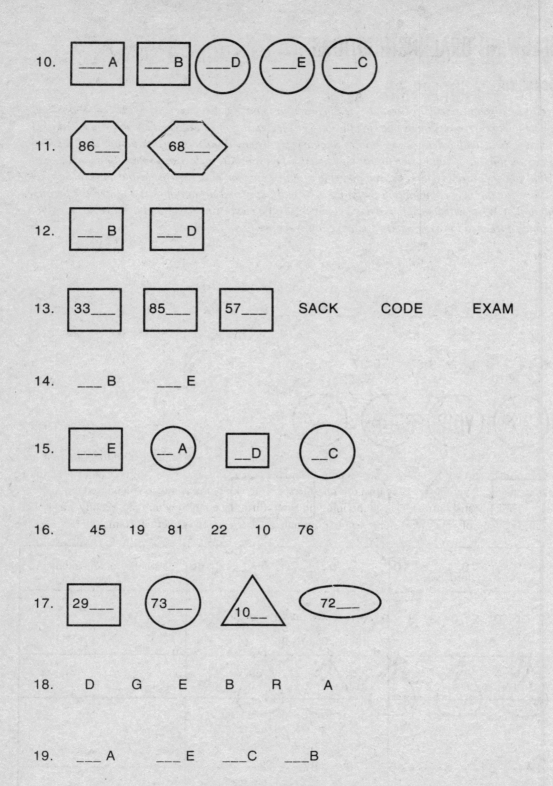

10. ___ A   ___ B   ___D   ___E   ___C

11. 86___   68___

12. ___ B   ___ D

13. 33___   85___   57___   SACK   CODE   EXAM

14. ___ B   ___ E

15. ___ E   __ A   __D   __C

16.   45   19   81   22   10   76

17. 29___   73___   10__   72___

18.   D   G   E   B   R   A

19. ___ A   ___ E   __C   __B

END OF EXAMINATION

Correct Answers for Model Examination 1

PART A—ADDRESS CHECKING

1. A	13. D	25. D	37. A	49. D	61. D	73. A	85. A
2. D	14. D	26. D	38. D	50. A	62. D	74. D	86. D
3. D	15. D	27. D	39. A	51. A	63. A	75. D	87. A
4. A	16. D	28. A	40. D	52. D	64. D	76. D	88. D
5. D	17. A	29. D	41. D	53. D	65. D	77. D	89. D
6. D	18. D	30. A	42. D	54. A	66. A	78. D	90. A
7. A	19. D	31. A	43. D	55. D	67. D	79. A	91. D
8. D	20. D	32. D	44. A	56. A	68. D	80. A	92. A
9. D	21. A	33. D	45. D	57. D	69. A	81. D	93. A
10. A	22. D	34. D	46. D	58. D	70. D	82. A	94. A
11. D	23. D	35. D	47. A	59. D	71. A	83. D	95. D
12. D	24. A	36. A	48. D	60. A	72. D	84. A	

ANALYZING YOUR ERRORS

This Address Checking Test contains 35 addresses that are exactly alike and 60 addresses that are different. The chart below shows what kind of difference occurs in each of the addresses that contains a difference. Check your answers against this chart to see which kind of difference you missed most often. Note also the questions in which you thought you saw a difference but in which there really was none. Becoming aware of your errors helps you to eliminate those errors on the actual exam.

Type of Difference	Question Numbers	Number of Questions You Missed
Difference in NUMBERS	2, 3, 8, 12, 14, 26, 32, 34, 35, 40, 43, 45, 52, 59, 67, 68, 72, 75, 76, 88, 91, 95	
Difference in ABBREVIATIONS	3, 9, 15, 25, 27, 33, 42, 46, 57, 61, 64, 77	
Difference in NAMES	6, 11, 13, 16, 18, 19, 20, 22, 23, 29, 38, 41, 48, 49, 53, 55, 58, 62, 65, 70, 74, 78, 81, 83, 86, 89	
No Difference	1, 4, 7, 10, 17, 21, 24, 28, 30, 31, 36, 37, 39, 44, 47, 50, 51, 54, 56, 60, 63, 66, 69, 71, 73, 79, 80, 82, 84, 85, 87, 90, 92, 93, 94	

PART B—MEMORY FOR ADDRESSES

Practice I

1. B	12. A	23. A	34. C	45. B	56. D	67. C	78. C
2. C	13. C	24. B	35. A	46. E	57. A	68. E	79. D
3. D	14. B	25. E	36. D	47. B	58. B	69. B	80. E
4. E	15. E	26. B	37. A	48. D	59. A	70. E	81. D
5. A	16. A	27. E	38. D	49. D	60. A	71. B	82. E
6. E	17. C	28. D	39. B	50. D	61. E	72. D	83. B
7. C	18. B	29. A	40. B	51. C	62. A	73. A	84. E
8. B	19. D	30. A	41. E	52. C	63. B	74. E	85. D
9. B	20. C	31. E	42. E	53. B	64. D	75. B	86. A
10. A	21. D	32. C	43. A	54. E	65. A	76. E	87. E
11. E	22. E	33. C	44. C	55. C	66. C	77. A	88. B

Practice II

1. A	12. A	23. E	34. B	45. D	56. D	67. C	78. A
2. E	13. A	24. C	35. C	46. B	57. C	68. B	79. D
3. C	14. B	25. B	36. A	47. E	58. A	69. C	80. B
4. D	15. E	26. C	37. E	48. E	59. C	70. E	81. C
5. B	16. B	27. C	38. A	49. C	60. D	71. E	82. C
6. B	17. D	28. C	39. A	50. E	61. A	72. C	83. A
7. D	18. C	29. A	40. E	51. C	62. D	73. E	84. D
8. E	19. D	30. D	41. B	52. E	63. D	74. E	85. A
9. C	20. D	31. B	42. A	53. B	64. B	75. B	86. A
10. C	21. A	32. D	43. D	54. D	65. A	76. A	87. E
11. E	22. A	33. D	44. B	55. A	66. B	77. D	88. E

Practice III

1. C	12. E	23. A	34. D	45. A	56. C	67. B	78. C
2. E	13. B	24. A	35. B	46. E	57. D	68. B	79. A
3. A	14. D	25. C	36. E	47. B	58. A	69. D	80. E
4. D	15. A	26. C	37. D	48. D	59. E	70. B	81. A
5. B	16. B	27. E	38. B	49. D	60. C	71. A	82. A
6. A	17. D	28. B	39. A	50. A	61. D	72. E	83. C
7. E	18. E	29. E	40. E	51. A	62. B	73. E	84. C
8. B	19. D	30. D	41. E	52. C	63. E	74. B	85. D
9. D	20. C	31. B	42. A	53. C	64. E	75. C	86. C
10. A	21. B	32. C	43. B	54. E	65. A	76. D	87. E
11. A	22. B	33. D	44. D	55. C	66. B	77. D	88. A

Memory for Addresses

1. E	12. E	23. B	34. D	45. E	56. C	67. C	78. E
2. A	13. A	24. B	35. B	46. A	57. D	68. B	79. B
3. C	14. D	25. D	36. E	47. E	58. C	69. A	80. B
4. D	15. D	26. B	37. B	48. A	59. D	70. B	81. B
5. B	16. C	27. E	38. D	49. A	60. E	71. C	82. D
6. C	17. B	28. A	39. E	50. B	61. A	72. A	83. B
7. C	18. D	29. E	40. A	51. E	62. D	73. D	84. C
8. E	19. B	30. C	41. B	52. B	63. C	74. E	85. C
9. A	20. E	31. A	42. C	53. B	64. D	75. C	86. D
10. A	21. C	32. D	43. D	54. C	65. E	76. E	87. A
11. E	22. A	33. C	44. A	55. B	66. E	77. E	88. E

PART C—NUMBER SERIES

1. D	4. E	7. B	10. C	13. E	16. A	19. C	22. E
2. D	5. C	8. A	11. A	14. C	17. E	20. B	23. A
3. A	6. E	9. D	12. B	15. B	18. D	21. C	24. B

Explanations

1. **(D)** The series really begins with 9 and consists of repeated numbers moving upward in order. The number <u>8</u> is inserted between each pair of repeated numbers in the series.
2. **(D)** The numbers repeat themselves and move up in order.
3. **(A)** 6 6 is a repetitive theme. Between each set of 6s, the numbers move up by +2.
4. **(E)** The full sequence is a number of sets of mini-series. Each mini-series consists of three numbers decreasing by – 6. Each succeeding mini-series begins with a number one lower than the previous mini-series.
5. **(C)** Two alternating series each increase by +1. The first series starts at 1 and the second series starts at 3.
6. **(E)** Two series alternate. The first series consists of repeating numbers that move up by +1. The alternating series consists of numbers that move up by +1 without repeating.
7. **(B)** The series proceeds 5 6 7 8 9 10, with the number 18 appearing between each two numbers.
8. **(A)** The first series ascends one number at a time starting from 8. The alternating series ascends by +2 starting from 1.
9. **(D)** The pattern is: – 2, – 2, ×2; – 2, – 2, ×2....
10. **(C)** The pattern is: – 8, – 7; – 8, – 7; – 8, – 7....
11. **(A)** Two series alternate. The first series ascends by +3; the alternating series descends by – 5.
12. **(B)** This is a tough one. The pattern is +2, ×2, – 2, ÷2; +2, ×2, – 2, ÷2....
13. **(E)** The pattern is: – 6, repeat the number; – 6, repeat the number....
14. **(C)** The pattern is: +5, – 4, repeat the number; +5, – 4, repeat the number....
15. **(B)** The pattern is: +2, +2, – 3; +2, +2, – 3....
16. **(A)** The pattern is: ×3, – 8; ×3, – 8; ×3, – 8....
17. **(E)** The pattern is: – 8, – 6; – 8, – 6; – 8, – 6....
18. **(D)** There are two alternating series. The first series descends by – 4 starting from 47; the alternating series ascends by +4, starting from 23.
19. **(C)** The pattern is: +9, +8, +7, +6, +5, +4, +3, +2, +1.
20. **(B)** Then pattern is: +1, +2, repeat the number; + 1, +2, repeat the number....
21. **(C)** This is really a times 2 series with the number 41 appearing twice after each two numbers in the series. Thus: $9^{×2}$ $18^{×2}$ $36^{×2}$ $72^{×2}$ 144.
22. **(E)** The sequence 13 15 17 repeats itself over and over.
23. **(A)** Two series alternate. The first series ascends by +4; the alternating series descends by – 3.
24. **(B)** The pattern is: ×2, +3, – 10; ×2, +3, – 10; ×2, +3, – 10....

PART D—FOLLOWING ORAL INSTRUCTIONS

Correctly Filled Answer Grid

1 Ⓐ ● Ⓒ Ⓓ Ⓔ	23 Ⓐ Ⓑ Ⓒ Ⓓ Ⓔ	45 Ⓐ Ⓑ Ⓒ Ⓓ Ⓔ	67 Ⓐ Ⓑ Ⓒ Ⓓ Ⓔ
2 Ⓐ Ⓑ Ⓒ Ⓓ Ⓔ	24 Ⓐ Ⓑ ● Ⓓ Ⓔ	46 Ⓐ Ⓑ ● Ⓓ Ⓔ	68 ● Ⓑ Ⓒ Ⓓ Ⓔ
3 ● Ⓑ Ⓒ Ⓓ Ⓔ	25 Ⓐ Ⓑ Ⓒ Ⓓ Ⓔ	47 Ⓐ Ⓑ Ⓒ Ⓓ Ⓔ	69 Ⓐ Ⓑ Ⓒ Ⓓ Ⓔ
4 Ⓐ Ⓑ Ⓒ Ⓓ Ⓔ	26 Ⓐ Ⓑ Ⓒ Ⓓ Ⓔ	48 Ⓐ Ⓑ Ⓒ Ⓓ Ⓔ	70 Ⓐ Ⓑ Ⓒ Ⓓ Ⓔ
5 Ⓐ Ⓑ ● Ⓓ Ⓔ	27 ● Ⓑ Ⓒ Ⓓ Ⓔ	49 Ⓐ Ⓑ Ⓒ Ⓓ ●	71 Ⓐ Ⓑ Ⓒ Ⓓ Ⓔ
6 Ⓐ Ⓑ Ⓒ Ⓓ ●	28 Ⓐ Ⓑ Ⓒ Ⓓ Ⓔ	50 Ⓐ Ⓑ Ⓒ Ⓓ Ⓔ	72 Ⓐ Ⓑ Ⓒ Ⓓ Ⓔ
7 Ⓐ Ⓑ Ⓒ Ⓓ Ⓔ	29 Ⓐ Ⓑ Ⓒ Ⓓ Ⓔ	51 ● Ⓑ Ⓒ Ⓓ Ⓔ	73 ● Ⓑ Ⓒ Ⓓ Ⓔ
8 Ⓐ Ⓑ Ⓒ Ⓓ Ⓔ	30 Ⓐ Ⓑ Ⓒ Ⓓ ●	52 Ⓐ Ⓑ Ⓒ Ⓓ Ⓔ	74 Ⓐ Ⓑ Ⓒ Ⓓ Ⓔ
9 Ⓐ ● Ⓒ Ⓓ Ⓔ	31 Ⓐ Ⓑ Ⓒ Ⓓ Ⓔ	53 Ⓐ Ⓑ Ⓒ Ⓓ Ⓔ	75 Ⓐ Ⓑ Ⓒ Ⓓ ●
10 Ⓐ Ⓑ Ⓒ ● Ⓔ	32 Ⓐ Ⓑ Ⓒ Ⓓ Ⓔ	54 Ⓐ Ⓑ Ⓒ Ⓓ Ⓔ	76 Ⓐ Ⓑ Ⓒ Ⓓ Ⓔ
11 Ⓐ Ⓑ Ⓒ Ⓓ Ⓔ	33 Ⓐ Ⓑ Ⓒ ● Ⓔ	55 Ⓐ Ⓑ Ⓒ Ⓓ ●	77 Ⓐ Ⓑ Ⓒ Ⓓ Ⓔ
12 Ⓐ Ⓑ Ⓒ ● Ⓔ	34 Ⓐ Ⓑ Ⓒ Ⓓ Ⓔ	56 Ⓐ Ⓑ Ⓒ Ⓓ Ⓔ	78 Ⓐ Ⓑ Ⓒ Ⓓ Ⓔ
13 Ⓐ Ⓑ Ⓒ Ⓓ Ⓔ	35 Ⓐ Ⓑ Ⓒ Ⓓ Ⓔ	57 ● Ⓑ Ⓒ Ⓓ Ⓔ	79 Ⓐ ● Ⓒ Ⓓ Ⓔ
14 Ⓐ Ⓑ Ⓒ Ⓓ Ⓔ	36 Ⓐ Ⓑ Ⓒ Ⓓ Ⓔ	58 Ⓐ Ⓑ Ⓒ Ⓓ Ⓔ	80 Ⓐ Ⓑ Ⓒ Ⓓ Ⓔ
15 Ⓐ Ⓑ Ⓒ Ⓓ Ⓔ	37 Ⓐ Ⓑ Ⓒ Ⓓ Ⓔ	59 Ⓐ Ⓑ Ⓒ Ⓓ Ⓔ	81 Ⓐ Ⓑ ● Ⓓ Ⓔ
16 Ⓐ Ⓑ Ⓒ ● Ⓔ	38 Ⓐ ● Ⓒ Ⓓ Ⓔ	60 Ⓐ Ⓑ Ⓒ Ⓓ Ⓔ	82 Ⓐ Ⓑ Ⓒ Ⓓ Ⓔ
17 Ⓐ Ⓑ Ⓒ Ⓓ Ⓔ	39 Ⓐ Ⓑ Ⓒ Ⓓ Ⓔ	61 Ⓐ Ⓑ Ⓒ ● Ⓔ	83 Ⓐ Ⓑ Ⓒ Ⓓ Ⓔ
18 Ⓐ Ⓑ Ⓒ Ⓓ Ⓔ	40 ● Ⓑ Ⓒ Ⓓ Ⓔ	62 Ⓐ Ⓑ Ⓒ Ⓓ Ⓔ	84 Ⓐ Ⓑ Ⓒ Ⓓ Ⓔ
19 Ⓐ ● Ⓒ Ⓓ Ⓔ	41 Ⓐ Ⓑ Ⓒ Ⓓ Ⓔ	63 Ⓐ Ⓑ Ⓒ Ⓓ Ⓔ	85 Ⓐ Ⓑ Ⓒ Ⓓ ●
20 Ⓐ Ⓑ Ⓒ Ⓓ Ⓔ	42 Ⓐ Ⓑ Ⓒ Ⓓ Ⓔ	64 Ⓐ Ⓑ Ⓒ Ⓓ Ⓔ	86 Ⓐ Ⓑ Ⓒ Ⓓ Ⓔ
21 Ⓐ Ⓑ Ⓒ Ⓓ Ⓔ	43 Ⓐ Ⓑ Ⓒ Ⓓ Ⓔ	65 Ⓐ Ⓑ Ⓒ ● Ⓔ	87 Ⓐ Ⓑ ● Ⓓ Ⓔ
22 Ⓐ Ⓑ ● Ⓓ Ⓔ	44 Ⓐ ● Ⓒ Ⓓ Ⓔ	66 Ⓐ Ⓑ Ⓒ Ⓓ Ⓔ	88 Ⓐ Ⓑ Ⓒ Ⓓ Ⓔ

Correctly Filled Worksheet

1. <u>75</u>   14 <u>9</u>   27   54   12

2. <u>38</u> B   ___ D   ___ C   ___ A   ___ E

3. 5:43   4:32   3:58   <u>6:27</u>   <u>16</u>

4. (<u>24</u> C)   (___ D)   (<u>40</u> A)   (___ E)

5. [33 ___]   △ 81 <u>C</u>   (17 ___)   [3 <u>A</u>]

6. 35 ___   16 ___   10 ___   52 ___   6 <u>E</u>   80 ___

7. 7 1 <u>0</u> 5 <u>0</u> 3 3 <u>0</u> 6 8 <u>0</u> 4 <u>0</u> <s>55</s>

8. (61 <u>D</u>)   (39 ___)   (45 ___)   (58 ___)   (47 ___)

9. 17   ✗   37   ✗   76   ✗   12   ✗

10. [___ A] [_I_ B] (**12** D) (___ E) (___ C)

11. (86___) <68 _A_>

12. [_79_ B] [___ D]

13. [33 _D_] [85 _E_] [57 _A_]   SACK   CODE   EXAM

14. _19_ B   ___ E

15. [_30_ E] (__ A) [**65** D] (__ C)

16.   45   19   81   (22)   10   76

17. [29 ___] (73 _A_) (triangle: 10 _D_) (ellipse: 72___)

18.   D   G   E   (B)   R   A

19.   ___ A   _49_ E   ___ C   ___ B

Score Sheet

ADDRESS CHECKING: Your score on the Address Checking part is based upon the number of questions you answered correctly minus the number of questions you answered incorrectly. To determine your score, subtract the number of wrong answers from the number of correct answers.

Number Right   –   Number Wrong   =   Raw Score

_____ – _____ = _____

MEMORY FOR ADDRESSES: Your score on the Memory for Addresses part is based upon the number of questions you answered correctly minus one-fourth of the questions you answered incorrectly (number wrong divided by 4). Calculate this now:

Number Wrong ÷ 4 = _____.

Number Right   –   Number Wrong   ÷   4   =   Raw Score

_____ – _____ = _____

NUMBER SERIES: Your score on the Number Series part is based only on the number of questions you answered correctly. Wrong answers do not count against you.

Number Right   =   Raw Score

_____ = _____

FOLLOWING ORAL INSTRUCTIONS: Your score on the Following Oral Instructions part is based only upon the number of questions you marked correctly on the answer sheet. The worksheet is not scored, and wrong answers on the answer sheet do not count against you.

Number Right   =   Raw Score

_____ = _____

TOTAL SCORE: To find your total raw score, add together the raw scores for each section of the exam.

Address Checking Score _____

\+

Memory for Addresses Score _____

\+

Number Series Score _____

\+

Following Oral Instructions Score _____

= _____

Total Raw Score _____

Self-Evaluation Chart

Calculate your raw score for each test as shown above. Then check to see where your score falls on the scale from Poor to Excellent. Lightly shade in the boxes in which your scores fall.

Part	Excellent	Good	Average	Fair	Poor
Address Checking	80–95	65–79	50–64	35–49	1–34
Memory for Addresses	75–88	60–74	45–59	30–44	1–29
Number Series	21–24	18–20	14–17	11–13	1–10
Following Oral Instructions	27–31	23–26	19–22	14–18	1–13

GLOSSARY

Auxiliary Route—A carrier that augments and supplements service and normally evaluates at less than 8 hours per day

Base Salary—*Basic Salary* with *COLA*

Basic Salary—Annual, daily, or hourly rate of pay as indicated by the salary schedule for the employee's assigned position; excludes *COLA*

Business Route—A *route* on which 70 percent or more of the possible deliveries are business addresses; see also *Residential Route*

Career Appointment—An appointment to the postal career service without time limitation

Carrier Technician—A full-time city letter carrier used to replace scheduled absences within a group of *routes*

Casual Appointment—A non-career limited term appointment to positions used as a supplemental work force

City Delivery—Delivery by carriers of mail addressed to residences and business places within the city delivery limits of the post office

COLA—See *Cost of Living Adjustment*

Collection Route—A *route* which consists primarily of stops for collection of mail

Cost of Living Adjustment (COLA)—Increase in pay based on increases in the Consumer Price Index (CPI) over a base month; this increase is specified in bargaining unit agreements

Entrance Examinations—Tests given to establish eligibility for employment

Foot Route—A city *route* served by a carrier on foot; see also *Motorized Route*

Grade—Each pay category

Inservice Examinations—Tests administered to substitute rural carriers and career postal employees to determine eligibility for advancement and reassignment; also used to establish qualification for enrollment in certain postal training courses

Merit Promotion Program—Provides the means for making selections for promotions according to the relative qualifications of the employees under consideration

Motorized Route—A city *route* on which a motor vehicle is used in collecting all classes of mail; see also *Foot Route*

Performance Test—A procedure in which the applicant is directed to carry out a certain work activity related to the position under consideration

Promotion—The permanent assignment, with or without relocation, of an employee to an established position with a higher grade than the position to which the employee was previously assigned in the same schedule or in another schedule

Quality Step Increase—An increase in addition to a periodic *step increase* granted on or before expiration of required waiting periods in recognition of extra competence

Rated Application—Applications and other required documents that provide a basis for evaluation against an established rating standard; based on this application, a final rating is established for each competitor

RCA—See *Rural Carrier Associate*

Reassignment—The permanent assignment, with or without relocation, to another established position with the same grade in the same schedule or in a different schedule

Register—A file of eligibles' names arranged in order of relative standing for appointment consideration

Residential Route—A foot or motorized *route* on which 70 percent or more of the deliveries are to residential customers; see also *Business Route*

Route—A scheduled course within a prescribed area, where a carrier performs his or her duties

Rural Carrier Associate (RCA)—A non-career position; RCAs do not receive benefits; to be eligible, one must pass the Rural Carrier Examination 460 and all prescreening requirements and must have an excellent driving record for the preceding five years; see also *Temporary Rural Carrier*

Step Increase—An advancement from one step to the next within a specific grade of a position; it is dependent on satisfying certain performance and waiting period criteria; see also *Quality Step Increase*

Temporary Appointment—A non-career limited term appointment up to, but not exceeding, one year in a position that includes the performance of duties assigned to nonbargaining units

Temporary Assignment—The placement of an employee in another established position, for a limited period of time, to perform duties other than those in the position description

Temporary Rural Carrier (TRC)—Substitute for rural carrier; may be appointed to a term not exceeding 359 calendar days, but cannot be employed for more than 180 days within the 359 calendar day period; there are no benefits for this position, and applicants must have an excellent driving record

TRC—See *Temporary Rural Carrier*

Vehicle Hire Contract—Use of privately owned vehicle for *city delivery*

Veteran Preference—Granted to eligible applicants to be added to the ratings on examinations

Notes

Notes

Notes

Notes

Notes

Notes

Notes

Notes